A FEAST

FOR

HUNGRY

SOULS

"*A Feast for Hungry Souls* is an outstanding read for any Catholic longing to get closer to Jesus. It contains a banquet of wisdom gleaned from the lives and writings of thirty of the greatest spiritual masters of the Church. Making careful introductions to the reader, Muto selects choice tidbits from the writings of each one, teaching you how to implement their timeless practices and delve deeper in your relationship with Christ by following their practical advice. If you want to experience friendship with Christ and to pray more fully, pick up a copy of this book!"

Emily Jaminet
Coauthor of *Divine Mercy for Moms* and *The Friendship Project*

"Only the saints and spiritual masters are our true guides in sustaining a Christian spiritual life. To prayerfully read this gift from Susan Muto is to be ushered into the deepest waters of Christian prayer and thought, a depth meant to refresh all, as there is no *elite* when it comes to the call to holiness."

Deacon James Keating
Director of Theological Formation
Institute for Priestly Formation

"What you are holding in your hands is a tour de force, an exquisite offering of Christian spiritual thought and exploration from the earliest Church Fathers, through the great mystics of the Church, both male and female, right up to the twentieth-century minds that have informed and enriched our faith. Their dogged pursuit of truth, love, mercy, and justice is revealed in their encounters with the Christ who is all of those things, ever-new, ever challenging. Rarely has a book been so perfectly titled as Susan Muto's *A Feast for Hungry Souls*: a smorgasbord of wisdom, instruction, and inspiration from which we are invited to feed, whether we are looking for a mere morsel or a full meal. This book is a banquet, and it should be included in the library of any Catholic who is intent on deepening their relationship to Christ Jesus."

Elizabeth Scalia
Editor at-large at Word on Fire Catholic Ministries

"While there are a number of introductions to the Christian spiritual masters, none are quite so accessible, informative, or helpful as Susan Muto's

A Feast for Hungry Souls. Resisting the urge to reduce the great figures of Christian spirituality to a series of cliches, Muto devotedly dives into the nuances of a wide range of spiritual masters from early Christianity through today. *A Feast for Hungry Souls* is that rare book, accessible enough for parish study while also possessing a bibliography rich enough to serve as the basis of an undergraduate or graduate textbook on spirituality."

Timothy P. O'Malley
Director of Education for the McGrath Institute for Church Life
University of Notre Dame

"As a lifelong student and teacher of the spiritual life, I have often been asked, 'What does someone who lived centuries ago have to say to me about how to live life in the twenty-first century?' Susan Muto answers that question. She has a unique ability to astutely name the 'soul sicknesses' of contemporary life and provide a spiritual antidote through wisdom gained through the experiences of ancient, medieval, and modern spiritual masters. This book is filled with insight, practical advice, and probing questions that will help readers grow in wholeness and holiness at every stage of the spiritual journey."

Patricia Cooney Hathaway
Professor of Spirituality and Systematic Theology
Sacred Heart Major Seminary

"As a Catholic educator in an era fraught with New Age sentimentalism, I endeavor to show my students that the deep interior life—imbued with prayer and enriched with the wisdom of holy men and women through the ages—is not a novel challenge to pursue. Rather, it has been a feature of the Christian life, fortified by the sacraments, for the past two thousand years. This magnificently promising work by Susan Muto will feed the soul of whoever urgently hungers for enriching spiritual nourishment."

Justin McClain
Theology teacher at Bishop McNamara High School
Forestville, Maryland

"This is a treasure trove of deep spiritual truths introducing some of the most important figures who shaped Christian spirituality."

From the foreword by **Haley Stewart**
Catholic blogger, podcaster, and author of *The Grace of Enough*

A FEAST

SPIRITUAL LESSONS FROM

FOR

THE CHURCH'S GREATEST

HUNGRY

MASTERS AND MYSTICS

SOULS

SUSAN MUTO

AVE MARIA PRESS AVE Notre Dame, Indiana

Scripture quotations are from the *New Revised Standard Version Bible: Catholic Edition*, copyright © 1989, 1993 National Council of the Churches of Christ in the United States of America. Used by permission. All rights reserved worldwide.

Selected texts are quoted by permission of the publisher or other copyright holder, as indicated in the acknowledgments on page 321.

Foreword © 2020 by Haley Stewart

Founded in 1865, Ave Maria Press is a ministry of the United States Province of Holy Cross.

www.avemariapress.com

Paperback: ISBN-13 978-1-59471-925-7

E-book: ISBN-13 978-1-59471-926-4

Cover background © jessicahyde/Getty Images.

Cover and text design by Brianna Dombo.

Printed and bound in the United States of America.

Library of Congress Cataloging-in-Publication Data
Names: Muto, Susan, 1942– author.
Title: A feast for hungry souls : spiritual lessons from the Church's greatest masters and mystics / Susan Muto.
Description: Notre Dame, Indiana : Ave Maria Press, 2020. | Includes bibliographical references and index. | Summary: "This introduction to thirty Christian masters represents the spiritual legacy of scholar of spiritual literature, Susan Muto. These voices from the ancient, medieval, and modern Church have been the focus of Muto's work for more than forty years, and the trusted guides of her own spiritual life. Now, they will help answer pressing spiritual questions, and satisfy the deepest cravings of the heart"—Provided by publisher.
Identifiers: LCCN 2019055478 (print) | LCCN 2019055479 (ebook) | ISBN 9781594719257 (paperback) | ISBN 9781594719264 (ebook)
Subjects: LCSH: Christian literature—History and criticism. | Spiritual life—Catholic Church. | Spiritual life—Christianity. | Christian saints—Biography.
Classification: LCC BR117 .M88 2020 (print) | LCC BR117 (ebook) | DDC 248—dc23
LC record available at https://lccn.loc.gov/2019055478
LC ebook record available at https://lccn.loc.gov/2019055479.

To Rev. Adrian van Kaam, C.S.Sp., PhD
(1920–2007)

The spiritual master
who inspired me to return
to the ancient, medieval, and modern
roots of my faith tradition

CONTENTS

PART TWO: MEDIEVAL MASTERS
(1100–1600)

PART THREE: MODERN MASTERS (1600–2000)

FOREWORD

"Why didn't anyone tell me about St. Ignatius of Antioch?" was my first thought when, as an undergraduate, I first encountered this disciple of St. John the Evangelist through his letters as bishop of one of the early Christian churches, written at the turn of the second century. "We have his writings about the Eucharist and the Church? We can just *read* what he wrote? Why haven't I heard his name before now?"

I felt both exhilarated and betrayed when I unearthed this treasure. I grew up in a faith tradition that did not highly value the development of Christian thought beyond the past couple of centuries. While I was familiar with recent bestsellers in Christian publishing, it wasn't until my college classes that I encountered some of the spiritual giants of the Christian tradition that you will encounter in this book: St. Augustine, St. Maximus the Confessor, and St. Gregory the Great.

Reading and rereading these ancient masters, I was hooked! My shallow theology and ignorance of Church history was challenged as the roots of the seeds of faith, planted in me so long ago, grew deep in the rich soil of two thousand years of the teachings of the Church fathers and mothers. I was amazed that such beauty and wisdom was mine for the taking. After years of "fast food" theology, I had been invited to a table creaking with the weight of a beautiful banquet. All I had to do was reach out and taste the rich meal before me.

Looking at today's landscape, we see a Church in crisis. One contributing (though certainly not the only) factor is the poor catechesis most Catholics have received. By constantly reaching for the novel and the trendy, we end up ignoring the rich tradition the Church and the saints have to offer us. The constant compulsion to seek cultural relevance has resulted in fast food theology, and Christians—especially younger generations—are hungry for real spiritual nourishment. But where do we turn? How do we even begin the journey of diving deep into the spiritual classics that have shaped Christian theology? Look no further.

A Feast for Hungry Souls is a treasure trove of deep spiritual truths introducing some of the most important figures who shaped Christian spirituality. Muto's extensive knowledge of these masters and mystics, based on decades of teaching and research, has enabled her to prepare a sumptuous banquet of spiritual truth, offering in small, accessible bites profound riches from these spiritual masters: desert fathers, doctors of the Church, mystics, medieval saints, modern contemplatives, and more.

In these pages you'll find the perfect starting point for diving into the meaty teachings of Christian spiritual masters from the past two thousand years. Not only does Muto familiarize the reader with these figures and their most essential teachings with clarity; she also offers resources by and about each spiritual master so that we can continue the feast beyond the pages of this book. Partaking of this creaking table will only whet your appetite to reach out for the resources Muto provides to befriend these spiritual masters and make them your companions on the way to a deeper spiritual life.

Haley Stewart

PROLOGUE

This book, like a slow-cooked meal, has been simmering in my heart for many years. I first began teaching the original works of the classical Christian writers in 1972. I created a six-semester cycle of courses leading my students from ancient to medieval to modern spiritual masterpieces. This book moves from those original appetizer courses to the main meal, featuring thirty of the classics I most love and want my readers to enjoy. We can only feed our spiritual hunger if we come to dine at the gourmet table of the mystics, bypassing the fast food of pop spirituality and taking the time to taste and savor these classical texts.

My hope is that this book will provide believers and seekers access to the lived experience and wisdom of spiritual masters whose works have passed the test of time. Their writings are essential reading for us who want to embrace our Christian life to the full. My aim over the years has been not only to educate readers intellectually but also to inspire them spiritually to grow in mind and heart closer to God.

The masters selected for this book have been helpmates to me in my personal life. The insights they gave me, the experiences they recounted, enabled me to go beyond the dynamics of human development to the farthest reaches of ongoing, in-depth spiritual formation. In my professional life, these thirty heroes and heroines of the faith gave me the courage to go from classrooms at the Epiphany Academy in my hometown of Pittsburgh, Pennsylvania, to diverse audiences around the world to unearth the contemporary relevance of these timeless treasures.

How can we pass this gourmet food for the soul on to future generations unless we know and live it daily? This is a question that burns in my heart. These masters offer excellent advice about how to follow Jesus to fresh pastures of discipleship and evangelization. I love the way they made the world a better place, and I appreciate how they inspire us to do the same.

By the time you reach the end of this book—read in continuity or as the Spirit moves you—I trust you will have found thirty friends who will fulfill time and again your hunger for God. Each of these thirty treasures is unique, and yet, taken together, they provide a wealth of resources for spiritual self-direction, direction-in-common, and one-on-one encounters. They offer time-tested and true ways to guard our hearts, deepen our faith, and create conditions that facilitate our inner and outer quest, our voiced and silent longing for spiritual maturity.

In an era when soul-sickness has reached epidemic proportions, it may well be that the Holy Spirit has laid upon us the duty to see to it that these classics never lie dormant on library shelves but that they become enlivening companions for laity, clergy, and religious of all faith groupings; for catechists, pastoral workers, and spiritual directors; and for chaplains, distinguished theologians, and people in the pew.

I especially offer this work of love to younger readers, who know that the time to avail themselves of the riches of the masters is now. Many have asked me to provide them with a kind of spiritual tool kit for how to live the Christian life as fully as possible in thought, word, and deed. I have done my best to answer this request, because our Christian youth are the hope of the Church. May God guard their hearts and give them the grace to be faithful followers of Jesus, transformed by God and these spiritual masters so that they in turn transform the world.

Helping me step-by-step to produce a work of this magnitude have been the faculty and staff of the Epiphany Academy of Formative Spirituality, notably our administrative secretary, Gerrie Mullooly, and my fellow researcher, Steve Geitgey. I am thankful for the support and guidance provided by Heidi Hess Saxton and all of her colleagues at Ave Maria Press. May these dear friends, along with countless supporters and students over the years, sense on each page of this book my undying gratitude to them and to the good God who gave us "so great a cloud of witnesses" (Heb 12:1).

PART ONE

ANCIENT MASTERS

(300–1100)

INTRODUCTION

ANCIENT MASTERS

What no eye has seen, nor ear heard, nor the human
heart conceived,
what God has prepared for those who love him.
—1 Corinthians 2:9

Who of us can know the mind of God? In this informational age, we seek answers to every question, yet we are so often lost in the drought-stricken climate of selfism, individualism, and functionalism. We risk losing respect for our human dignity, for our eternal calling in the Lord, and for the fulfillment of God's plan in our lives. All too often, we seek to master the mystery rather than allowing the mystery to master us. Our sense of the sacred suffocates under the weight of noise pollution, talking heads, and wariness of any authoritarian voice or self-revelatory reflection.

No wonder exposure to the teachings of these ancient masters may be a shocking experience. Popular psychology lauds self-actualization and shudders at the thought of self-mortification, preaching revenge and eschewing forgiveness until we find it unbearable to sit with our own thoughts. Still, the ancients remind us, there are times when words must give way to silent presence to the mystery.

Out of this depth of inner stillness come prayers, sighs, and songs celebrating every experience from the glory of new birth to the shadow of death. These masterful texts remind us to acknowledge our creaturehood and never delude ourselves into playing god. They teach us that our deepest identity is reducible not to what we do but to the essence of who we are. Only from this

3

transcendent perspective can we resist the temptation to live by untruths that neglect the splendor of the whole and Holy to whom we bow in adoration.

I

QUIET YOUR HEAD AND
HEAR WITH YOUR HEART

TEACHINGS FROM THE
DESERT TRADITION ON THE
FLIGHT TO FREEDOM

Abba Theodore of Scetis said, "A thought comes to me
which troubles me and does not leave me free; but not being
able to lead me to act, it simply stops me progressing in virtue; but a vigilant man would cut it off and get up to pray."
— *The Sayings of the Desert Fathers*, 68

In a world dominated by superficial chatter and uncommitted togetherness,
there weaves a narrow way, slender as a thread, through the desert tradition.
It is revealed to us in Psalm 46:10: "Be still, and know that I am God!" The
quest for solitude, to be alone with the Alone, manifests itself in all people
seeking to find the meaning of life; it is as natural an instinct as solidarity,
or reaching out to find communion with like-minded others.

The essential purpose of withdrawing from the world, or, better still, of
fleeing the emptiness of a merely worldly existence, is to free the seeker to
find God, whether in the wilderness or in the hermitage of the heart. The
seeker longs to experience God, to know God not just intellectually but also
intimately and personally.

5

The pursuit of this relationship with the Divine leads souls through a radical detachment from self-gratification to the way of total abandonment to the mystery. Abnegation of self liberates us to seek God directly, to quiet our minds in order to hear with our hearts. In this state, we no longer rely on sensible consolations and virtuous accomplishments or even on spiritual exercises and satisfying meditations, as sure signs of salvation. We do not reject these gifts when they come, but we do not actively seek them out—we feel detached from any gratification, human effort, or satisfaction that threatens to replace our reliance on grace.

The desert tradition teaches us to bind ourselves to what is lasting, good, and true. It instructs us in inner silencing and self-awareness, repentance and continual abandonment to God, humility and self-renunciation for Christ's sake. The masters of the desert remind us of the Gospel truth that we are to be in this world but not of it since "the world and its desire are passing away, but those who do the will of God live forever" (1 Jn 2:17).

Meet the Masters

During the reign of the Emperor Constantine (312–337), hundreds of seekers fled to the deserts of Egypt and Syria and other remote places such as Nitria, Scete, and Gaza. They sought a way to live in fidelity to their own baptism and in the fellowship Christ modeled in the breaking of the bread. Above all, they wanted to pursue an inner life of prayer, resulting in loving service to their neighbor. And they turned to the teachings and traditions of the Desert Fathers and Mothers to show them the way.

Exemplary in this movement is the life of St. Anthony of Egypt (250–375), who believed that bodily austerity, practiced with moderation, promoted a compassionate form of Christian living.[1] Solitude was meant to foster solidarity. He taught those who followed him to flee to the desert not out of hatred for the world but to seek words of truth by which to live their lives in service of the Lord and in love and harmony with others.

So edifying was Anthony's teaching that he found it almost impossible to handle the crowds who made their way across the desert, wanting to discuss their personal and spiritual problems with him. He escaped to an oasis in a mountainous region near the Red Sea and spent the remainder of his life seeking solitude while still being available to serve others.

Desert living flowed into two streams. The one was eremitical, the hermit life preferred by St. Anthony. The other was cenobitical, the community model pioneered by St. Pachomius (290–346). Both ways became part of Christian culture, representing a spiritual force still found today in every contemplative and apostolic community. In the desert—be it a retreat center, a hermit's cell, or a house of prayer—the seeker learns how to escape the traps of self-indulgence through total abandonment to the unfathomable mystery of which the prophet Hosea spoke, when God says: "Therefore, I will . . . bring her into the wilderness, and speak tenderly to her. From there I will give her her vineyards, and make the Valley of Achor a door of hope. There she shall respond as in the days of her youth, as at the time when she came out of the land of Egypt" (Hos 2:14–15).

Around the same year of Anthony's flight to the desert, Church history records the rise of the Arian heresy, which denied the divinity of Christ and was condemned at the Council of Nicaea in 325. The rise and fall of this heresy were closely bound up with the development of the eremitical life, which defended the humanity and divinity of Jesus Christ. At the time of Origen and Clement of Alexandria—both defenders of the faith—hermits, whose lives were the best witness to Gospel values, began to drift westward, propagating in Italy and France the ideals of primitive Egyptian monasticism as lived in Palestine and Asia Minor. Within a century, life based on the Egyptian model of solitude and solidarity had become an almost universal part of Christian culture. Its common theme was the complete abandonment of "everything" for "nothing"—that is to say, for no-thing but for God, who is our All in all.

FLEE TO BE FREE

Desert Fathers such as Evagrius Ponticus and John Cassian held fast to the goal of freeing ourselves from attachment to all that is not God. The core of our freedom equates with the awareness that God alone can fulfill our deepest longings. Did not Christ himself spend forty days in the desert prior to the start of his public life? He taught us from experience how to resist the devilish temptations to power, pleasure, and possession. In the fullness of his humanity and his divinity, he showed us the way to *flee* (from illusory promises of fulfillment) to be *free* (to pursue God in poverty of spirit and purity of heart).

In imitation of Christ, the Desert Fathers and Mothers asserted in their timelessly true sayings, narratives, and counsels that life in a dissipated, disbelieving world is like a shipwreck from which we must swim away to save our own lives. The tenets held up by the world as exemplary were a formula for spiritual, if not physical, death and disease. This flight *from* decadent society was a flight *to* communion with God and others. Only in the desert, guided by grace, might the seeker find the true self by rejecting the false self, fabricated by a fallen and obtuse ego.

The literature of the desert formed a genre comprised of sayings about how to unlock the prison of pride into which we have thrown ourselves by the immoral choices we have made. We must find a way, say the ancient ones, to smash the idols that preoccupy our attention and cause us to forfeit our love relationship with the Lord. Defacing the divine image in us are sins such as succumbing to selfishness, choosing to be loveless and unforgiving, and refusing to conform to Christ's unsparing efforts to redeem us.[2]

The story is told, for example, of Abba Agathon, who met a crippled man by the roadside; he asked the holy man rather abruptly to take him into the town where Agathon was heading to sell products that the brothers had produced to support the community. Each time Agathon sold an article, the beggar demanded that the holy man buy something for him to eat or drink. At the end of the day, the crippled man then demanded a ride back to their original meeting place. Then the cripple said, "Agathon, you are filled with divine blessings, in heaven and on earth." Raising his eyes, Agathon saw no man; it was an angel of the Lord, come to try him.[3]

Other obstacles desert dwellers overcome with the help of grace include a dissipating lassitude that overlooks the least sign of progress and refuses to focus on the blessing in every limit; an unwillingness to admit that conversion has to be ongoing; and a resistance to signals of transcendence, telling us to unlock the prison of pride into which we have thrown ourselves. Worst of all, we may refuse to smash the idols that preoccupy our attention and cause us to lose our living relationship with God through prayer and presence. Missing the mark through sin, succumbing to selfishness, and choosing to be loveless are some of the many ways in which we deface the image of God in ourselves and discount the divine design we were destined to fulfill in the desert of deep longing.

Those who sought the guidance of teachers such as Agathon or John the Dwarf came to see that the conditions for the possibility of following Jesus had to be emptying the self of willfulness and bowing in obedience to the will of the Father.

> It was said of Abba John the Dwarf that he withdrew and lived in the desert at Scetis with an old man of Thebes. His abba, taking a piece of dry wood, planted it and said to him, "Water it every day with a bottle of water, until it bears fruit." Now the water was so far away that he had to leave in the evening and return the following morning. At the end of three years the wood came to life and bore fruit. Then the old man took some of the fruit and carried it to the church saying to the brethren, "Take and eat the fruit of obedience." (*Sayings*, 1:73)

To quiet our mind and hear with our heart, here are some counsels the desert tradition teaches us to follow:

+ Flee from the demons of dissonance, dissipation, and distraction and flee to God in solitude, silence, and peace.
+ Experience a heightened sense of repentance or compunction of heart.[4]
+ Do not become so absorbed in a functionalized world or in the pursuit of fame and gain that you deny the truth that you are a weak, wounded, finite creature in need of God's grace.
+ In moments of quiet contemplation, realize how agitated and distracted you are and try to be present to God in the here and now.
+ Abandon the self-deception of treating temporal goods as if they were timeless.

In a word, the desert leaves no room for dishonesty. Hardship is part of this limited life, yet it is also a stepping-stone to complete acceptance of our finitude. Like the first apostles, we have to let go of the safety nets of our own contriving, embrace the Cross, and join Christ in proclaiming that we are a new creation.

The Lord asks us a question in the desert we cannot ignore: Do we want to live the life of the spirit in the abstract, as if it were reducible to an impersonal outline of rules and regulations, or do we want to abide in communion with him in the deserts of everydayness where he himself lived? The answer the masters give us is never to veer erratically from one extreme to another, as from a perfectionistic model of spirituality to the flabbiest sort of laxity, or from too much discipline to none at all. The solution is not to cultivate any extreme but to practice moderation; it is to engage in the kind of compassionate asceticism that guards our heart while encouraging us to care for others as Christ cares for us.

In the desert, we learn to follow the guidance of the Holy Spirit, who teaches us to watch and wait, not to question the changing nature of our call until we receive some inkling of what God asks of us. It is our sacred duty never to stop praying for peace, for transformation, for the fullness of joy God wants to grant our soon-to-be-liberated spirits.

FIND YOUR INNER DESERT

As our capacity for reflective dwelling increases, we may discover that we are becoming present to the Divine Presence, not only in moments of meditation but also in the midst of our daily tasks. We are less inclined to become irritable and agitated when our best-laid plans go astray. We look for meanings that might otherwise be lost in the rushing streams of labor and leisure. We try to slow down and sip the wine of ordinary living. Why rush when we can wait upon the Lord with "patience, kindness, holiness of spirit, genuine love, truthful speech" (2 Cor 6:6–7)?

When the burden of discipleship becomes exhausting, we can do as Jesus did and go off to a quiet place to pray. In moments of physical, functional, or spiritual dryness, we can call out to the Father, echoing Jesus' words, "My God, my God, why have you forsaken me?" (Mt 27:46). The pain of feeling deserted may be unavoidable at times, but to take up this cross is to discover, much to our amazement, that in this felt absence God may be more present to us. Naked faith convinces us that God is near. The self-emptying and detachment characteristic of the desert experience are part of the painful process of purification. The closer we come to God, the more we uncover the attachments we have not yet shed and the harm they are doing to our inner and relational growth. Whatever threatens to deplete us can be transformed by grace into another reason not to lose hope. God's purpose is that "the wilderness and the dry land shall be glad, the desert shall rejoice and blossom" (Is 35:1). Now is the time to listen anew to desert messengers and to take the risk of entering into a solitary encounter with God, all the while knowing that we cannot predict the outcome:

> One day when Abba John was going up to Scetis with some other brothers, their guide lost his way for it was night-time. So the brothers said to Abba John, "What shall we do, abba, in order not to die wandering about, for the brother has lost the way?" The old man said to them, "If we speak to him, he will be filled with grief and shame. But look here, I will pretend to be ill and say I cannot walk anymore; then we can stay here till the dawn." This he did. The others said, "We will not go on either, but we will stay with you." They sat there until the dawn, and in this way, they did not upset the brother. (*Sayings*, 17:76)

Seekers who go to the desert are as ordinary as the pilgrims with whom I once traveled to the Holy Land. All of us have the same problems: our bills come due; our faucets leak; people we thought we could trust betray us; our children disappoint us; our colleagues complain; our health fails; our prayer life becomes arid and routine. We are everyday folks who enjoy the carefree nature of youth, the responsibility of adulthood, the sobering reality of aging, and the solitude of death.

No wonder Jesus preferred parables and living examples as his modes of teaching. With one story he could lead his listeners to expose their fears and dreams, their griefs and hopes. He shows us in the breaking of the bread that the world is not an alien place but the Father's domain. Every day he asks us if we are willing to undergo our own desert initiation and become living witnesses to the truths he teaches.

This symbolic martyrdom is the foundation of our spiritual life. Like soldiers who have trained long and hard to carry out a difficult mission, so must we go through the training that results in the disciplining of our reluctance to be abandoned to the will of God. In the desert we learn to wait upon the Lord, convinced by *faith* that the dry land of doubt does give way to the lush garden of *hope*. Sustained by the Spirit, we become channels through whom the Triune God calls the world out of darkness into the light of liberating *love*.

Left to our own resources, we could never cope with the demands of radical conversion. As the desert alters our customary perceptions of life, so, too, does it compel us to reflect on our story. Mysteriously, in the darkness of unknowing and in the throes of spiritual dryness, we trust that God is moving us *from* the illusion of self-sufficiency, *through* layers of self-aware-ness, *to* new insights that break open the providential meaning of our journey as a whole.

In every desert experience, we walk on the razor's edge between fol-lowing the Triune God and succumbing to the ways of the world with its counterparts, the flesh and the devil.[5] To cite but one example of such a commitment: we feel compassionate toward evildoers, but we make no compromise with evil. In short, we live *in* the world without being *of* the world. We accept the reality that we must be willing to combat, not only externally but in the secret places of our heart, our own persistent lack of faith, hope, and love.

Consider the reply of Abba Theodore of Perme, when a brother asked him what the chief work of a monk ought to be:

> So the old man said, "Suppose you hear it said that I am ill and you ought to visit me; you say to yourself, 'Shall I leave my work and go now? I had better finish my work and then go.' Then another idea comes along and perhaps you never go; or again, another brother says to you, 'Lend me a hand, brother'; and you say, 'Shall I leave my own work and go and work with him?' If you do not go, you are disregarding the commandment of God which is the work of the soul, and doing the work of your hands which is subordinate." (*Sayings*, 11:64–65)

Our readiness to serve others depends on our willingness to die to every form of domineering condescension. Only then can we respect the innate dignity and worth of others. Having relinquished under the desert sun all remnants of vainglory, we give the Spirit free rein to teach us the truth that our faith does not "rest on human wisdom but on the power of God" (1 Cor 2:5). The desert experiences we have undergone grant us a glimpse of who we and others really are. While fleeing to an actual desert may be impossible, we can always retire to the hermitage of our heart. The inner peace we now enjoy changes our focus from one of frantic pursuit of spiritual highs to the calm demeanor of desert disciples willing to go wherever the Beloved deigns to lead us. In that quiet place, we are free to encounter the Divine Presence and to grow in compassion.

> Abba Macarius was asked, "How should we pray?" The old man replied, "There is no need at all to make long discourses; it is enough to stretch out one's hands and say, 'Lord, as you will, and as you know, have mercy.' And if the conflict grows fiercer say, 'Lord, help!' He knows very well what we need and he shows us his mercy." (*Sayings*, 19:111)

Reflect Now

1. When do you feel most in need of taking time for silence and solitude?
2. Do these times of quiet increase your awareness of the necessity of repentance and forgiveness? What other fruits do solitude and silence bear in your life?
3. How do you cope with the spiritual aridity that often accompanies a desert experience?

Read More

Catherine de Hueck Doherty, *Poustinia: Christian Spirituality of the East for Western Man* (Notre Dame, IN: Ave Maria Press, 1975).

Peter H. Görg, *The Desert Fathers: Saint Anthony and the Beginnings of Monasticism*, trans. Michael J. Miller (San Francisco: Ignatius Press, 2011).

Anselm Gruen, *Heaven Begins within You: Wisdom from the Desert Fathers*, trans. Peter Heinegg (New York: Crossroad, 1999).

2

RUN AWAY FROM EVIL AND RUN TOWARD THE GOOD

In your prayer seek only after justice and the kingdom of God, that is to say, after virtue and true spiritual knowledge. Then all else will be given to you besides.

—Evagrius Ponticus, *Chapters on Prayer*, 61

In the desert of divine direction, we experience our heart as a veritable battlefield where virtue clashes with vice. The soul-sickness caused, for example, by envy, anger, avarice, and lust can only be healed by exposing every semblance of self-deception while validating the victory of Christ, the Divine Physician, over the vices that would separate us from God.

The Evagrian system of spirituality may be ancient, yet it is also highly relevant to contemporary life. Evagrius addresses such questions as *Why do I feel so empty when I have so much? What is the best way to escape the noonday devil of discouragement? What would it be like to experience the peace of Christ that surpasses understanding?*

MEET THE MASTER

Evagrius Ponticus (ca. 345–399) elevated the desert tradition to a level of learning and prayer that brought the need to guard our heart to the forefront of Eastern and Western monasticism. Strengthening this quest for Christian maturity are such values as fleeing from worldliness with a heart at once full of longing to see God face-to-face and empty of any illusion that by our own efforts we can grasp this beatific vision. Evagrius teaches us that for prayer to become constant, it must be nourished by the reading of holy scripture and the writings of the spiritual masters. For our spirit to ascend to God, we must practice docility and vigilance, alert to the prowling and devouring spirit of evil while confirming Christ's victory over the prince of this world.

Evagrius upheld in his writings and teachings four passages to the imitation of Christ common to the desert tradition: from the darkness of sin to the light of salvation; from the visible order of creation to the invisible order of God's loving embrace; from restless disquiet to the peaceful focus of contemplative prayer; and from sinful selfishness to self-giving love.

To Evagrius we can attribute what appears to be the first complete system of Christian spirituality, detailing the obstacles to and the conditions for elevating our whole being (body, mind, and spirit) to intimacy with the Trinity. Plagued though we may be by untamed passions, we are still capable of living in conformity to Christ. To do so is a matter not of body-denying asceticism but of spirit-filled faith and fruitful prayer. Our task is not to craft our own path to holiness but to give ourselves over to the gentle demands of Christ's word and to trust in his promises. To those who sought his counsel, Evagrius would say:

+ Avoid discouragement.
+ Guard against the demon of unchastity.
+ Train yourself like a skilled athlete to run to God and to revere him at all times.
+ Cultivate deep humility.
+ Curb temptations with short prayers and utterances of the name of Jesus.

The seminal works of Evagrius, *The Praktikos* and *Chapters on Prayer*, present two main themes leading to Christian perfection: how to develop a life of virtue by way of detachment from vice, and how to progress in the life of prayer through the peace of contemplation.[1] *The Praktikos* is the most widely known of his works and the most influential due to its treatment of the ascetical life. His reflections on mysticism, found in *Chapters on Prayer*, lead us into the inner sanctuary of the knowledge of God. In this work, as in *The Praktikos*, Evagrius enumerates the conditions for steady progress in prayer, including the necessity of spiritual discipline and the willingness to renounce whatever hinders our perseverance to live in a state of contemplative awe and adoration oriented to beholding the Blessed Trinity.

Evagrius was as brilliant a teacher and theologian as he was an austere, God-fearing hermit. His influence and reputation complemented those of great saints and defenders of the faith like Gregory of Nyssa. Prior to his own conversion, he gave in to the temptations associated with worldly recognition and success. Despite his quest for virtue, he allowed self-gratification to rule his life, especially when he fell in love with the wife of a Roman prefect. This episode, though short-lived, plunged him into near despair and launched his lifelong struggle with what he would codify as the eight capital sins, lust being among the worst of them.

Lest he risk losing his soul on this battlefield between vice and virtue, Evagrius knew he had to leave Constantinople and set sail for the Holy Land. He arrived at the monastery in Jerusalem. There he met Melania, superior of the women's community on the Mount of Olives, and Rufinus, head of the men's community. This stay marked the most significant part of his life so far—the movement from worldly fame to monastic freedom. Though disturbing thoughts continued to plague him, he found an ideal way to deal with them that in due time would become the basis of his teaching on prayer, detachment, and the ascetical life.

The year 383 marked the decisive turning point of his journey from impurity to purity of heart. While in Jerusalem, Evagrius was tempted once again to indulge in promiscuous behavior and to become, as he described it, intoxicated with vainglory to the point of "spiritual sickness." Being a monk at heart, he obeyed Melania's directive to seek *metanoia*, or conversion of heart. God gave him the grace to make a new start. He settled in the

Egyptian desert with a group of monks influenced by the Greek thinker Origen.[2] In short order, he himself was acknowledged as a master of discernment, asceticism, and the mystical life. He pointed to *apatheia* as the core of his teaching since it means living in the peace of the Lord, freed from evil thoughts and the inclinations they spawn.

By the time Evagrius died in 399, his counsels on spiritual living, *The Praktikos* and *Chapters on Prayer*, were recognized then, as they are now, as storehouses of wisdom representing the finest teaching of the desert tradition.[3]

MAKING ASCETICISM THE GROUND OF MYSTICISM

For Evagrius, the monastic life was a kind of bloodless martyrdom. The dedicated study and personal discipline it espouses is the foundation of the life of prayer to which it draws the soul mystically. His gifted combination of psychological and spiritual self-reflection and insight enabled Evagrius to describe, analyze, and define both the deadly sins and the stages of the soul's journey to God, a journey anyone who wants to mature in the spiritual life must follow.

According to Evagrius, the ascetical way of keeping *prakitiké* (the commandments) is the only way to purify the unruly *logismoi* (the sources of sin). Through the knowledge gained by coping with the obstacles to contemplative presence, we reach with the help of grace a state of *apatheia* (passionless tranquility and deep calm):

> Stand guard over your spirit, keeping it free of concepts at the time of prayer so that it may remain in its own deep calm. Thus he who has compassion on the ignorant will come to visit even such an insignificant person as yourself. That is when you will receive the most glorious gift of prayer. (*On Prayer*, 69:66)

This rest in God gives rise in turn to *agape*, or self-giving love, that draws us closer to the heart of the Trinity.[4] In summary, the soul attains *apatheia* through the practice of virtues (*prakitiké*) and the struggle to overcome temptations and subdue the passions. Once the soul has attained some level of *apatheia*, it ceases to be the captive of its own passions; it may then receive the grace of penetrating discernment that enables it to appraise its own stumbling blocks to spiritual progress and to help others do the same.

The soul then proceeds by degrees from natural contemplation (*theoria*), using the senses and reason, to progressive contemplation (*theologia*), in which the intellect rises beyond forms and figures to behold in faith the heavenly luminosity of the living God. This graced encounter leads the soul into the realm of pure, imageless prayer. *Theologia*, as described by Evagrius, is not so much an *activity* that we *do* as it is a state of *being* pertaining to who we *are*.

The main barriers to this ascent to God are the capital sins or eight vices, named by Evagrius as gluttony, lust or impurity, avarice, anger, dejection (*acedia*), listlessness or sadness, vainglory or self-esteem, and pride.[5] Evagrius was the first spiritual master to identify *acedia* as the fiercest demon of them all, the noonday devil, who preys on the monk's peace of mind. To defeat him is to forecast victory over the other vices.[6]

HEEDING EVAGRIUS'S PRACTICAL ADVICE

Significant as his hermit's life of solitary detachment was, Evagrius knew from experience that it had to be complemented by the establishment of a community of Christians willing to persevere in prayer and to share material and spiritual goods. Seeking the solitude of the desert must be seen not as an end in itself but as a way of learning how to break apart the shell of our superficial securities and open up to the abyss of sin we all carry within us.[7]

Be God-Centered. Our embrace of this practice forces us to face how much our heart has been ruled by disordered impulses and passions typical more of a world-centered than a God-centered existence. Only when we relinquish what we deemed to be essential for our happiness do we begin to make real progress in the life of prayer. By means of this resolute clinging to God, we redirect our desires to their proper end; we let go of the disordered attachments to which we have clung and shift our attention from a self-centered perspective to a God-centered desire to obey God's will, motivated by love, not fear. Having discovered that nothing this world has to offer can take the place of God, we are able to forget "what lies behind and [strain] forward to what lies ahead" (Phil 3:13). Having detached ourselves from erroneous ideas devoid of docility, we are made ready by grace to contemplate the body of truth revealed by faith.

Be Tranquil. Characteristic of this liberation from the tyranny of the unruly passions that once enslaved us is the oft-repeated goal of *apatheia*, which is not a state of apathy, or insensibility, but a tranquil, undisturbed condition of the soul. It brings to full flowering the virtue of obedience, which bears fruit in humility and compunction of heart. As Evagrius reminds us:

> Remember your former life and your past sins and how, though you were subject to the passions, you have been brought into *apatheia* by the mercy of Christ. Remember too how you have separated yourself from the world which has so often and in so many matters brought you low. "Put this also to my credit (says Christ) that I preserve you in the desert and put to flight the demons who rage against you." Such thoughts instill humility in us and afford no entrance to the demon of pride. (*Praktikos*, 33:25)

Be More like Christ. The goal we seek is a return to the *synergy*, or the likeness to Christ lost by sin. On this battlefield of the heart, torn between our longing for peace and our combat with the "demons," Evagrius senses the need to further delineate the various forms these temptations, or *logismoi*, take. This Greek word points to his understanding of the passions and roaming thoughts that incline us to sin. Arising as they do within the human heart, the *logismoi* are the root causes of our disordered desires. They trigger the impulses that block our longing for God. As Evagrius describes each:

1. *Gluttony* cajoles us to forget our ascetical efforts, and thus victory over it is the first step in the repression of all the other *logismoi*.
2. *Impurity* leads us to lustful desires and actions.
3. *Avarice* causes us to resist the call to practice poverty of spirit.
4. *Sloth* tempts us to give up the pursuit of perfection since it deprives us of the fulfillment of our own will.
5. *Anger* evokes wrath and irritability in the face of injury.
6. *Acedia* makes us feel disgusted with the demands of the spiritual life.

7. *Vainglory* binds us to the need for public recognition of whatever good we do.

8. *Pride* causes us to live in the illusion that we can save ourselves without the constant help of God.

Be Vigilant. It does no good to try to stomp out our passions violently; rather, Evagrius advises us to exercise patience and be vigilant, allowing God to do the work of reformation in us. In other words, asceticism is not a question of rigid self-control but a quest for deeper faith and a response to prayer. Monks never imagine that they are the artisans of their own holiness; they simply give themselves up to Christ and trust in his saving work. The struggle against pride and the demons of ignorance that sustain it is the work of Christ in us *before* it becomes our work of cooperating with his grace.

Evagrius returns to the truth of his own experience: that the end stage of a virtuous life is *apatheia*, or liberation from the "lesser gods" that have dominated our lives. The virtues taught by Evagrius begin to free us from the debilitating effects of the eight *logismoi*, but we ought not to conclude that the state of *apatheia* to which we are led by grace implies a kind of emotionless or passionless existence. Because our emotions and passions have been calmed to such a degree, our interior life is open to new depths of prayer and loving service of the Lord. With *apatheia* comes a lessening of distractions in prayer, a feeling of calm amid the challenges of everyday life, and the absence—awake and asleep—of disordered emotions. Patience regarding our progress in the life of the Spirit facilitates the eight conditions that best effect these results. They are:

1. *Faith,* the starting point and the source of perseverance, which enables us to engage in the asceticism of detachment and to give up gluttony both physically and spiritually.

2. *Continence,* which helps us to overcome impurity and to resist the impulses of all lustful passions.

3. *Fear of the Lord,* which quells avarice and replaces it by reverence for God's will and trust in his providence.

4. *Patience,* which counteracts sadness or dejection, modifies our attraction to self-gratification, and increases our endurance of the crosses God asks us to carry.

5. *Tranquility*, which reduces anger and other volatile patterns of behavior.
6. *Peace*, accompanied by joy, which combats *acedia* and sloth.
7. *Hope*, or the expectation of true and lasting good, which redeems us from the despair bred by vainglory.
8. *Humility*, which weans us slowly but surely from the deceptions of pride and frees us from being dominated by deformed passions that are always opposed to charity.

Facilitating this integration are such experiences as avoiding distractions; fleeing from the emptiness of a merely worldly existence; taking time to be alone with the Alone; engaging in an intentional battle between vice and virtue; living without anxiety; overcoming discouragement; guarding against the demon of unchastity; cultivating deep humility; and especially, at times of temptation, making use of short prayers the moment we become conscious of the slightest sign of inward turmoil. In the state of unrest, our thoughts move aimlessly through our heads. We recall the past, anticipate the future, and plan what to do next. We see faces and places in unending succession. We lack the power to gather ourselves in one spot and to do God's will here and now rather than on our own timetable.

A sure mark of Christian maturity in the teaching of Evagrius is that prayer is not to be seen as a repression of passions but as a gentle, persistent act of detachment from the distractions associated with them. It is not a practice we do at special moments to seek nearness to God; it is who we *are to be* all the time. It is a ceaseless state of adoration in which the words and meanings of prayer are oriented to dedicating our first and last thoughts to God.

Growth in prayer and Christian perfection leads to a deeper regard for the dignity of our neighbor. Our whole life, every act and gesture, becomes a hymn of thanksgiving to God not only for what we have been given but also who Christ calls us to be. For Evagrius, grace works through nature: "At times just as soon as you rise to pray you pray well. At other times, work as you may, you achieve nothing. But this happens so that by seeking still more intently, and then finally reaching the mark, you may possess your prize without fear of loss" (*On Prayer*, 29:59).

John Cassian interpreted the doctrine of Evagrius for the Latin world; he pruned away some of the more severe strains of Evagrian teachings while retaining the essentials of the asceticism of the master—complete with its orientation to purity of heart as the pathway to contemplative prayer and its outflow in charitable acts. He validated Evagrius's key conclusion: that we must run away from evil and run toward the good.

Although the writings of Evagrius were replicated in different strains and in diversified forms throughout the Roman Empire, they also found their way into Syria, Armenia, and Persia. Above all, it was the Syrian Church that embraced the spirituality of Evagrius most completely. His works were widely circulated and copied, and many commentaries were written on the works of Evagrius by Syrian theologians.

In the Russian Orthodox tradition, his *Chapters on Prayer* are preserved in the spiritual body of work known as the *Philokalia*. Pseudo-Dionysius borrowed some of the basic elements of Evagrian theology, and through his writings those teachings influenced the Christian mystical writers of the Middle Ages, proving that the spiritual writings of Evagrius Ponticus are infused with such a longing for God that their influence on faith formation is as valid for our time as it was in his own.

Reflect Now

1. How would you describe the battlefield in your own heart between virtue and vice?
2. Do you see a connection in your life between tranquility (*apatheia*) and self-giving love (*agape*)?
3. What have you found to be the best way to liberate yourself from the tyranny of unruly passions that have dominated your life and hampered the full flowering of your growth in prayer?

Read More

Benedict XVI, *Great Christian Thinkers: From the Early Church through the Middle Ages* (Minneapolis: Fortress Press, 2011).

Douglas Burton-Christie, *The Word in the Desert: Scripture and the Quest for Holiness in Early Christian Monasticism* (New York: Oxford University Press, 1993).

Luke Dysinger, *Psalmody and Prayer in the Writings of Evagrius Ponticus* (London: Oxford University Press, 2005).

3

SEEK THE LORD AND LET YOURSELF BE FOUND

GREGORY OF NYSSA ON THE SOUL'S ASCENT TO GOD

Hope always draws the soul from the beauty which is seen to what is beyond, always kindles the desire for the hidden through what is constantly perceived. Therefore, the ardent lover of beauty, although receiving what is always visible as an image of what he desires, yet longs to be filled with the very stamp of the archetype.

—Gregory of Nyssa, *The Life of Moses*, 114

For St. Gregory of Nyssa (ca. 335–395), the ascent to God is as natural as our looking upward to the stars. What makes us humans different from any other form of life on earth is our longing to go beyond what we know to that unknown realm of longing for God. Our goal is to seek the Lord and let ourselves be found. We remain humble, knowing that we cannot propel ourselves on this way of ascent. Only God can reveal what it means to move ceaselessly upward, toward the heavens, forgetful of what is past and hopeful for the new graces that are to come.

MEET THE MASTER

Having played a prominent role in the second ecumenical council at Constantinople in 381, Gregory became known as one of the most creative theologians and mystics of the fourth century. His writings continue to strengthen the two lungs of Christianity, the Eastern and the Western Church. Among his most notable accomplishments is the formulation of the Church's Trinitarian doctrine.[1] In his mystical masterpiece, *The Life of Moses*, he presents an itinerary of the soul's ascent to God, suggesting that we are always in the process of being perfected, ceaselessly straining toward those things that are still to come.[2]

The spiritual ascent, symbolized by God's revelations of himself to Moses, begins with the dawning of faith; enters into the cloud that hovered over Mount Sinai, where what transpired between God and his messenger will never be fully known; and ends in the experience of God's presence in the darkness of incomprehensibility, which gives way paradoxically to the deepest light:

> For this reason we also say that the great Moses, as he was becoming ever greater, at no time stopped in his ascent, nor did he set a limit for himself in his upward course. Once having set foot on the ladder which God set up (as Jacob says), he continually climbed to the step above and never ceased to rise higher, because he always found a step higher than the one he had attained. (*Life*, Book II, 227:113–14)[3]

While the movement toward God follows the trajectory of Gregory's doctrine of *epectasis* (perpetual progress), it is to be expected that on this ascent we may lose our footing and plunge downward; we may believe we have reached the summit when we still have a long way to go.[4] Any boasting erodes the humility needed by earnest climbers; they thank God for not abandoning them, knowing with each step they take that they must be properly equipped and that they can do nothing by themselves alone.[5]

St. Gregory was the younger brother of St. Basil of Caesarea (330–379), and both of them were friends of St. Gregory of Nazianzus (329–389), the third person who formed the trio of Cappadocian Fathers of the fourth century. It was the rule of Basil that provided the basis for monastic life and practice in the Eastern Church and the teaching of Gregory of Nyssa that mounted one of the staunchest defenses of Christianity against the Arian heresy, which denied the fully human, fully divine nature of Jesus Christ.[6]

Besides his ability to synthesize mystical theology and philosophical reflection, Gregory had gifts for pastoral leadership and preaching that caught the attention of his brother Basil, who was the archbishop of Caesarea and who decided to name Gregory bishop of the town of Nyssa in his district so that he might help him in his struggle against the growing influence of the Arians. So effective was Gregory's defense of the true faith that he incurred violent opposition by the Arian bishops, who falsely accused him of misappropriating funds and had him deposed in 376.

After the death of the Arian emperor Valens in 378, Gregory returned to Nyssa and continued the fight to counter Arianism and its denial of the full equality of Father, Son, and Holy Spirit. He composed as well numerous Christian classics, including *On Virginity*, which proves that purity of heart is the foundation for the soul's union with God; *On Perfection*, which deals with the need to perfect our nature by living a virtuous life of thought and action; *The Life of Macrina*, a brief account of his sister's chosen vocation of virginity as the most simple yet heroic of virtues; and a commentary on the Song of Songs.[7]

Toward the end of his mission on earth, Gregory retired to a monastery near Constantinople where he practiced to everyone's edification his own teachings on asceticism and mysticism. Until his death in 395, he continued to epitomize post-Nicaean teaching on the mystery of the Trinitarian life and on all that he and Basil and their friend Gregory of Nazianzus had accomplished as defenders of the centerpiece of the Christian faith: the full humanity and the full divinity of Jesus Christ.

WE ARE ALWAYS ASCENDING

Drawn as he was to the infinite, inexplicable mystery of the Trinity, combined with the humbling truth of God becoming God-with-us, Gregory came to a unique description of the spiritual life as one of constant progress along a lifelong trajectory of ascent to God, or the pursuit of increasing, ever more virtuous perfection. Due to our fallen nature and our limited human condition, we never arrive, so to speak, but are always arriving. This progress toward divinization involves three stages: moving from the darkness of ignorance, through illumination, to the "divine darkness" of our relationship with the infinite and incomprehensible God.[8]

In *The Life of Moses*, Gregory draws upon the spiritual sense of the scriptures to reveal the metaphor of the soul's journey to God from enslavement to evil to freedom to pursue the good. He transforms the biblical narrative of the exodus event into a spiritual allegory depicting the place from which we must depart, the horizon to which we are heading, and the terrain we must traverse. The journey from slavery to salvation begins through the purifying power of radical detachment. We recall that Moses stands in awe before the bush that burns but is not consumed. Gregory says that this life-changing event signifies the calling and initial enlightenment of Moses's soul by God. He is told to take off his shoes (Ex 3:5), which represent, according to Gregory, "the dead and earthly covering of skins"—that is to say, what Paul calls "the flesh," the desires and passions of our fallen nature, "which . . . must be removed from the feet of the soul. When we do this the knowledge of the truth will result and manifest itself" (*Life*, Book II, 22:59–60).

Because the spiritual life entails an ongoing process of growth, we soon discover that true enjoyment consists in never ceasing to ascend to that "kindred Deity," who draws that which is his own to himself. Our Creator implants this longing in us, but many obstacles stand between us and union with God. Disobedience marred our likeness to God, but his image is etched on our soul. He gives us the redeeming grace we need to overcome the disordered desires that lead us to sin: "Since human nature was fashioned by the divine hands, and beautified with the unwritten characters of the Law, the intention of the Law lay in our nature in turning us away from evil and in honoring the divine" (*Life*, Book II, 215:110).

Once we expose these destructive thoughts and passions to the light of God's love and God's law, the truth of his Great Commandment penetrates into the depths of our being and begins the slow but steady process of their reform. In cooperation with the grace of God, we look, as it were, in the mirror of our interior life and see with utter candor what we must free ourselves from to be free for God.

To accomplish this, says Gregory, there may be times of both fight and flight. He tells us: "If, therefore, we by ourselves are too weak to give the victory to what is righteous, since the bad is stronger in its attacks and rejects the rule of truth, we must flee as quickly as possible from the conflict . . . to the greater and higher teaching of the mysteries" (*Life*, Book II, 16:58). This flight to freedom includes times of faltering and wandering from the path of holiness. The enemy will attack us through the return of old temptations, impulses to descend to lower satisfactions, and troubling images, all of which God will help us to subdue.

When these relapses occur, we may become downhearted, feeling that we are failures in the spiritual life; but ongoing battles like these do not indicate a falling away from faith: quite the contrary! For Gregory, we can only return to the land of likeness to God through a never-ending process of defeating vices and progressing in virtue. Gregory attributes our winning this battle to the presence and power of God in Christ, our Divine Defender. He makes it possible for us to drive away the destroyer, inviting us to put the blood of the Lamb on the entrance to the doorposts of our heart. This precious blood moves our whole being upward on the wings of grace. We "lay aside every weight" and "run with perseverance the race that is set before us" (Heb 12:1). In his interpretation of the passage from this earthly life to the life of heaven, Gregory says:

> For leaving behind everything that is observed, not only what sense comprehends but also what the intelligence thinks it sees, it keeps on penetrating deeper until by the intelligence's yearning for understanding it gains access to the invisible and the incomprehensible, and there it sees God. This is the true knowledge of what is sought; this is the seeing that consists in not seeing. (*Life*, Book II, 163:95)

CONFORMING TO GOD'S LOVING PLAN

Despite these advances toward the promised land, Gregory does not hide the fact that "the gnawings of desire are frequently active even in the faithful" (*Life*, Book II, 277:125). Never ought we to grow discouraged, for the

mystery of iniquity is no match for the mystery of the Cross. The nourishment we seek comes not from our own efforts to guarantee fulfillment but
from the free dispensations of divine grace. Though we may be caught at
times in an avalanche of sinful leanings, we learn to accept this struggle as
part of God's loving plan for us. Such recognition encourages gentleness with
ourselves and a corresponding avoidance of self-styled perfectionism. We
admit our limits and see them as blessings in disguise. We acknowledge in
humility how precious we are in the eyes of God, who draws us, despite the
inherent stubbornness of sin, to the liberating mountaintop of perfection.

In fact, Gregory adds, "The one limit of virtue is the absence of a limit"
(*Life*, Book I, 8:31). The nourishment we receive from reading holy scripture
and from living the life of discipleship moves us from irrational, deformed
eros to true, agapic love, where we do good not because we hope for reward
but because we have unbounded affection for the commandments God gave
us. We want to listen to what God asks of us and continue our journey to the
promised land with renewed intensity: "What then are we taught through
what has been said? To have but one purpose in life: to be called servants of
God by virtue of the lives we live" (*Life*, Book II, 315:135).

If the goal of this sublime way of life, ever ascending upward to God, is
to become God's servants and friends, then the first and foremost mark of
spiritual maturity is to live simply, freed from the weight of "evil append-
ages" (*Life*, Book II, 317:136). Restored in us are the *imago dei* and the
dignity bestowed on us by our Maker as we imitate our Beloved Savior
and conform to God's loving plan. Second, perfection of life, which aims to
complete the soul's ascent to God, must be grounded in the moral teachings
of the Church, that is to say, mysticism must flow forth from the firm soil
of asceticism.

One of the earliest of Gregory's ascetical treatises is *On Virginity*, written
in 370. In it he presents a picture of his brother Basil as the ideal model
of the ascetical-mystical life for laypeople and monks. He says that "it is
necessary for the one who wishes to learn the strictness of this life to be
taught by one who has achieved it."[9] Anyone who seeks to maintain the
virtue of virginity must have the witness of a convincing teacher. As Virginia
Woods Callahan notes, virginity is "the central virtue through which man
perfects himself and reaches his goal which is participation in the purity and

incorruptibility of God. It is the mediating force which brings God down to man and lifts man to God."[10]

Gregory insists that virginity ought not to be confined to bodily purity; it is to be seen in every activity since it is a necessary door to a holier life. He sees the entire divine economy, the whole chain of salvation, in the light of virginity. This chain reaches from the Three Persons of the Blessed Trinity and the angelic powers of heaven to humankind as its last link. Christ is the "archvirgin," and the Mother of Christ, Mary, the most striking example of virginity: "For what happened corporeally in the case of the immaculate Mary, when the fullness of the divinity shone forth in Christ through her virginity, takes place also in every soul spiritually giving birth to Christ."[11]

While not everyone is given the charism of physical virginity, all who follow Christ are called to virginity of the spirit. Such purity of heart cannot be reached by ascetical disciplines only; it is a gift given to us by grace, enabling us to partake in the glory of God.

Gregory posits that though the choice of celibacy puts us close to attaining the ideal of virginity, marriage is a state of life that must also be held in high esteem because, among other things, it releases us from the danger of caring only for ourselves. And yet Gregory also knew that, because the duties associated with marriage and family so often draw married couples to give the lion's share of their time to more secular pursuits, a celibate calling facilitates the pursuit of spiritual ideals more freely and inclusively. Gregory avoids the subtle dualism of those neoplatonic trends that would assume that spiritual pursuits mean freedom from the body or that virginity is by definition a holier state than nonvirginity. In this and other treatises, Gregory maintains a delicate interplay between the spirit and the body by never losing sight of the Incarnation of the Lord.

To assimilate ourselves to God is to live as far as possible the Christ-life of perfect virtue, but how can this be?[12] There is only one answer: we have been ransomed from the darkness of sin by Christ, our Liberator. Though our nature is fallen, our final destiny is secure. Since, in Gregory's words, we are the imprint of Christ's substance, we must accept in serenity that the journey to Christian maturity means first to be "filled with the blessings of peace, and then to communicate it to those who have need of it."[13]

Pursuing higher levels of virtue, we ascend toward the mountain of the ineffable knowledge of God and the contemplation of our true spiritual nature. The nearer we are to God, the more we see that he is incomprehensible, since God always transcends anything we can know of him. Christ, who is the power and wisdom of God, the protector and Savior of us all, encompasses everything divine and human in himself. The way we catch a glimpse of heavenly realities is through the symbols offered by the Church to those who have eyes to see, whose hearts are purified of sin, and whose thoughts regarding doctrine and faith are sound and steadfast. Communion with and conformity to God calls for a constant ascent since "all of us, with unveiled faces, seeing the glory of the Lord as though reflected in a mirror, are being transformed into the same image from one degree of glory to another; for this comes from the Lord, the Spirit" (2 Cor 3:18). For Gregory, the spiritual life is a never-ending orientation to the transcendent. We are constantly being drawn upward, but because of our limited human condition, we never arrive; we are always arriving.

Reflect Now

1. In what way does the exodus event, as a movement from enslavement to freedom, pertain to your life?
2. When relapses in the ascent of your soul to God occur, how do you handle them?
3. Where do you turn for spiritual nourishment when you feel the onrush of spiritual hunger? On which of the Christian classics have you begun to feast?

Read More

Hans Urs von Balthasar, *Presence and Thought: Essays on the Religious Philosophy of Gregory of Nyssa* (San Francisco: Ignatius Press, 1995).
Harvey D. Egan, *Soundings in the Christian Mystical Tradition* (Collegeville, MN: Liturgical Press, 2010).

John R. Willis, ed., *The Teachings of the Church Fathers* (San Francisco: Ignatius Press, 2002).

4

SAY YES TO GRACE AND CHANGE YOUR LIFE

AUGUSTINE OF HIPPO ON CONVERSION OF HEART

So I hurried back to the spot where Alypius was sitting, for I had put there the volume of the apostle when I got up and left him. I snatched it up, opened it, and read in silence the chapter on which my eyes first fell: "Not in rioting and drunkenness, not in chambering and impurities, not in strife and envying; but put you on the Lord Jesus Christ, and make not provision for the flesh in its concupiscences." No further wished I to read, nor was there need to do so. Instantly, in truth, at the end of this sentence, as if before a peaceful light streaming into my heart, all the dark shadows of doubt fled away.

—Augustine, *The Confessions of St. Augustine*, 202

The restless heart is an image everyone understands. It comes to rest only when we say yes to God's gracious call and choose to change our life. *The Confessions of St. Augustine* may surprise us by how familiar the events described sound. Who of us has not chosen passing pleasures over lasting love? Professional fame over life-changing faith? Resistance to grace over compunction of heart?

Falsehood is not foreign to any of us. Untruth stalks us like a pack of hungry wolves. We need help to pass safely through the shadowy woods of our oft-darkened world to the safe pasture of conversion to Christ.

MEET THE MASTER

The candid, detailed story of the conversion of St. Augustine, bishop of Hippo (354–430), reveals a man whose powerful intellect bowed to the force of faith and whose stubborn will gave way to the primacy of love.[1] Augustine's honorary title is Doctor of Charity. God's love for us and our love for God explains why "our heart is restless until it rests in [God]" (*Confessions*, Book 1, 1:1, 43). Until his conversion, Augustine admits to having confused lust with love. This turn to purity of heart meant replacing the short-term satisfaction of sensuality with a long-term relationship with the Triune God whom he adored.

Having turned away from God in favor of his own independence, Augustine fell captive to the pride that defaced humility and made it impossible for him to find the truth. When the time was right, God used the torrent of his passion to swallow up the stubborn fortifications of his pride; he experienced his own moral impotence and his need for redemption. His conversion did not entail a dualistic separation of body and spirit but a wholistic integration of sensuality and spirituality, of vital energy and intellectual clarity.

For Augustine, the converted heart is the symbolic center where body, mind, and spirit meet under the guidance of grace and transformation of heart becomes a reality. Augustine confesses that only when his heart broke open in repentance could God reach out and heal him, stirring his will to love and attracting him to good works. Augustine says that nothing is closer to God's "ears than a contrite heart and a life of faith" (*Confessions*, Book 2, 3:5, 67).

It was not until Augustine's heart became a barren land that he knew he had no place left to go but to God. With Christ as his helper and redeemer, he fled from his loveless ways and began a new life freed from "the gnawing cares of favor-seeking, of striving for gain, of wallowing in the mire, and of scratching lust's itchy sore." He says, with tears of compunction, "I spoke like a child to you, my light, my wealth, my salvation, my Lord God" (*Confessions*, Book 9, 1:1, 205–6). The prodigal son had returned at last to his Father's arms. Having said yes to grace, he changed his life—a lesson each of us must learn, however hard it may be.

We identify with Augustine, who admits to being a poor student in his early years, not because he lacked intelligence but because he failed to apply himself to serious study. Though he advanced to the head of the class at his new school in Carthage in 371, his motive for studying, as he confesses, was not a pure love of learning but a prideful desire to become a famous teacher. In Carthage, he fell prone to bad habits, ranging from sexual promiscuity to heretical beliefs. Following the death of his father Patricius in 372, he consorted with a mistress, who later bore him a son named Adeodatus. Between 372 and 373, Augustine read the writings of Cicero and chose to pursue the study of philosophy. Though an unvoiced longing for truth led him to the scriptures, he put them aside because of their unpolished style and turned instead to the Manicheans, who maintained that reason alone, literally mind over matter, could free people from error and lead them to the farthest reaches of spiritual awareness.

The religion of Mani, the founder of Manicheism, captivated Augustine. This false form of belief expressed a revulsion for the material world and became the rationale for ultra-ascetic practices. The body and the "dark side of life" (evil) were closely connected in Mani's mind. His adherents consisted of two classes or grades. Absolute celibacy was required only of the higher grade, the elect. Mani denied the Old Testament presupposition of the goodness of the material order of things and of their Maker. He summarily deleted texts in the New Testament that assumed either the order and goodness of matter or the inspiration and authority invested in them by virtue of the Old Testament accounts of creation. He interpreted reality from a dualistic perspective; cast his doctrine in a complex, elaborately pantheistic mythology; and explained the origin of evil as a primeval and ongoing conflict between Light and Dark.[2]

Augustine was involved with the Manicheans for nearly ten years. Their influence on him lingered until an episode that marked the start of his conversion. In 373, at the time of Augustine's greatest intellectual errors, Ambrose became the bishop of Milan. When at last the two men met, the bishop's calm, open demeanor revealed to Augustine the cauldron of mental and emotional turmoil that his own life had become. And as they continued to speak together, the bishop's wise counsel began to dispel the doubts Augustine felt. "And when I opened up my heart to receive the eloquence with which he spoke, there likewise entered, although only by degrees, the truths that he spoke" (*Confessions*, Book 5, 14:24, 131). Brick by brick, the wall of resistance he had built around himself began to crumble. Due in great measure to the force of his mother St. Monica's fervent prayers for her wayward son, he reached the point of admitting that nothing but faith could satisfy his quest for truth. Low as he had sunk, he never lost hope.

By 383, wearied by the dualistic philosophy of the Manicheans, Augustine went to Rome to establish an independent school of rhetoric. His ideals for critical and creative learning were high, but his attempts at instruction were short-lived since his students failed to pay their tuition. More by default than by desire he accepted a commission to teach in Milan. There his mother saw an opening to challenge her son to practice in private what he preached in public. She was with him in that city when he agreed to cease living out of wedlock. Even though he decided to leave his mistress while caring for the son she bore by him, he was still troubled by doubt and lustful desires as this oft-quoted sentiment reveals: "God make me chaste, but not yet."

Having met the bishop of Milan, to whom St. Monica introduced him, Augustine felt inwardly drawn to this man of prodigious erudition who was at the same time a beloved shepherd of wayward souls like his own. Here was a true disciple of Christ, as comfortable in the pulpit as in the corridors of political and academic power, as aristocratic as he was apostolic. Fluent in Greek, he acknowledged his debt to Plotinus, yet he did not allow pagan philosophy to override his conviction that it could not guide the seeker to the full truth. Only the Gospel of Jesus Christ could do that.

So inspiring were the personal life and powerful preaching of Ambrose that Augustine began to read the Bible, no longer with the arrogant intention to argue against it, but with a disposition of humble submission to the wisdom of the Word. Especially attractive to him were the epistles of another convert, Paul of Tarsus. Later a passage from his letter to the Romans would cause Augustine to banish his old self, put on Christ, and lead a life converted to the whole truth of Christianity.

In 385, when Augustine's mother came to Milan, she witnessed with joy the efficacy of her prayers. Her son had separated from his mistress and had started on a path compatible with the destiny God had in mind for him. Though his conversion was neither a simple process nor quickly accomplished, there were signs that a major change was in the offing. Augustine felt discontented with philosophical speculation that had no way of resolving the mystery and meaning of life and death. Nothing he found there satisfied the longing of his heart. Then one day in the month of September, 386, as he walked in his garden with his friend Alypius, Augustine heard what he thought was a child's voice chanting, "Take up and read." Finding the book of Paul's epistles open, his eyes fell on this passage from Romans 13:13–14: "Not in rioting and drunkenness, not in chambering and impurities, not in strife and envying; but put you on the Lord Jesus Christ, and make not provision for the flesh in its concupiscences" (*Confessions*, Book 8, 12:29, 202). At that moment, he tells us, all hesitation ceased, all doubts vanished. Alypius then picked up the book and found these words from Romans 14:1: "Now him that is weak in faith take unto you" (*Confessions*, Book 8, 3:30, 203). The two of them ran to tell Monica the good news so she could rejoice with them. At the age of thirty-two, her son had at last come home, not to the fleshpots of this world but to the rule of faith, not to the company of heretics but to the fatherhood of countless spiritual children who would come to rely on his wisdom and guidance.[3]

In due time, Augustine made his homecoming journey to Hippo with the idea of founding a monastery there. There was a scarcity of clergy in Africa in 391, and holy men were often conscripted for the priesthood by popular demand. When the people of Hippo witnessed Augustine's faith, they clamored for his ordination. Since he had no such desire, Augustine protested but to no avail. He was ordained in 392 and appointed as an aide to Bishop Valerius, whom he later succeeded. His chief duty as a priest seems to have been writing and delivering sermons, of which over four hundred have been preserved.

From 400 to 416, in addition to his pastoral duties Augustine devoted himself to writing his books on the Trinity, composing several commentaries on the scriptures, and preaching on the mystery of the Triune God. He reflected on what it means to baptized believers to be, so to speak, a little trinity in the Divine Trinity. In his masterwork *The City of God*, he traces the story of the human race from the creation of Adam and Eve through the fall of man to the birth of Christ and the establishment of the Church, especially at the time of the Roman Empire. He meditates upon salvation history not merely as a timeline but as the story of God's love for creatures as sinful as himself. Augustine's post-conversion gratitude for God's providential plan, culminating in our eternal happiness in heaven, grew stronger with each passing year of his life.

Along with his reputation as a prolific writer and leader of the Church in Hippo, Augustine emulated Ambrose's passion to be a humble pastor and an exemplary servant of the poor. He felt that it was his duty to cleanse the Church of heretical teachings, like the forms of agnosticism he had once adopted, and to prevent further erosion of doctrinal truths. He directed his attention to the Pelagian notion that human efforts were sufficient for salvation. He maintained that without the transforming grace of God, we are powerless to save ourselves.[4] He regretted his own history of abusing free will prior to his conversion. Had God not intervened to save him from the self-destructive paths he had chosen to follow, he would have been lost. Never would he forget how he looked everywhere for God, only to find him in his own heart.

Augustine died at the age of seventy-six in 430. A year before his death, the Vandals invaded Rome and threatened to destroy the fabric of religion and culture in Africa. Their attempts failed in great measure because of the bulwark of faith Augustine had built. Although Hippo fell captive the year he died, no invasion could close the floodgates of theology and spirituality released by the pen of this powerful Father and Doctor of the Church.[5]

GOD'S INDWELLING PRESENCE

Once Augustine realized that the Lord's dwelling place was within his own heart, his groaning ceased and his suffering made sense. Sinner that he was, he had sought God in all the wrong places: in Manichean dualism, which drew a dividing line between matter and spirit; in Donatist perfectionism, which demanded of him a sinless life before he could be loved and forgiven by God; and in Pelagian efforts to save himself by works devoid of faith in a merciful Savior. All such promises of self-salvation left Augustine's spirit arid. He looked for love outside himself and failed to see that God had all the while been inhabiting his own interiority:

> Too late have I loved you, O Beauty so ancient and so new, too late have I loved you! Behold, you were within me, while I was outside: it was there that I sought you, and, a deformed creature, rushed headlong upon these things of beauty which you have made. You were with me, but I was not with you. (*Confessions*, Book 10, 27:38, 254)

This retrospective look at his life's journey revealed to Augustine the meaning of every happening that comprised his fascinating history. For example, early in *The Confessions*, he recalls a boyhood episode of stealing some pears, saying, "For I stole a thing of which I had plenty of my own and of much better quality. Nor did I wish to enjoy that thing which I desired to gain by theft, but rather to enjoy the actual theft and the sin of theft" (*Confessions*, Book 2, 4:9, 70). That God loved him anyway, despite his being a runaway inflated with conceit, may explain why in so much of his spirituality he identifies with the scriptural accounts of the prodigal son and the publican praying in the Temple. These passages symbolized his lifelong struggle with the "demon of vainglory," which by his own admission was the central cause of his blindness. The only reason he wanted to distinguish himself as an orator was "for a damnable and inflated purpose, directed towards empty human joys" (*Confessions*, Book 3, 4:7, 81). As his personal testimony reveals, God thwarts the proud and exalts the humble: "I strove towards you, but I was driven back from you, so that I might taste of death, for you resist the proud" (*Confessions*, Book 4, 15:26, 109).

Almost at the exact moment when intellectually Augustine was convinced of his own ability to pierce the essence of truth, God thwarted his hubris and cast him into the throes of shameful disillusionment. The world of rhetoric, riddled as it was with heresy, almost made him a skeptic, denying that he could know anything for sure. By the time he encountered Bishop Ambrose, grace had reduced him to abject compunction of heart, to such brokenness of spirit that God could at last find room to insert in a soul darkened by doubt the light of faith:

> Yet even now, says the LORD,
> > return to me with all your heart,
> with fasting, with weeping, and with mourning;
> > rend your hearts and not your clothing.
> Return to the LORD, your God,
> > for he is gracious and merciful,
> slow to anger, and abounding in steadfast love,
> > and relents from punishing. (Jl 2:12–13)

CHANGING OUR HEARTS AND LIVES

For Augustine, the heart is not merely an organ that registers the way we feel; it is the center of our being where the battle between the good that we would do and the evil that we would rather not do rages in us until tears of compunction give way to full conversion. Only when we surrender to God do lesser goods lose their power over us. Only then can we begin the lifelong task of loving God with our whole being and our neighbor as ourselves.[6]

The heart is also "God's field" (see *Confessions*, Book 2, 3:5, 67), the place where God fertilizes the soil of our free will and attracts us through the action of grace to himself. God, says Augustine, is the "God-of-my-heart," the one who knows me through and through and who is my companion on the long road to self-knowledge through humility. As Augustine laments, "For where could my heart fly to, away from my heart? Where could I fly to, apart from my own self?" (*Confessions*, Book 4, 7:12, 100–101). This stark description of the divided heart, separated from its ground in God, gives way to the realization that God is nearer to us than we are to ourselves. After his conversion, Augustine experienced a cessation of alienation and a restoration of peace within his heart because of his surrender to the Lord, to whom he says: "Not with doubtful but with sure knowledge do I love you, O Lord. By your Word you have transfixed my heart, and I have loved you" (*Confessions*, Book 10, 6:8, 233).

Augustine found that the treasure he had sought was awaiting him from within. We catch a glimpse of God in contemplation, but our desire for the Godhead, for the fullness of the Trinity, can never be satisfied in this lifetime. We grow from longing to deeper longing and with Augustine "sing songs of love to you, groaning with unspeakable groanings on my pilgrimage, and remembering Jerusalem, with heart lifted up towards it" (*Confessions*, Book 12, 16:23, 317).

The story of Augustine's conversion follows a fascinating from-through-to pattern of decision and action. He moves *from* following people famous for their philosophical expertise but without faith; from succumbing to perilous pitfalls of desire; and from loving his own way, however blinding it might be. Then he moves *through* a recognition of how the providence of God had a hand in every event of his life; through doubt in his erring ways and attention to people of faith such as Monica and Ambrose; through the humiliation of watching his false systems of belief crumble under the piercing light of faith; and through the epicenter of a crisis of transcendence. Finally, he moves *to* peace and deeper faith; to a change of heart that requires an ongoing yes to God; to transformation of mind and will in love for God and others; and to the freedom of following his call in response to the inspiration and direction of the Holy Spirit.

The latter dynamic becomes the propelling force of Augustine's whole-hearted service of the Church. He experiences God with utter certainty, yet this taste only results in his Spirit-filled desire to know God more intensely than he could ever have imagined. God's Word has so transfixed his heart that nothing can compare to it, not even the "limbs made for the body's embrace" (*Confessions*, Book 10, 6:8, 233). Now the conversion of his heart proceeds from inward recognition of God to outward care and concern for others. Augustine had had enough of the pain of loneliness into which sin had plunged him. It had closed the door of his heart to God and neighbor, resulting in a nightmare of self-encapsulation.

Perhaps that explains why the first commitment Augustine made after his conversion was to form a community of friends in the Lord. His rule of love outlined a life of prayer and study, readying its adherents to care for the physical, intellectual, and spiritual needs of others. The contemplative scholar had become an active pastor, who pleaded for clemency for accused persons; who acted as a just and merciful judge in local disputes; who provided shelter for widows and orphans; and who enabled countless seekers to find the light of the Divine in what was once the darkness of their own sinful lives. His conversion, though a personal event, had profound ecclesial and social implications. Augustine was so in union with his faith community that in one of his sermons he said, "I am unwilling to be saved without you." Possession of God yields a nearness to God and others, whereas profession of sin means a distancing from God resulting in broken relationships, disunity, and distrust. We journey together with the Lord into a land of union and communion, governed by the rule of charity that has become the contemplative-active focus of our existence.

GOD IN PURSUIT OF US

The Confessions is the story of our pursuit of God made possible because from the beginning of time God has been in pursuit of us. Like Augustine, for us to grow in Christian maturity means to look appreciatively at all the events that have moved us from a self-centered to a God-centered life. Change of heart can only become a reality when we let our hearts be broken open by the reality of God. The solution to self-encapsulation is service of others in love.[7] By the grace of God, our once-hardened heart, aloof from sharing, becomes a servant's heart loving the least of these as Christ taught us to do.

In Book 9 of *The Confessions*, we find a profile of Christian maturity under the heading "The New Catholic." Ours is, as Augustine's was, a soul set free from the bondage of sin. The worldliness of the world has no more hold over us. We give thanks always and grow in the art and discipline of ceaseless prayer. In the first chapter of the final book of *The Confessions* (Book 13, 1:1, 335), Augustine reminds us that we long for God because God has breathed that longing into us. Trusting, as Augustine did, in God's prevenient grace prevents us from regressing to the spiritual immaturity associated with discouragement and the dejecting thought that our sins are unforgivable. Augustine was made new by the mercy of God, and so are we. He teaches us from experience the one biblical truth we must never forget: "You do not draw near to any but the contrite of heart, and you are not found by the proud, not even if they could number with curious skill the stars and the sands, and measure the constellations, and plot the courses of the planets" (*Confessions*, Book 5, 3:3, 115).

Because Augustine wrote *The Confessions* from a post-conversion per-spective, he was able to see in the light of grace the meaning of all that happened to him and how God used believers to turn his life around. He did not see, but they did, how much his will was enslaved to sin and what God would do with him once he was set free. He found that the treasure he sought awaited him within his own interiority. That is why his conversion story and his defense of the faith are as fresh today as when he first gave his restless heart to God. To experience the dwelling place of the Lord in the core of our being, we must counter pride with humility; allow our hearts to be broken open by the reality of God; and change self-seeking into selfless love for God and neighbor.

REFLECT NOW

1. Do you feel a need for ongoing conversion of heart? Why might this be so?
2. What helps you to develop a disposition of humble submission to the goodness, truth, and beauty of God's Word?
3. In what way do chastity and obedience facilitate your Christian com-mitment to sacrifice and service?

READ MORE

Don Brophy, *One Hundred Great Catholic Books: From the Early Centuries to the Present* (New York: Blue Bridge, 2007).

Peter Brown, *Augustine of Hippo* (Los Angeles: University of California Press, 2000).

Romano Guardini, *The Conversion of Saint Augustine*, trans. Elinor Briefs (Chicago: Henry Regnery, 1960).

5

REJOICE ALWAYS AND GIVE THANKS

To keep the thought of God always in your mind you must cling totally to this formula for piety: "Come to my help, O God; Lord, hurry to my rescue" (Ps 69:2). . . . This short verse is an indomitable wall for all those struggling against the onslaught of demons. It is an impenetrable breastplate and the sturdiest of shields. Whatever the disgust, the anguish, or the gloom in our thoughts, this verse keeps us from despairing of our salvation since it reveals to us the One to whom we call, the One who sees our struggles and who is never far from those who pray to him.

—John Cassian, *Conferences*, 132–33

To keep the thought of God always in our mind, to rejoice always and to give thanks, mark the beginning of our quest to pray unceasingly. When we become discouraged, we must cry silently or aloud, "God, come to my assistance; Lord, make haste to help me." The battle between virtue and vice that goes on in our heart is not easily overcome, but we can find solace in the advice given by St. Paul: "Do not be overcome by evil, but overcome evil with good" (Rom 12:21). We can begin to unmask the deceptions in our spirit by not merely *saying* prayers but *becoming* living prayer.

MEET THE MASTER

According to John Cassian (365–435), the spiritual life often begins with an experience of ego-desperation in which God strips us of every expression of selfish sensuality. He shows us the way to persevere in prayer and practice purity of heart. He learned these essentials of the desert tradition by becoming a disciple of great masters of prayer such as Evagrius Ponticus, under whose tutelage he lived and from whom learned the obstacles to and conditions for ceaseless prayer. He was also discipled by the desert masters, among others, Abba Moses and Abba Isaac.[1] These monks taught him that prayer must be grounded in a genial, realistic sense of everydayness, combined with the virtues of discretion, common sense, and moderation.

In addition to his influence on Eastern monasticism, Cassian's impact extended to Western spirituality. For example, St. Benedict of Nursia acknowledges the contribution of Cassian by recommending that his *Conferences* be read to the community each evening before Compline. Legend has it that St. Thomas Aquinas kept a copy of this book at his bedside for nightly reading, and Thomas à Kempis frequently cites Cassian's works in *The Imitation of Christ*. St. Teresa of Avila also mentions the *Conferences* in her autobiography. In his *Introduction to the Devout Life*, St. Francis de Sales indicates his indebtedness to the thought and practice of Cassian, all of which explain why, when he died, John had already attained the reputation of being a saint who lived what he taught and who wanted us while we were on earth to catch a glimpse of the kingdom of heaven.[2]

Cassian had a particular fondness for psalmody, not merely sung in the Divine Office but assimilated into the marrow of our being. There it gave birth to prayer so loving and intense that it transformed the heart and evoked a passion for the unseen disclosed already in this life. The Liturgy of the Hours, repeated reverently, taught the monks all they needed to know about their relationship with God, about the meaning of their failures and progressions in the spiritual life. By the cadence of chant and the raising of the mind and heart to God in song, they were able to discern what they felt within themselves and why they needed to etch these verses on their hearts by means of meditative reading and attentive listening to scripture.

Cassian's integration of scriptural wisdom, desert theology, and acute psychological insight was taught to him by the monks and masters from whom he learned the essentials of Christian discipleship. In his *Conferences* he adopts a question-and-answer dialogue focused on practices that unveil the link between virtuous living and unceasing prayer. The dominant image in *The Institutes* is that of the monk as an athlete who has gone into the desert to do battle with demons, that he may be led to the humility and obedience that came to fruition in the life of Jesus.[3] This connection between action and contemplation can best be seen in the perfection of charity. Cassian sees prayer not as an activity in which we engage to gain merits to earn our place in heaven but as a disposition of the heart that grows deeper day by day. To repent of habits of sin, to rejoice always and give thanks, to rely on the transforming power of grace—all of these conform our will to God's will in imitation of Christ.

Cassian taught that the ascetical disciplines associated with the struggle to overcome vices and exercise virtues come to fruition in the mystical life thanks to the grace of God. In contrast, Cassian's contemporary, Pelagius (344–420), erroneously claimed that the value of Christ's redemptive work was important in regard to instruction and example but that the proper direction of our will, tempered by the practice of asceticism, was sufficient to gain eternal life.[4] His interpretation of free will became known as Pelagianism, which held that the strength of the human will is sufficient to attain salvation without the aid of grace. Cassian, on the other hand, says that "before we pray, we must hasten to drive from our heart's sanctuary anything we would not wish to intrude on our prayers . . . but we will not be able to fulfill this injunction unless the mind within us is cleansed of the contagion of sin, is devoted to virtue as its natural good, and feeds continuously on the contemplation of the all-powerful God" (*Conference* 9, 3:102–3).

PRAYING WITH A PURE HEART

According to Cassian, "three things keep a wandering mind in place—vigils, meditation, and prayer. Constant attention to them and a firm concentration upon them will give stability to the soul.... [It] cannot be obtained except by a continuous effort made not for the sake of ambitiousness but because of the requirements of [one's] present way of life" (*Conference* 10, 14:139).

Cassian brought the practice of prayer without ceasing into dialogue with the scriptural counsel, "Be pleased, O God, to deliver me! O LORD, make haste to help me!" (Ps 70:1). God hurries to our rescue by means of such a formula for growing in prayer and Christian piety. We can repeat it as frequently as possible, whether we are at rest or preoccupied with countless tasks:

> This verse should be the first thing to occur to you when you wake up. It should precede all your thoughts as you keep vigil. It should take you over as you rise from your bed and go to kneel. After this it should accompany you in all your works and deeds. It should be at your side at all times ... write it upon the threshold and gateway of your mouth .. . place it on the walls of your house and in the inner sanctum of your heart. It will be a continuous prayer, an endless refrain when you bow down in prostration and when you rise up to do all the necessary things of life. (*Conference* 10, 10:136)

For Cassian, ceaseless prayer ought to be the central dynamic of our spiritual journey. It is the inspiration for growth in intimacy with the Lord because it facilitates inner stillness or tranquility of heart; it grants patience with our progress and encourages us to continue this practice, especially amid temptations by the fiercest demon of all, dejection, that can cast our soul into despair.[5] Cassian helps us to understand the sources of dejection so that we will not be caught off guard when it arises in our hearts, perhaps because of hidden anger due to the fact that our desire for some gain has not been realized.[6]

Embedded in both the *Conferences* and *The Institutes* is Cassian's reflection on the virtue of godly sorrow or repentance. He links repentance to the experience of compunction, which refers to our being inwardly pierced by sorrow for sin, combined with the joy of forgiveness, leading often to the point of tears as well as to shouts of joy. Compunction grants us the grace of reevaluating the direction our life has taken and of opening our hearts in profound silence or inarticulate sighs to the merciful presence of the Lord.

If ceaseless prayer and repentance are central to Cassian's spirituality, so, too, is renunciation or detachment. He says this virtue takes three forms. The first has to do with letting go of the riches of this world, which is to say, by not making them ultimate sources of our peace and joy, a prerogative that belongs only to God. Then it is necessary to renounce our past sins and vices and the erratic passions that despoil our conformity to Christ. Finally, to be really free we need to defocus our gaze on the visible as the only knowable reality and focus instead on cultivating a passion "for the unseen" (*Conference* 3, 6:85). These detachments from what is less than God have the effect of drawing us toward meditation on the things of God and onward to the practice of contemplation. Succinctly and with great clarity Cassian says, "With renunciation we can reach perfection. Bound to worldly riches we are visited with everlasting death" (*Conference* 3, 8:90).

GOD IS WITH US WHEN WE PRAY

Neither outward acts, however devout they may be, nor the mere observation of rules can lead us to oneness with the Trinity. To attain this depth of holiness, it is necessary to commit ourselves to the pursuit of unceasing prayer. We must erase the thoughts that despoil purity of heart as well as the vain acts that weaken virtuous living. Victory over vice is the key to finding our true self in God, whom we know loves us with a pure, sincere, and unbreakable bond of affection.

Cassian wants us to muster the courage to confront the zigzag motion that disrupts our hearts on a daily basis. No one expressed this dilemma better than the apostle Paul, who said, "I do not understand my own actions. For I do not do what I want, but I do the very thing I hate" (Rom 7:15). We feel this tension every time we act as beloved disciples of the Lord one minute and the next fall away from God's will through habitual sin. What heals this split in our hearts is not a denial of our fallen condition but the exercise of godly sorrow. Only then can we move, under the gentle prodding of grace, from the arid soil of seemingly endless inner conflict to the fertile soil of lasting peace.

Our greatest help on this journey are the three theological virtues of faith, hope, and love. Cassian shows how much they sustain us and why we ought to draw upon them daily for the strength we need to imitate Christ:

> For it is *faith*—with its fear of the judgment and punishment to come—which brings about the decline of sin's contagion. It is *hope* which draws our mind from the things of the present and which in its anticipation of heavenly rewards spurns all the pleasures of the body. And it is *love* which fires us to long for Christ, to be zealous for the fruit of the spiritual virtues and to detest utterly whatever is contrary to these virtues. (*Conference* 11, 6:144; italics mine)

The result of these three infused gifts is to move us from slavery to sin to a reclaiming of our true identity as children of God. We leave behind the complexity of disobedience to go toward the simplicity of submission to the will of God, resulting in pure prayer, so concentrated on giving praise and glory to God that we "will be joined to him in a never-ending unshakeable love, and it will be such a union that our breathing and our thinking and our talking will be 'God'" (*Conference* 10, 7:129–30).

The lasting fruit of contemplation and its outflow in service to others prevents any deviation from our longed-for goal of union with God. Along the way, the Holy Spirit may illumine the scriptures to such a degree that their meaning appears to be revealed to us in practice before we comprehend it intellectually. The words are alive and active like a sharp-edged sword that cuts through bones and marrow (see Heb 4:12). By the grace of God, we attain the purest kind of prayer, which "centers on no contemplation of some image or other. It is masked by no attendant sounds or words. It is a fiery outbreak, an indescribable exaltation, an insatiable thrust of the soul. Free of what is sensed or seen, ineffable in its groans and sighs, the soul pours itself out to God" (*Conference* 10, 11:138).

As we rise on the wings of grace to this high point of love, we realize that the main task we face is not to try to understand the mystery that has embraced us but "to cling always to God and to the things of God" (*Confer-ence* 1, 8:42). Even at this height of intimacy with the Trinity, we recognize that we are always in need of redemption. Humble admission of sin protects us from ever forgetting that we are dependent on God for everything.

Cassian offers many avenues to amend our life and correct our faults, from the formative reading of holy scripture to the practice of monastic moderation and hospitality. Unceasing prayer, together with purity of heart, frees us to ponder supernatural truths unknown or unattended to when we were preoccupied with worldly attachments. To pray unceasingly, we must keep the thought of God always in our mind while humbly asking the Lord under all circumstances to hasten our rescue. In this way we move from merely saying prayers to becoming living prayer.

Now our goal is to maintain the peace of Jesus amid the ministry he asks us to do. This rhythm of unceasing prayer and charitable action can be sustained by means of meditation on holy scripture, psalmody, and continual reflection on the prayer that Jesus taught us (see *Conference*, 9, 18–25:111–16). Its interiorization enhances our ability to conform to Christ to such a degree that the love of the Trinity hidden in our heart comes to fruition in daily life: "Not to be jealous, not to be puffed up, not to act heedlessly, not to seek what does not belong to me, not to rejoice over some injustice, not to plan evil—what is this and its like if not the continuous offering to God of a heart that is perfect and truly pure, a heart kept free of all disturbance?" (*Conference* 1, 6:41).

REFLECT NOW

1. Do you agree that ascetical discipline must underpin the practice of contemplative prayer? Why or why not?
2. Have you felt in your heart the battle between the good you want to do and the evil you end up doing?
3. Do you experience repentance as a healing balm made up of two com-mingled ingredients: the sorrow of sin and the joy of forgiveness? Why is compunction so important to a Christian's spiritual life?

READ MORE

Owen Chadwick, *John Cassian* (London: Cambridge University Press, 1968).

John J. Levko, *Cassian's Prayer for the 21st Century* (Scranton, PA: University of Scranton Press, 2000).

Alister E. McGrath, *Christian Spirituality: An Introduction* (Malden, MA: Blackwell Publishing, 1999).

6

REMAIN AT
THE SAME TIME
CONTEMPLATIVE
AND ACTIVE

BENEDICT OF NURSIA ON
BALANCING WORSHIP AND WORK

First of all, every time you begin a good work, you must pray
to God most earnestly to bring it to perfection.
—Benedict, *The Rule of Benedict*, 20

How often have we felt as if we were living a split existence? Worship on
Sunday, work on Monday. The answer is to live not an either-or but a both-
and way of life, consisting of *ora* (prayer) and *labora* (labor) in ongoing
interaction with one another. We want the Martha in us on kitchen duty
to be in partnership with the Mary resting at the Lord's feet. This ebb and
flow from contemplation to action is the rule that governed St. Benedict's
life. It helps us at every moment to serve the Lord with a blessed balance of
functionality and spirituality.

MEET THE MASTER

St. Benedict (ca. 480–550) was born in Norcia, a village high in the mountains, northeast of Rome. By the time he wrote his Rule, around 530, he realized that he had been called by the Lord to establish a school of love and service where every good work would begin with prayer.[1] Labor without leisure leads to busy modes of efficiency devoid of deeper meaning, just as religious services with no intention of serving the community can be a source of isolating individualism, resulting in a "Jesus-and-I" piety devoid of Christian care.

Serving God prayerfully with the zeal of accomplishing good works is the only sure way to abide by Gospel values. Then we can apply ourselves to fulfilling the Divine Will in all that we are and do: "Never swerving from God's instructions, then, but faithfully observing God's teaching in the monastery until death, we shall through patience share in the sufferings of Christ that we may deserve also to share in the eternal presence" (*Prologue*, 29).

Benedict assures his monks that if they want to dwell on earth as a foretaste of heaven, they must go forward by means of good deeds or this outcome will elude them. He introduces the entire Rule with these words: "Listen carefully, my child, to my instructions, and attend to them with the ear of your heart" (*Prologue*, 19). To listen is to obey the authority of the abbot, who is obliged to pray and work in obedience to the Lord himself. A monk has to be a good listener, emulating Jesus, who paused in prayer and silent presence to the Father. Only then did he teach the people, assuage their hunger, and heal their ills.

Benedict warned his monks that without prayerful listening they risked the endless drifting of purposeless days, betraying their vocation to become workmen in God's workshop. Listen! Obey! These are the indispensable dispositions at the root of spiritual vitality. To be still is the best way to prevent ourselves from debasing other people and substituting mere functionalism for quiet, dedicated service.

Throughout the Rule, Benedict shows that good actions flow from converted hearts, which is to say that outer work (*labora*) is always the result of inner prayer (*ora*). Without a doubt, Benedict composed his Rule from the wisdom of experience. For three years he lived at Subiaco in a solitary cave, devoting himself to prayer and conversation with God. So many sought his guidance that he had to erect twelve cells in the valley. In each of them a number of monks lived under a superior while he himself directed the community as a whole and introduced young monks to the monastic life.[2] These tiny seeds produced the tree of Benedictine spirituality that spread throughout the West in a monastic heritage as alive today as it was in its earliest era. The master transmited to his disciples not abstract doctrine but a way of life. His life-giving word, encompassing the Rule's seventy-three chapters, unlocks the secret design of sanctity and service God intends for all of us:

> This is advice from one who loves you; welcome it and faith-
> fully put it into practice. The labor of obedience will bring
> you back to God from whom you had drifted through the
> sloth of disobedience. This message of mine is for you, then,
> if you are ready to give up your own will, once and for all,
> and armed with the strong and noble weapons of obedience
> to battle for Jesus, the Christ. (*Prologue*, 19)

By 529, in response to the number of monks that continued to gather around him, Benedict relinquished his solitude and moved to Monte Cassino, once the site of a pagan temple dedicated to Apollo. Here he wrote the Rule that became the cornerstone of Benedictine life, in which contemplation becomes the ground of action and ongoing conversion of heart.[3]

Benedict taught that the customs, observances, and settings of the common life must all incarnate total abandonment to God. Benedict details examples of his juridical genius from kitchen service (chapter 35 of the Rule), to the times for meals (chapter 41), to clothing and footwear (chapter 55), to the reception of visiting monastics (chapter 61).

While the majority of ancient rules were written for a single monastery, Benedict wrote for several foundations dispersed in different regions and provinces. This need may account for the Rule's universality and its appeal to monks of diversified backgrounds, ranging from simple serfs to members of the nobility, from manual laborers to learned scholars.

St. Gregory the Great captures the heart of the Benedictine tradition in the *Dialogues*, written in 593.[4] There he describes how and why Benedict fled from the moral decay of Rome to find freedom in solitude. The seedbed of his holiness was established in Subiaco, where he spent days and nights in prayer, doing battle with the demons, practicing virtue, and performing good works. St. Gregory devotes the second book of the *Dialogues* to St. Benedict, painting a picture based not so much on recorded historical facts as on the miracles that revealed the depth of his communion with Christ and the breadth of his ability to attract so many followers. So successful was Benedict that he soon became the victim of envy and jealousy among some early followers. As Gregory tells it, they balked at adhering to the depth of conversion their abbot expected of them. So upset were they that they tried to poison his wine at a meal; no sooner had Benedict made the Sign of the Cross over the pitcher than it shattered.

St. Gregory also tells of what happened to a monk named Placid, who fell into a lake and drifted away from shore into deeper water where he would have drowned. Back in the monastery, Benedict somehow knew what had happened. He blessed another monk named Maurus and sent him to rescue Placid. Maurus immediately sought out the soaked Placid and pulled him to safety. Only then did Maurus realize that he had been running on the surface of the water! Upon hearing of the rescue, Benedict refused to take credit for the miracle. Instead, he attributed it to Maurus's obedience. Yet Placid claimed that when he was being brought to shore, he saw the abbot's cloak draped over his head.

Thanks to the *Dialogues*, we also learn of the last conversation between Benedict and his twin sister, Scholastica, a holy nun who lived in a convent not far from her brother's monastery in Monte Cassino. Three days before her death, she asked God to allow her brother, contrary to the Rule, to extend their visit all night long so that they could continue to converse about their mission on earth and the joys awaiting them in heaven. Benedict declined, reminding her that monks were required to return to the monastery before darkness fell. But God heard his sister's prayers. A raging storm flared up, making it impossible for Benedict to hasten homeward. As their night together gave way to the dawn of a new day, the siblings listened to God in the love they shared. As to her request, Scholastica simply said, "When I appealed to you, you would not listen to me. So I turned to my God and he heard my prayer."[5]

The day she died, as St. Gregory tells us in the *Dialogues*, Benedict saw his sister's soul soar heavenward. So earnestly did he pray for her that, dark as it still was, he beheld a shaft of light shining down on him from above. In this single ray, more brilliant than the sun, he saw what appeared to be a vision of the whole world united in one beam. Such, he concluded, was his beloved sister's parting gift to him: "Surely it is no more than right that her influence was greater than his, since hers was the greater love."[6]

REAPING THE LASTING FRUITS OF CONTEMPLATIVE LIVING

Why the Rule had such an influence on the Church from the time of its composition through the Dark Ages and in many forms of monastic life today may lie in the foundational virtues that comprise its teaching: stability, obedience, humility, and charity. Conversion to this Gospel way of living begins when we give up our own will and guard our hearts from the tendency to waywardness, disobedience, vainglory, and a lack of love.

In the first chapter of the Rule, Benedict describes four kinds of monks. The first are *cenobites*, who seek the highest ideals of holiness in accordance with the prescribed ways of living that anchor them to their monastic family. Their dedication to the Gospel has been so interiorized that they edify all whom they encounter without calling undue attention to themselves. *Hermits*, or *anchorites*, are those who stand on the front line of the battle with evil in all its insidious forms. Because they lead intensely disciplined lives, God makes them competent enough to engage in lonely combat with the powers of darkness. Contrast them to the *sarabites*, who live in little groups without serious guidance and who are prone to please themselves. Guideless as they are, they hide their self-serving ways from authority figures and think they can even hide from God. *Gyrovagues* represent the collapse of the monastic ideal. They end up as wanderers who produce no spiritual fruit no matter in what monastery they live.

True to the ideals of monastic life defined in the first three chapters of the Rule, cenobites and hermits submit to the obligations inherent in the vowed life and to the authority invested in the abbot, whereas sarabites and gyrovagues ignore the requirements of stability and obedience in favor of getting their own way and forfeiting the necessity of charitable giving. A disciple who refuses to obey lawful authority and to practice the Great Commandment cannot expect to follow Christ.

In the fourth chapter of the Rule on the tools for good works, Benedict rehearses the commandments to love and not kill, to be generous and not steal, and to speak the truth and not bear false witness as the most nourishing spiritual food we can enjoy for a lifetime. Good works such as clothing the naked and visiting the sick are the fruits of a life grounded in prayer, where the love of Christ comes before all else. There can be no room in such a heart for wrongful thoughts or deceptive lies. Sarcasm dies and cynicism shrinks when we cultivate habits of holy reading, compunction, and good conduct: "Do not aspire to be called holy before you really are, but first be holy that you may more truly be called so" (*Rule*, 4:55).

Since the forces of disobedience have plagued humanity since the Fall, it comes as no surprise that Benedict devotes the whole of chapter 5 to what it means to follow the will of God and to identify with his beloved Son. As Benedict reiterates in this chapter, the key to ongoing conversion is unhesitating obedience. This yes to the Father is the chief characteristic of the life of Christ. Through docility we become an instrument of God—a helper, never a hindrance, to our own and others' spiritual progress.

Insofar as we succumb to the foul fruits of disobedience, we risk incurring the habit of sin and a laissez-faire attitude toward wrongdoing. Presumption upon the mercy of God takes the place of obedience and self-control. What follows is a spirit of rebellion against our superiors and the disruption of community life, especially by unrestrained speech (see chapter 6) and constant grumbling. We make judgments about others or act in a demeaning fashion toward them. We focus on our own importance and judge others through the lens of our own lack of integrity. We might go so far as to make a hypocritical confession and shun reproof, become defensive about our sins, or seek to justify them.

THE LADDER OF SPIRITUAL MATURITY

The centerpiece of Benedictine spirituality is humility, to which Benedict devotes the whole of chapter 7 of the Rule. No matter what we do or experience, no matter how engaging or mundane a task, humility enables us to view the whole of life from a divine perspective. In this chapter Benedict proves that this virtue is essential to becoming a true follower of the Master. Without humility, meddling in others' affairs becomes second nature, as does the secret assertion that we are wiser than they are. Singularity or the proud esteem of our self-justified ways replaces community concern. Boasting and talkativeness, silly mirth, levity of mind, bouts of unreasonable joy or profound sadness, and curiosity regarding what is not our concern—all such foul fruits go counter to the school of love Benedict initiated. However nourished we may be by scripture and the masters, Benedict felt that only on the day of judgment will the Workman's (Christ's) work be complete, for then we shall rest in humble adoration of the Workman whose work we are.

It is only by keeping the exercise of humility in the forefront of our consciousness that we move from self-exaltation to a state of likeness to Christ in our internal and external life. Even a brief review of chapter 7 reveals Benedict's ability to trace our advance from the beginning stages of discipleship to the summit of conformity to Christ as active contemplatives and contemplatives-in-action.

1. *Holy fear.* The first step or mark of Christian maturity is keeping the fear of God always before our eyes, which helps us to avoid sin and monitor our decisions and deeds from God's perspective. Holy fear inspires us to reevaluate our actions in regard to both prayer and community participation. According to Benedict, we must always be fearful of allowing selfish motives to weaken the influence of God's Word in our everyday life.

2. *Surrender of the will.* The second step emphasizes that we should not love our own will, or take pleasure in the satisfaction of selfish desires; rather we must imitate Christ's actions and say with the Lord: "I have come ... not to do my own will, but the will of him who sent me" (Jn 6:38). We must avoid any behavior that is not inspired by humble cooperation with the infinite grace that enlightens our finite nature.

3. *Obedience.* The third step requires submission to our superiors (a bishop, a pastor, or a spiritual director, to give a few examples) in imitation of the obedience of Jesus to his Father's will. As we read in Philippians 2:8, he "became obedient to the point of death—even death on a cross." Obedience counters the notion of personal autonomy and the egocentric assumption

that "I am the captain of my ship and the master of my fate." All such illusions erode the spiritual maturity essential for discipleship.

4. *Endurance in suffering.* Exercised in favorable as well as unfavorable circumstances, obedience forecasts the fourth step: being willing to embrace suffering and endure it for Christ's sake. This step requires that we deny ourselves for the sake of carrying life's crosses in the certitude that they will draw us to deeper intimacy with the Lord.

5. *Unguarded confession.* The fifth step reminds us of the importance of not concealing from our confessors any of our sinful thoughts and wrongdoings. A humble confession, full of integrity, allows us, as Psalm 36 says, to make known our ways to the Lord and hope in him. Then, too, Psalm 31 reminds us that we will experience God's forgiveness to the degree that we acknowledge our faults and offenses.

6. *Humble toil.* The outcome of these first five steps happens on the sixth rung of the ladder of humility, which enables mature Christians to be content with the lowest and most menial tasks. The desire to be insignificant and no better than a beast of burden before the Lord cancels all prideful attempts to be the boss! Tasks we once found to be annoying or tedious have a profound meaning when we consider ourselves no more than useless servants (see Lk 17:10).

7. *Utter dependence upon God's providence.* The seventh step interiorizes this feeling of unworthiness and deepens the awareness of our depending on God for everything. We see every opportunity for being humbled, even for being humiliated, as a blessing that enables us to let go of all self-centeredness and to put on the mind of Christ (see 1 Cor 2:16).

8. *Looking together toward Christ alone.* The eighth step reveals a penchant in our heart to efface ourselves by pointing instead to Christ. We foster a wise blending of solitude and togetherness, of silence and speaking, of worship and work.

9–11. *Control the tongue, eschew careless words, and speak with gentleness.* The ninth, tenth, and eleventh steps of humility urge us to control our tongue and temper our tendency to be too talkative. We first listen and only then do we speak. St. Benedict cautions that an excessive need for words does not always produce charitable results. He also warns us not to engage in derisive laughter or cynical humor. Rather we are to speak gently with patience and modesty, never murmuring or complaining under our breath. Is it any wonder that putting empty speech and idle gossip to rest permits the hearing of God's voice at all times and in all places?

12. *Walk in the truth.* On the twelfth rung, in both thought and action, we walk in the truth of who we are and do what God wills in daily life. To follow this classical master's steps of humility leads to a transformation of heart and a change of life that comprises a blueprint for Christian maturity in our own and every age. To paraphrase St. Benedict's prayer in chapter 72, "May we value nothing whatever above Christ himself and may he bring us all together to eternal life."

REFLECT NOW

1. What do you try to do on a daily basis to find the balance between worship and work?
2. Why is the virtue of humility the key to Christian maturity? Why is it so essential for companionship with Christ?
3. What situations and relationships in your life benefit most from obedience and conformity to Christ?

READ MORE

Michael Casey, *A Guide to Living in the Truth: St. Benedict's Teaching on Humility* (Ligouri, MO: Liguori Publications, 1999).

Dwight Longenecker, *St. Benedict and St. Thérèse: The Little Rule & The Little Way* (Huntingdon, IN: Our Sunday Visitor, 2002).

Adalbert de Vogüé, *Reading Saint Benedict: Reflections on the Rule* (Kalamazoo, MI: Cistercian Publications, 1994).

7

LIVE IN AWE OF THE MYSTERY

PSEUDO-DIONYSIUS ON
THE WAY OF UNKNOWING

My argument now rises from what is below up to the transcendent, and the more it climbs, the more language falters,
and when it has passed up and beyond the ascent, it will
turn silent completely, since it will finally be at one with him
who is indescribable.
—Pseudo-Dionysius, *The Complete Works*, 139

Life is a mystery. No matter how much we know, there is so much more that
eludes us. We live between two awesome unknowables: birth and death.
When we face the great unknown, we can cower in fear or rise up in faith.
In awe and adoration, we believe though we do not see.

That is why mystical theology is often associated with the way of
unknowing; it expresses our ultimate inability to explain God's ways. We
are at a loss for words to pierce the unknown depths of God's mystery; it
transcends all knowledge. It is a light in the darkness that the darkness can
never grasp. Our only response is to abandon ourselves to God, whose ways
will forever baffle us.

Reason gives way to faith, which opens up new doors of perception,
beyond the visible to the Invisible. We leave behind what we know and cross
the threshold to behold a mystery that surpasses all knowledge and draws us

into the heart of pure love. As Pseudo-Dionysius confirms, at this threshold between knowing and unknowing language falters, and we fall into silence, for who can describe what awaits us beyond the realm of words?

MEET THE MASTER

Pseudo-Dionysius (fifth or sixth century), an enigmatic yet profoundly influential master of mystical theology, may have been a Syrian monk who wrote under the pseudonym of Denys or Dionysius the Areopagite, whom Paul the apostle refers to as one of his first-century converts (Acts 17:34). His writings stress the utter inability of the human mind to penetrate the impenetrable abyss of the mystery of God.

Emphasis on this truth stems from one aspect of mystical theology known as the *via negativa*, the negative or apophatic way, which focuses on the nature of the soul's ecstatic union with God beyond the reach of every rational process. One of its main proponents is Pseudo-Dionysius, who formulated in a more systematic way the experience of the soul entering into what he calls the "dazzling darkness" of presence to the Divine Presence. His book, *The Mystical Theology*, was translated into Latin in the ninth century and came into general vogue in the twelfth century.[1] The author of *The Cloud of Unknowing*, which dates from fourteenth-century England, acknowledges his indebtedness to Dionysius.[2] Traces of his influence are prominent in the writings of St. John of the Cross, who says: "It is noteworthy that, however elevated God's communications and the experiences of his presence are, and however sublime a person's knowledge of him may be, these are not God essentially, nor are they comparable to him because, indeed, he is still hidden to the soul."[3]

In the context of the *via negativa*, the soul acknowledges the impotence of every human attempt to penetrate the veil that stands between us and God, before whose allness our human nothingness bows in humility. Beyond all attempts to name God, says Pseudo-Dionysius, God remains unknowable, a being beyond being who resides in the dark reality of the superessential nature of the Godhead that will always and forever defy definition.[4] Awe overtakes us as we pass in wonder beyond anything we can perceive or know into the darkness of unknowing. Being lifted into the realm of pure faith leaves us speechless. Reason gives way to receptivity to the mystery of the Trinity. The paradox is that we, who want to know everything, thank God for leading us beyond what our mind can grasp by revealing how little we really know.

Even the cleverest concepts cannot exhaust the unknown depths of the Divine.[5] The fear expressed by Pseudo-Dionysius in *The Mystical Theology* is that our knowledge of created things may evoke the temptation to "learned arrogance," which destroys "learned ignorance." It is this quality of incomprehensibility that keeps us humble and that lets us know God in love beyond thought.

The way of unknowing relies not on abstract concepts but on communion with the living God; it leads not to an absence, to an utter emptiness, but to a new kind of fullness. The Unknowable God, known to the disciples of his Son, Jesus, is not an impersonal force but a presence whose love is without measure. In this ecstatic experience of meeting One God in Three Persons, we pass from particulars to universals, arriving at the superessential darkness, which outshines and obliterates the light shed by sensible things. With Pseudo-Dionysius we pray:

> Lead us up beyond unknowing and light,
> up to the farthest, highest peak
> of the mystic scripture,
> where the mysteries of God's Word
> lie simple, absolute and unchangeable
> in the brilliant darkness of a hidden silence.
> (*The Complete Works*, 135)

Interest in the *via negativa* has been revived in our day, thanks to a renewed exploration of the meaning and practice of contemplative prayer. As people grow more disillusioned with scientism, functionalism, and pragmatism, they may sense in themselves a readiness to leave the realm of logical analysis and plunge into the abyss of needing not to penetrate the mystery but to meet God in love and humility. Reason represents only one wing of truth; the other is faith. In the Dionysian sense, it enables us to "[belong] completely to him who is beyond everything . . . [we are] supremely united by a completely unknowing inactivity of all knowledge, and [we know] beyond the mind by knowing nothing" (*The Complete Works*, 137).[6]

KNOWING GOD

The way of unknowing leads not to the terror of empty spaces but to living in awe. It leads us to know God, even though we can never comprehend God's essence with our created intellect. God remains an infinite mystery to reason alone, yet reveals himself to us as Father, Son, and Holy Spirit, as a Trinitarian unity of Creator, Redeemer, and Sanctifier. God is at one and the same time transcendent and immanent. While always being above and beyond us, God draws us into a relationship of intimacy that is more real to us than we are to ourselves.

There will always remain about the Godhead an "irrational residue," which escapes analysis and cannot be expressed in concepts. The unknowable depth of things constitutes their true, indefinable essence, making it impossible for us to define God in words, concepts, or structures. The mystery we contemplate is beyond all earth-bound attributes:

> It suffers neither disorder nor disturbance and is overwhelmed by no earthly passion. It is not powerless and subject to the disturbances caused by sense perception. It endures no deprivation of light. It passes through no change, decay, division, loss, no ebb and flow, nothing of which the senses may be aware. None of all this can either be identified with it nor attributed to it. (*The Complete Works*, 141)

The Dionysian texts also extend the meaning of the word *mystical* to any interior experience of the Divine as a mystery within us and yet beyond us. In this sense, the Holy Eucharist is preeminently mystical in its proclamation of the fullness of the Gospel promise that bread and wine become the Body and Blood of Christ. Reason may prompt us to discover the bond between us and God, but, at a certain point, we come up against a barrier beyond which reason cannot go. Of all that we know and can say about God, to our finite tongue God remains infinite and indescribable. All particular expressions of God's perfection, however lofty they may be, are inadequate to describe the reality of who God is in his essence.

ABIDING WITH THE MYSTERY

According to Pseudo-Dionysius, our natural way of knowing through our senses must be complemented by a divine way of knowing in which God alone is the object of our faith and the agent of our transformation. While we know God's attributes by meditation on God's actions, there will always be about God a mystery that escapes our analysis. By accepting the darkness of our ignorance and not being discouraged by it, we reach what is above reason or verbal expression. At this profound moment of awe-filled abiding with the Divine Presence, we are brought by grace to the threshold of a peace that surpasses understanding, to a totally gifted moment of intimacy with God and inner harmony with self and others.

Intellectual conceptualizing allows us to know ourselves as participating in the Divine, but the only gift that lifts us beyond feeling and beyond reasoning is faith. Our soul needs to be freed from multiple distractions so that we can be free to worship God in spirit and truth. The pure of heart who see God accept their utter inability to know the mind of God. We remain in awe like poor beggars, beseeching God for guidance:

> My advice to you . . . is to leave behind you everything perceived and understood, everything perceptible and understandable, all that is not and all that is, and, with your understanding laid aside, to strive upward as much as you can toward union with him who is beyond all being and knowledge. By an undivided and absolute abandonment of yourself and everything, shedding all and freed from all, you will be uplifted to the ray of the divine shadow which is above everything that is. (*The Complete Works*, 135)

To truly know God, in a union transcending all knowledge, we must let go of what may be known by our senses or our understanding. We must renounce overattachment to the world of created things so that we can gain access to the *un*created. This renunciation frees us from perceiving only what eyes can see, ears can hear, or tongues can taste. While these touches may offer us hints of the Infinite, the problem is that we may be tempted to attach ourselves to them rather than go beyond them to a realm of loving knowledge of the ineffable, which transcends thought. This kind of knowing is felt intuitively, even if it defies reason or understanding.

Only if we abandon all that is not of God (what is impure) may we receive the grace we need to scale the supreme heights of sanctity. The word "impure" refers not to bodily chastity only but also to pride, arrogance, and unwarranted fear. "Impure" can be the reasons, the proofs, we try to attach to the Divine. It is only through the purifying of our heart, which symbolizes the whole of us, of useless words and egocentric desires that our soul can be readied to penetrate the darkness wherein God, who is beyond all created things, makes his dwelling: "The more we take flight upward, the more our words are confined to the ideas we are capable of forming; so that now as we plunge into that darkness which is beyond intellect, we shall find ourselves not simply running short of words but actually speechless and unknowing" (*The Complete Works*, 139).

Language returns to silence, and we dwell in the awesomeness of our being created in love while remaining aware that the "Cause of all is above all. . . . It is not a material body, and hence has neither shape nor form, quality, quantity, or weight. It is not in any place and can neither be seen nor be touched. It is neither perceived nor is it perceptible. It suffers neither disorder nor disturbance and is overwhelmed by no earthly passion. . . . It passes through no change, decay, division, loss, no ebb and flow, nothing of which the senses may be aware" (*The Complete Works*, 140–41).

As we temper our inordinate desire to know, to possess, and to control the mystery, we are better able to behold all creatures, ourselves included, as we really are; we see persons, events, and things in God, and hence we honor their true being. This unknowing does not mean uncertainty about the existence of God; rather it articulates in each of us the realization that no finite knowledge can disclose in full the Infinite God or penetrate the dazzling darkness where the Divine dwells. God invites us in unknowing to stretch toward the loftiest point to which faith can lead us. By relinquishing all the knowledge we possess, however lofty it may be, we proceed in faith toward a knowing that exceeds our understanding while granting us a glimpse of all that we can ever hope to know.

To be united with God is to praise him as the cause of all that is, was, and will be. We become ever more God-conscious while still remaining our creaturely self. As Pseudo-Dionysius says, by Divine Paternity all things abide in God and God abides in all things. By Divine Filiation, all things proceed from God and God passes into all things. By Divine Spiration, God penetrates all things and all things return to God. These three divine principles (Abiding, Proceeding, and Penetrating) correspond to the Three Persons in One God: Father, Son, and Holy Spirit (the Undifferentiated Godhead).

Ultimate Reality transcends our finite symbols and images of God. The Godhead we adore in awe is richer than any description we can formulate. God is the preeminent cause of all things, but he himself is not any of them. Pseudo-Dionysius reiterates the importance of negation since by it we deny all sensible attributes of God as being equatable with God's own self. God remains outside the limits of time and space, though by virtue of the Incarnation, God comes to us in time and space. God is beyond any finite spatial or sensible experience we might have, yet God comprehends the sensations we humans receive.

God is the Giver of immortal life to our body and soul. God's love flows through our whole being in such a way that the outer, material world is not at odds with our inner, spiritual world. The *via negativa* is in no way dualistic. It does not imply a rejection of matter or of creation; rather it surpasses these distinctions due to the force of love that draws creation, even the lowest of beings, to the Creator.

In brief, the way of negation leads not to the false conclusion that God is an aloof, uncaring force but to the revelation that God is love, a love "beyond every limitation ... [and] beyond every denial" (*The Complete Works*, 141). In unknowing, we come to know the divine-human personhood of Jesus Christ through whom we experience intimacy with the Trinity while forever being in awe of its mystery.

REFLECT NOW

1. Have you ever felt in your mind and heart the utter inability to penetrate the impenetrable abyss of the mystery and majesty of God?
2. Have you ever found yourself at a loss for words to express your love for God?
3. Do you recall a time when it felt as if you were being swept up in awe of God's presence? In wordless wonder and adoration?

READ MORE

Ronald F. Hathaway, *Hierarchy and the Definition of Order in the Letters of Pseudo-Dionysius* (The Hague: Martinus Nijhoff, 1969).

John D. Jones, *The Divine Names and Mystical Theology* (Milwaukee: Marquette University Press, 1980).

Paul Rorem, *Biblical and Liturgical Symbols within the Pseudo-Dionysius Synthesis* (Toronto: Pontifical Institute of Medieval Studies, 1984).

8

COMMIT YOURSELF TO CLIMB UP TO GOD

JOHN CLIMACUS ON THE PATH TO PARADISE

If the sight of the one we love clearly makes us change completely, so that we turn cheerful, glad, and carefree, what will the face of the Lord himself not do as he comes to dwell, invisibly, in a pure soul?
—John Climacus, *The Ladder of Divine Ascent*, 287

Is there a shortcut to heaven? Not really, but let's give John Climacus credit for making the effort to map a path to paradise. So excellent is the result that his ladder has passed the test of time and inspired seekers of truth throughout the Christian world. On it he shows us that the evil thoughts and actions that encumber us must be corrected by penitence, unceasing prayer, and a charitable life. Little is known about this master personally, but his presentation of the ascent to God has become a spiritual classic in both the Eastern and Western Churches.

What inspires us to make this climb up to God is the desire to be more conformed to Christ, but this commitment is not for the faint of heart. John Climacus directs us, so to speak, to put on the boots of faith, the slacks of surrender to God's will, and the cap of selfless love. With one foot in front

of the other, we progress upward to God on the rungs of humility and simplicity, of gratitude and joy. When Christ calls, it is time to forget our fears
and follow him to the peaks of contemplative union, knowing that this goal,
however lofty, is within our reach.

MEET THE MASTER

John Climacus (579–649) saw himself as a disciple of the desert tradition,
as evidenced by his blending of Eastern and Western insights in his masterpiece, *The Ladder of Divine Ascent*, also called *The Stairway to Paradise*. It
became standard reading for Orthodox monks as well as a popular guide for
believers throughout the Christian world, for whom it became an enduring
spiritual classic.[1] John's central image parallels the Old Testament patriarch
Jacob's dream of a ladder extending from earth to heaven, on which angels
ascended and descended (Gn 28:10–19).[2]

The Ladder consists of thirty chapters or steps (paralleling the years of
the hidden life of Jesus of Nazareth prior to his public ministry). Each of
them features a virtue meant to lead us upward to conformity to Christ,
contrasted to a vice that threatens to undermine our spiritual life. John says
of this traditional way of thinking: "The holy virtues are like the ladder of
Jacob and the unholy vices are like the chains that fell off the chief apostle
Peter. The virtues lead from one to another and carry heavenward the man
who chooses them. Vices on the other hand beget and stifle one another"
(*Ladder*, 152).

We might be tempted to ask what relevance writings from such a different era and set of circumstances could have for us today. What could a
seventh-century text written for monks in the Eastern Church say to those
of us living in this complex twenty-first-century Western world? John provides the answer:

> God is the life of all free beings. He is the salvation of all,
> of believers or unbelievers, of the just or the unjust, of the
> pious or the impious, of those freed from the passions or
> caught up in them, of monks or those living in the world, of
> the educated or the illiterate, of the healthy or the sick, of

> the young or the very old. He is like the outpouring of light,
> the glimpse of the sun, or the changes of the weather, which
> are the same for everyone without exception. (*Ladder*, 74)

At age sixteen, at the monastery of St. Catherine on Mount Sinai, John entrusted himself to a superb director, Abbot Martyrius. After the death of his tutor, he retired to a hermitage in Tholas, five miles from the monastery. There he remained a solitary for forty years. He was then elected by popular acclaim abbot of the monastery at Mount Sinai, where he composed his famous guidebook dedicated to the pursuit of holiness and detailing how to excel in discipleship whatever vocation we espouse, since "a Christian is an imitator of Christ in thought, word, and deed, as far as this is humanly possible, and believes rightly and blamelessly in the Holy Trinity. A friend of God is the one who lives in communion with all that is natural and free from sin and who does not neglect to do what good he can" (*Ladder*, 74).

So thorough was John's presentation of the ascent to God that from the ninth century onward, *The Ladder* was translated into many languages, including Arabic, Latin, Slavonic, Russian, Italian, Spanish, French, and English. It made a particular impact on the Orthodox church and its venerated elders, notably St. Symeon the New Theologian (949–1022), who confirms that the whole of his life reflected the influence of *The Ladder*. It seems fair to say that this book is to the Christian East what *The Imitation of Christ* by Thomas à Kempis is to the West.

In addition to offering a personal testimony to John's own transformation in Christ, it contains a synthesis of the wisdom and experience of the monastic teachers who preceded him; it represents a first, and remarkably successful, attempt to produce a directory of monastic spirituality. John succeeds in integrating into the steps he presents on the path to paradise the Evagrian classification of the eight evil thoughts: those affecting beginners in a fallen state with sins of the "old man" (gluttony, lust, and avarice); those attacking entrance to the middle way with inward temptations (dejection, anger, and despondency); and those deforming the spiritually initiated with the seedbeds of all the vices (pride and vainglory).

The directorial gifts of John Climacus reveal that he was adept at uncovering the depths of self-deception and the subtle ways in which we try to escape the consequences of sin. The lessons taught in *The Ladder* indicate that our natural impulses are not corrupt in themselves; rather they have to be redirected toward God in openness to his commandments with no selfish wants blocking the way. The only avenues by which to overcome this downward descent are to pray without ceasing, to exercise continual compunction, and to overcome selfishness by the self-gift of a charitable life.

We can be confident that if we are striving upward to reach the Divine, God is reaching downward to draw us to himself: "If you wish to draw the Lord to you, approach him as disciples to a master in all simplicity, openly, honestly, without duplicity, without idle curiosity. He is simple and uncompounded. And he wants the souls that come to him to be simple and pure. Indeed you will never see simplicity separated from humility" (*Ladder*, 216).

BECOMING THE LORD'S TRUE FRIEND

John Climacus was both a man of letters and a mystic aware of the vanity that entraps us when we are overly attached to power, pleasure, and possessions. The course of action he proposes to souls on the battlefield between virtue and vice starts with our squelching the flame of self-idolatry, not by harsh measures like engaging in excessive mortifications but by showing compassion for our own and others' wounded condition. He names among the causes of this affliction the capital sins of gluttony (step 14) and lust (step 15). In his role as abbot, he accepted the responsibility of pointing out to the brothers of the community the obstacles they would encounter on the path to paradise and the conditions that would enhance their ascent.

John identifies the deformations that erode our Christian character and suggests how to reform them, often by countering them with the opposite virtue. It is important to note that one step is not left behind as we ascend to another. The virtues we acquire support our struggle against the vices we reject. This battle continues throughout our lifetime.

The inspiration to climb the ladder, John reminds us, comes to us from our longing to seek conformity to Christ. As challenging as this goal of grace is, we can always rely on the comforting truth that God is our "great collaborator" (*Ladder*, 109) and that we benefit from his outpouring of mercy and forgiveness. God judges us by our intentions, and because of his love for us, "he only demands from us such actions as lie within our power" (*Ladder*, 253).

To begin, we must put aside "the capacity to make [our] own judgment" (*Ladder*, 92). Given the fact that the initiative for our being transformed belongs to God, this posture of obedience is not a technique by which we achieve upward mobility based on our own efforts, however heroic they may be. Obedience calls for openness to the leading of the Holy Spirit; it is an expression of our willingness to deny ourselves, take up our cross, and follow Jesus.

The rungs of John's ladder, though distinct, are all in some way a manifestation of Jesus' yes to the will of the Father (see *Ladder*, 91–92). To begin half-heartedly only increases the likelihood of our giving up and retreating rather than facing the challenges to come. In his usual down-to-earth fashion, John notes that a good beginning is the only way to forecast a good ending: "It is detestable and dangerous for a wrestler to be slack at the start of a contest, thereby giving proof of his impending defeat to everyone. Let us have a firm beginning to our religious life, for this will help us if a certain slackness comes later. A bold and eager soul will be spurred on by the memory of its first zeal and new wings can thus be obtained" (*Ladder*, 76).

The practical steps we take to become a true friend and servant of the Lord are common to all believers and yet respectful of each one's unique personhood. Surrender to God's will results in obedience, without which no progress is possible.

What John Climacus contrasts is not our physical self versus our spiritual self but the selfish sensuality that corrupts us versus the selfless love that is incorruptible. In cooperation with grace, we gain the capacity to distinguish between blockages to our upward ascent and the conditions that facilitate it. Directing us throughout this divine ascent must be the desire for sanctification of body, mind, and spirit in a harmonious synthesis. John details in one step after another how to discern which spirits move us toward an enlightened understanding of God's will and which retard this process.[3]

The thread that weaves together the various strands of *The Ladder of Divine Ascent* is John's targeting of the vice of all vices, vanity, since it is embedded in everything we do: "Like the sun which shines on all alike, vainglory beams on every occupation. What I mean is this. I fast, and turn vainglorious. I stop fasting so that I will draw no attention to myself, and I become vainglorious over my prudence. I dress well or badly, and am vainglorious in either case. I talk or I hold my peace, and each time I am defeated. No matter how I shed this prickly thing, a spike remains to stand up against me" (*Ladder*, 202).

John confirms that the best way to overcome vainglory is "to remain silent and to accept dishonor, gladly" (*Ladder*, 205). Only when we bind ourselves to the immaterial fetters of the Spirit can we hope to loosen ourselves from the bonds of inordinate attachments to people, events, and things. He tells us that he ate what was allowed by his monastic vows and partook of sleep only in such measure as to prevent his mind from being distracted. Praying and productivity helped him to subdue despondency, or "tedium of the spirit" (*Ladder*, 162). He devoted his life in solitude and in community to producing a blueprint for Christian maturity, culminating in an unfailing ability to distinguish between good and evil and to enjoy union with the Trinity in purity of heart and poverty of spirit.

CLIMBING TO GOD WITH COURAGE, COMMITMENT, AND COMPASSION

Though we may have begun to climb the ladder, there is always the danger of regressing to our old life. This temptation can be cloaked under apparently selfless and compassionate motivations. John cautions that we must be careful that the attempt to lift others up does not result in our own fall: "Many set themselves the aim of rescuing the indifferent and the lazy—and end up lost themselves" (*Ladder*, 85). He also stresses, "If you have left the world, then do not begin to reach out for it" (*Ladder*, 86).

We must have the courage to deny our unredeemed self (our fallen nature) "for the sake of what is above nature" (*Ladder*, 74). By "nature," he means not our physical being but those disobedient decisions that darken our understanding and separate us from God. If we do not renounce these wrongful choices, they will hamper us from following God's will. Unless we let go of dissonant attachments, we may carry too much baggage to climb all thirty rungs of the ladder to union with God. As John says, "Those bearing chains can still walk. But they often stumble and are thereby injured"

(*Ladder*, 78). We must free ourselves of such attachments, lest they prevent us from answering the Master's call: "In this world when an emperor summons us to obedience, we leave everything aside and answer the call at once. . . . Someone caught up in the affairs of the world can make progress, if he is determined. But it is not easy" (*Ladder*, 78).

This letting go involves not simply a renunciation of that which is not of God but also a radical detachment from those things—not necessarily bad in themselves—that distract us and divide our heart. The problem that plagues us is being too attached to things that are transitory and mutable, grasping on to possessions so tightly they gain control over us. Rather than leave everything behind, we must discern between what is good and what is evil and choose, when all is said and done, what is of eternal value.

Accompanying renunciation is what John Climacus names "exile." What he means is escape from the desires of the ego-self, whether for attention or achievement or simply for something that substitutes for God. Already by the age of nineteen, John had begun his exile to the monastery, where he found the way to open his heart to God and to teach others what he had first lived himself.

Underlying the virtues of both renunciation and exile is the spirit of obedience. John describes it as "the burial place of the will, and a death freely accepted" (*Ladder*, 92). He says that "to obey is, with all deliberateness, to put aside the capacity to make one's own judgment. The beginning of the mortification both of the soul's will and also of the body's members is hard. The halfway stage is sometimes difficult, sometimes not. But the end is liberation from the senses and freedom from pain" (*Ladder*, 92).

Such a "resurrection of lowliness," or humility, is not an emotional response based on shame but a renewal of our baptismal commitment. It reminds us that our days are "like an evening shadow" (Ps 102:11) and that our life is "like grass; . . . the wind passes over it, and it is gone" (Ps 103:15–16). Recalling the brevity of life can prevent us from placing too much trust in our own plans. Life is not under our control. When we remember our mortality, we grow in humility. We accept the limits of our finitude and rely wholly on the infinite mystery and majesty of God. We hear anew Christ's promise to us: "I am the resurrection and the life. Those who believe in me, even though they die, will live, and everyone who lives and believes in me will never die" (Jn 11:25–26).

Much as he would have liked to remain solitary, John affirmed the divine commission that he was to guide and heal sinners such as himself in need of redemption. Having felt the weight of his own sin, he knew how necessary it was to move from rash judgment to compassion: "To pass judgment on another is to usurp shamelessly a prerogative of God, and to condemn is to ruin one's soul" (*Ladder*, 157). A compassionate person tends to look at the positive attributes of another, recognizing that God is at work in everyone's life. As he says: "A good grape picker chooses to eat ripe grapes and does not pluck what is unripe. A charitable and sensible mind takes careful note of the virtues it observes in another, while the fool goes looking for faults and defects" (*Ladder*, 157).

The point is not to remain oblivious to others' faults but to foster their reformation. In this way, compassion softens our tendency to be judgmental. We show others the mercy we have received from God; we treat their faults with the same gentleness with which we would desire them to treat ours.

John exemplifies another facet of compassion by showing that the best way to avoid harmful speech and the sins it evokes is to guard against excessive talkativeness, which he calls "the throne of vainglory . . . a sign of ignorance, a doorway to *slander* . . . [and] the end of vigilance." He advises us to practice the monastic virtue of silence, saying, "The lover of silence draws close to God" (*Ladder*, 159). A gentle word of encouragement warms a person's heart and strengthens us for the unending battle with the inner and outer foes of God. He also warns us that gluttonous and greedy obsessions breed spiritual insensitivity and a lack of compassion. Therefore, he counsels us, "Control your appetites before they control you!" (*Ladder*, 167). Such restraint yields the benefit of a life without anxiety, drawing us from loss of hope to the virtues of courage, commitment to Christ, and compassion.

The underlying disposition enabling these virtues is abandonment to the will of God. The one who is poor in spirit "accepts what comes his way as if from the hand of the Lord." When we see possessions in this light, we become "a son of detachment [who] sets no value on what he has" (*Ladder*, 189). Only then can the things of this world become true blessings, for just as gluttony and avarice make the heart insensitive, so the dispositions of poverty and chastity (rather than possessiveness and defilement) alert us to the godly value of people, events, and things. We see others as messengers of God's goodness, truth, and beauty. Such awe-filled attentiveness to the transcendent can only occur if we "strive first for the kingdom of God and his righteousness" (Mt 6:33), rather than pursuing what will never satisfy our spiritual hunger.

Honesty toward ourselves and recognition of our limits helps counteract pride, which John divides into two sources of sin: vainglory, which relates to the self, and pride, which relates to others: "A vainglorious man is a believer—and an idolater. Apparently honoring God, he actually is out to please not God but men. . . . The fast of such a man is unrewarded and his prayer futile, since he is practicing both to win praise" (*Ladder*, 202).

When our primary concern becomes how we look to others and how admired we are for our spirituality, we drift far away from humility. As John observes, "Vainglory induces pride in the favored and resentment in those who are slighted" (*Ladder*, 203) rather than encouraging us to give God the credit. Concern for appearances may cause us "to pretend that we have some virtue which does not belong to us." Such personal vanity can also lead to pridefulness toward others, lording our supposed superiority over them by "the humiliation of our neighbor, [and] the shameless parading of our achievements" (*Ladder*, 207).

The cure for this two-headed sin of pride is candid and courageous self-appraisal; it shows us that we, too, are full of faults and limitations, and it keeps us from being puffed up with a false sense of our own attainments. Coupled with obedience, such docility becomes the wellspring of the virtue of humility, identified by John as a sacred vine that gives us "a solid understanding of the will of God in all times, in all places, in all things: and it is found only among those who are pure in heart, in body, and in speech" (*Ladder*, 229).

REACHING THE SUMMIT OF THIS DIVINE ASCENT

John Climacus's highest rungs address those virtues enabling the life of contemplative union with God. The first of these is stillness. To discern the will of God, we must be attentive to his voice in the midst of daily life. A noisy, overly distracted life closes us to God's presence and God's still, small voice in the core of our being. John stresses that even our bodily posture may encourage us to "put on the appearance of those at prayer. For among the weak the mind often conforms to the body" (*Ladder*, 277).

These practices bring with them the blessing of *dispassion*, a virtue that reflects a life of continuous intimacy with God. In describing dispassion, John directs us not to confuse it with contrived serenity. True dispassion means abiding in the Divine Presence; ours becomes a constant Godward focus, freeing us from the swings of emotion that result when we set our heart on lesser things. Dispassion does not result from a lack of involvement with the world, but from being with God in the world.

At the summit of the ladder are the three theological virtues of faith, hope, and love. Love keeps us focused on God and on our neighbor, revealing that "he who loves the Lord has first loved his brother, for the latter is proof of the former." Hope "causes us to look forward to the reward of love" (*Ladder*, 288). Faith lets us face the situations in which we find ourselves with trust in the presence and promises of God. Together, these virtues bring us to the peace and joy of Jesus, not only in our illumined heart but also in our relationships with others.

Loving contemplation of the Godhead is the last rung of the ladder. To reach it with the help of grace is worthy of any struggle or sacrifice we may have to endure. Though few souls may arrive at this height of contemplation, all can experience being on the way since love is a "resemblance to God, insofar as this is humanly possible" (*Ladder*, 286).

John Climacus is at pains to show us that *The Ladder* ought to be read not as a series of progressive steps to perfection but as an interconnected group of counsels meant to shake us out of our complacency and bring us to a liberating life of virtue, freed from vice and its consequent loss of hope. On this ladder we learn to recognize the wily tricks of isolated individualism and the autonomous pursuit of self-idolatry, as opposed to the humility of our having been made in the image of God.

Climbing the rungs of *The Ladder* helps us to let go of our false self and to put on the form of Christ, which constitutes our true self.[4] Only then can we ponder what to retain and what to renounce; how to withstand demonic assaults; how to avoid entanglements with the world in its worldliness; what style of life to choose, whether to live in solitude or under the protection of a faith community; and how to practice gentleness and firmness on the way to becoming mature followers of Christ.

John proves that the role of the spiritual master is to direct us inward, not to feats of immoderate mortification but to purity of heart. To progress on the stairway to perfection, we must approach it not with modes of mastery but with a life of surrender to the mystery. John wants us to see that the way to overcome sinfulness is not repression but reorientation. Neither is the answer repudiation of the body; it is rather a reintegration of body, mind, and spirit.

Even though our likeness to God has been marred by sin, we remain God's creation, women and men made in his likeness and called to share in the glory of the risen Lord. The aim of transformation in Christ is to transfigure, not suppress, our incarnate reality; to educate, not eradicate; to make the earthly a true mirror of the heavenly. The resulting life of prayer is "action without end, wellspring of virtues, source of grace, hidden progress, food of the soul, enlightenment of the mind, an axe against despair, hope demonstrated, sorrow done away with" (*Ladder*, 274).

John Climacus grounds his notion of perpetual progress in the conviction that our growth in virtue and love has no end point in this life. On earth, we may be perfected in Christ, but we never become perfect. Rather we advance from one facet of transforming love and light to the next. Just as love between a married couple ought to grow more intimate and never become static, so the love between the persons of the Trinity and the human soul ought always to deepen. Step by step, John guides our ascent toward the summit of Christian life: contemplative union with God. Every vice we reject reveals the depths of self-deception and the subtle ways in which we try to escape the consequences of sin. Every virtue we cultivate leads us upward and onward in conformity to Christ.

John ends *The Ladder* with an affirmation of what is higher than any momentary ecstasy or mystical revelation, higher than any knowledge we may acquire on our approach to the summit of love, and that is "the face of the Lord Himself . . . [who] comes to dwell, invisibly, in a pure soul" (*Ladder*, 287).

REFLECT NOW

1. What steps have you taken in what may be an overly complex life to acquire the virtue of simplicity?
2. Do you find a tug-of-war in your heart between anger and meekness, greed and generosity, pride and humility?
3. Do you agree that renunciation of self-centered encapsulation is the key to personal and spiritual liberation?

READ MORE

Guigo II, *The Ladder of Monks: A Letter on the Contemplative Life and Twelve Meditations,* trans. Edmund Colledge and James Walsh (Garden City, NY: Image Books, 1978).

J. R. Martin, *The Illustration of the Heavenly Ladder of John Climacus* (Princeton, NJ: Princeton University Press, 1954).

Elias G. Matsagouras, *The Early Church Fathers as Educators* (Minneapolis, MN: Light and Life, 1977).

9

LEARN HOW TO BE WITH AND FOR OTHERS

MAXIMUS THE CONFESSOR ON THE MEANING OF LOVE

If the life of the mind is the illumination of knowledge and this is born of love for God, then it is well said that there is nothing greater than love.

—Maximus the Confessor, *Selected Writings*, 36

What is the meaning of love? This question intrigued Maximus the Confessor, who rejected a worldly career to answer the call to the monastic life; to defend the early Church against heresy; and to show new believers the unconditional love God has for them. He believed that to be like God ("deification") and to love one another as Jesus loves us is our destiny.

Proclaiming this truth led him to write a hundred short chapters on love, showing us in each of them what it means to be and become model Christians. If love means laying down our life for our friends, as Jesus did, then it goes beyond any pedestrian emotion; it means forfeiting our willfulness and following God's will with hearts open to the meaning of suffering and self-sacrifice. Such love of God and neighbor defeats hate and proves to be stronger than death.

MEET THE MASTER

St. Maximus (ca. 580–662) hailed from a distinguished family in Constantinople, who saw to his education in grammar, rhetoric, theology, and philosophy. The years of his life in the East parallel those of St. Gregory the Great's pontificate in the West. Among the Fathers and Doctors of the Church, Maximus has been identified not only as a seminal thinker and a practical spiritual master but also as a gifted, bicultural theologian. He spoke with equal fluency the language of spirituality representing the mystical genius of the East and the language of doctrinal truth representing the analytical genius of the West.

Prior to his entering a monastery near Carthage in 613, Maximus played an important role in the imperial court, becoming secretary of the emperor Heraclitus in 610. Political power held no attraction for him. He loved solitude and the hesychast (Jesus Prayer) tradition. As a monk and a respected theologian, he found himself embroiled in the defense of the faith due to the controversy caused by two heretical movements: monophysitism, which denied the humanity of Christ (according to this heresy, Jesus had only one nature, and that was divine); and monothelitism, which insisted that Christ had a divine but not a human will.

Against these untruths, Maximus maintained that human nature without a human will is an unreal abstraction: if Christ does not have a human will as well as a divine will, he is not truly man; and if he is not truly man, the Christian message of salvation is rendered void. What we see in Christ, our Savior, is a human will, genuinely free yet bound by obedience to the divine will; it is this voluntary cooperation of manhood with divinity in Christ that restored the integrity of human nature, enabling us to make our own wills obedient to the will of God and so to attain salvation.

Integral to this doctrine is what Maximus referred to as a *technique of opposition to sin* that entails control of the passions and the proper use of free will. The *technique of cooperation with grace* enhances our contemplative presence to the Trinity and involves the practice of the virtues, especially that of self-mastery, which leads to growth in agapic love. As Maximus says, in the best-known work of his *Selected Writings*, called *The Four Hundred Chapters on Love*, "The one who has genuinely renounced worldly matters and serves his neighbor without pretense through love soon frees himself of all passion and is rendered a sharer of divine love and knowledge."[1]

The fruit of this restraint is detachment, which readies us to devote ourselves to a God-oriented appreciation of creation and unceasing prayer as an antidote to possessiveness and its destructive influence on our capacity for self-giving love. Maximus is firm on this point: "The one who truly loves God also prays completely undistracted, and the one who prays completely undistracted also truly loves God. But the one who has his mind fixed on any earthly thing does not pray undistracted; therefore the one who has his mind tied to any earthly thing does not love God" (*Love*, 2,1:46).

The key word in this text is "tied." Any inordinate attachment puts us at risk of idolatry, be it of a person, a thing, or an event. Our love is deflected from its proper end, God in his glory. Love, freed from selfishly clinging to what is less than God, restores unity within our heart and peace with others. Thanks to the harmony already established between us and God by Baptism, Penance, and Eucharist, Maximus felt himself to be a worthy spokesperson for the wisdom he had received from "the writings of the Holy Fathers." He says at the start of *The Four Hundred Chapters on Love*, "I went through [them] and selected from them whatever had reference to my subject, summarizing many things in few words so that they can be seen at a glance to be easily memorized" (Prologue, 35). He asks us to read each chapter with an uncomplicated mind, rooted in fear of the Lord, and motivated mainly by love, without which no true knowledge of God, self, and others can ever be found.

In line with the masters of the contemplative life that preceded him, Maximus expounded a doctrine of charity, centering on the love of Christ, our incarnate Redeemer, whose sacrifice on the Cross overcame the sinful results of self-love. In *The Four Hundred Chapters on Love*, he shows that charity is the virtue that defines our Christian life and enables us to experience our "adoptive filiation" in the family of the Trinity. This relationship accounts for that graced bond of union with God that constitutes what the Greek Fathers term "deification."[2] It represents the ultimate fulfillment of our created capacity for God, though it is not attainable by our natural powers alone.

For Maximus, all activity of the Godhead has been bestowed on the Church through the power of the Holy Spirit. The three agents of this deification, according to the tradition he adopted, are the Church itself; the mystagogy of the Church; and entrance to this mystery through the sacraments of Baptism, Penance, and Eucharist.

The Church, born of the water and blood issuing from the pierced side of Christ, keeps whole and intact the revealed knowledge of God given to us by the Holy Spirit. Progress in faith can never come to us by the "enlightenment" promised by a gnostic or heretical sect. A full and willing participation in the redemption brought about in us by the Body of Christ and the one, true faith it proclaims counters such falsehoods.

Mystagogy refers to our being brought by grace into unity as a body worthy of serving its head, Christ Jesus our Lord. It sheds light on oral or written explanations of the mystery hidden in scripture and celebrated in the liturgy. And by entering into the holy and august rites of the Church, we are given access to the fullness of that revelation.

Baptism is the first and most fundamental sacrament. It represents the restoration in us of a provisional sinlessness, which can be preserved if we keep the commandments. The power to condemn sin is conveyed to the baptized, not merely as an individual path to Christian perfection but for the benefit of humankind. *Penance* brings us from the chaos caused by sin to the calming experience of reconciliation with God. *Eucharist* is the "connatural" food of the soul, transforming us into other Christs. Bread and wine become his Body and Blood at the moment of consecration. Christ's compassion for wounded humanity is the model of the ascetical struggles we undergo to become the "new creation" Christ intends us to be (2 Cor 5:17).

Maximus not only sees traces of the Trinity in creation; he also sees within us an image of the Triune God—in our minds, in our words, and in our spirit. For Maximus, the summit of the spiritual life consists of union with the Blessed Trinity through the following gifts:

+ *Perfect simplicity*, by conforming us insofar as possible with the substantial unity of the Godhead;
+ *Perfect goodness*, by habitual practice of the virtues, especially faith, hope, and charity, in imitation of the total benevolence of the Trinity; and

✦ *Perfect love,* by putting off divisive self-centered modes of disobedience and adhering to the unitive will of God.

In the Incarnation, God in his Word became one of us in all things but sin. God made us that we might become sharers in his divinity, but it is God's grace alone that deifies us and makes possible our participation in the work of redemption. The fullest effect of this deification can be seen in our growth in love. As Christ loved us and died for us, so we ought to be ready to live and die for one another. The agent of this transformation is the Holy Spirit, who invites us to emulate in every way the love the Lord has for us. Such was God's deifying plan: that his only begotten Son would show us the way to become sons and daughters of God.

Just as serious sin—deliberately disobeying God's revealed will or knowingly embracing heretical teachings—leads to separation from God, so intentional obedience leads to keeping the commandments and to union with God. Maximus paid a high price for his obedience as well as for his unwavering faith in the fully human, fully divine will and nature of Jesus Christ. So brilliant was his articulation of the true faith that he became the target of animosity. He was put on trial in 655, where every effort was made to accuse him of political crimes. The real issue, however, was his refusal to communicate with the See of Constantinople as long as the emperor and the patriarch clung to heretical beliefs.

He was exiled for six years and brought to trial again. In the last year of his life, he was imprisoned in Constantinople, where the same heretics he castigated condemned him to be scourged and to have his tongue cut off and his right hand amputated as a symbol of his commitment as a "confessor," or witness to the true faith. He died on August 13, 662, as he had lived, proclaiming Christ as his Savior and suffering persecution for the Lord's sake.

MIRRORING DIVINE LOVE IN OUR HUMANITY

The story of divine love extended from God to us and from us to God overflows in our love for others and in our fulfillment of the Great Commandment. Since all that is preexists in God prior to its coming into existence, nothing ought to be contrary to God's intent. God himself ought to be the aim and end of all creative action. In us creatures, there is a natural desire for the enjoyment of God. We long to be *informed* as to the object of our love and to be *conformed* to God as an image is to its archetype. This desire, freely chosen, involves no destruction of our free will. For the spiritual person, neither sense nor reason operates on its own but only insofar as it contributes to and is under the influence of the higher power of the contemplative mind; its operations are moved by and toward their end, who is God.

The problem we face is that our natural desire for God attaches itself to sensible things. Instead of choosing the good and advancing toward God, unbound to inordinate attachments, we succumb to passions like lust and anger with all of their unstable fluctuations. We replace what is superior with what is inferior. And yet, as Maximus insists, we cannot be our own end. The perfection of self-actualization can only be attained through a complete handing over of our self-determination to God. Only in obedience and submissiveness to God's will can we be free.

Is there any remedy for the sickness of soul caused by self-love that puts us at war not only with ourselves but with one another? Maximus says that the solution resides in the "compenetration" in our soul of the work of Christ (grace) and of asceticism (cooperation with grace), as when we see someone in distress and take pity on them, or as when we are moved to do a good deed and act in charity, or as when we discern good from evil and choose the good.

What moves us in the opposite direction—to choose what is evil—are our passions, as when we crave food outside the time of hunger or lash out in anger in response to another's offense: "When the passions hold sway over a mind, they bind it together with material things, and separating it from God make it to be all-engrossed in them. But when love of God is in control, it releases it from the bonds and persuades it to think beyond not only things of sense but even this transient life of ours" (*Love*, 2,3:46). The demons go on the attack when they detect our carelessness and lack of vigilance and find openings to further arouse these unruly passions. Our will itself becomes our worst enemy every time we prefer self-love over loving God and others.

These obstacles are seen by Maximus not as condemnations of our nature but as openings to realign our spirit, heart, mind, and will with our Savior. He reverses our understanding of the meaning of hardships and removes the sting of physical and spiritual death. While the disobedience of the first Adam ended in bondage, the obedience of Christ, the second Adam, freed, restored, and deified our whole personhood.

This new "generation of the Spirit" enables us to observe the commandments, to condemn sin, and, if need be, to suffer and die for what we believe. The principal motive behind the struggle to overcome out-of-control passions, set aflame by the capital sins, is the desire to know, love, and serve God that is inherent in our makeup and that cannot be eradicated. According to Maximus, this desire to mirror Divine Love in every facet of our humanity is so much a part of us that it arouses in everyday life a longing for the eternal mystery: "When the mind is completely freed from the passions, it journeys straight ahead to the contemplation of created things and makes its way to the knowledge of the Holy Trinity" (*Love*, 1,86:45).

The lasting fruit of contemplation is charity. The heart of the spirituality of St. Maximus is love or, as he might say, the voluntary disposition of goodwill. The same love that we have for God must be extended to others in word and deed. Love delivers us from wickedness and leads us to prefer good over evil: "The work of love is the deliberate doing of good to one's neighbor as well as long-suffering and patience and the use of all things in the proper way" (*Love*, 1,40:39). The soul then becomes the abode of the Holy Spirit and receives, so to speak, the power of knowing the divine nature through love. By this power, Christ is born anew, becoming incarnate once more through those whom he redeems.

LET THE WILL TO LOVE HAVE ITS WAY

The will to love ought to have dominion over all that we are and do. It is a naturally given, inherent gift of God to us, albeit wounded in its potency for obedience and total surrender to God. Since we cannot be our own end, the perfection of our true self can only be attained through a complete handing over of our powers of self-determination to God.

Living in love detaches us from excessive possessiveness; it tempers mistaken notions of ownership and the irrational affections that support them. Constantly calling on God for help prevents us from trusting in our own strength. Humility reverses the arrogant consequences of the passions of pride and becomes, as Maximus says, "the benefactor and pilot of our life" (*Love*, 1,48:40). It prevents us from sinking into spiritual immaturity with its unloving consequences, such as slander and the ultimate treachery of feeling hatred for our brothers and sisters.

Maximus says that the peak of Christian maturity occurs when we purify the hatred and unforgiveness in us and try to live in peace, knowing that "love and self-mastery free the soul from passions; reading and contemplation deliver the mind from ignorance; and the state of prayer places it with God himself" (*Love*, 4,86:85).[3] He adds this astute advice: "Do not, because you changed from love to hate, disparage today as bad and vicious the one whom yesterday you praised as good and honored and virtuous, and blame your brother for the evil hate within you. Rather, continue in those same praises even though you are still full of hurt, and you will easily return to the same saving love" (*Love*, 4,27:78).

In an endearing metaphor, Maximus highlights the need for the mind devoted to Christ to be detached: "As a little sparrow whose foot is tied tries to fly but is pulled to earth by the cord to which it is bound, so does the mind which does not yet possess detachment get pulled down and dragged to earth when it flies to the knowledge of heavenly things" (*Love*, 1,85:44–45). His advice pertaining to how to grow in love for others is also linked with detachment: "Be as eager as you can to love every [person], but if you cannot do this yet, at least do not hate anyone. And you cannot do this unless you scorn the things of this world" (*Love*, 4,82:84).[4]

For Maximus, prayerfulness is the chief motivator of virtue. He says that "all virtues assist the mind in the pursuit of divine love, but above all does pure prayer. By it the mind is given wings to go ahead to God and becomes alien to all [lesser] things" (*Love*, 1,11:36). Growth in the knowledge of God comes through love and humility since "the one who ceaselessly devotes his energies to the interior life is temperate, patient, kind, and humble. Not only this, but he is also contemplative, united to God, and prayerful" (*Love*, 4,64:82).

THREE ATTRIBUTES OF GOD'S PRESENCE

The prolonged exercise of self-mastery over pleasure allows us to become spiritually mature by advancing in divine things, recognizing our own dignity, and directing that for which we long to God. Complementing this link between knowledge of God and self are the three attributes of God's presence we must foster throughout our life: utter simplicity, utter goodness, and utter love.

Utter simplicity. For Maximus, the purpose of the commandments, the Beatitudes, and the Lord's Prayer is to simplify our thoughts and bind us to God. The aim of reading and contemplating is to render our minds clear of any images or forms that would decenter our attention from God. Simple centering ensures undistracted prayer.

Utter goodness. How can we help but marvel when we consider that immense ocean of goodness that is beyond astonishment? How can we not be struck when reflecting on how and whence rational and intelligent nature came to be, and when there was no matter at all previous to its creation? And what kind of power is it that brought all that is into being? Such is the all-powerful goodness of God that is beyond the mind's powers of discernment.[5]

Utter love. Christians benefit most from their belief in the revelation that "God is love" (1 Jn 4:8). Love is that disposition of our soul by which we prefer no other being to the being and knowledge of God. It is impossible to reach this depth of love if we retain any ultimate attachment to earthly things. Love is begotten of detachment; detachment of hope in God; hope in God of patient endurance and long-suffering; and self-mastery of fear of God and faith in the saving power of the Lord.

St. Maximus the Confessor never separates the meaning of love from its effective unfolding in the life of the Church. When we are loving members of the Body of Christ, we enjoy harmony of virtue, attunement to divine inspiration, and purity of heart. We master our passions and follow God's will in simplicity and love. We become messengers of the great plan of God, strengthened by a peaceful state of soul resistant to vice, freed from the passions, choosing good over evil, and rejoicing "unceasingly in divine love" (*Love*, 1,34:38).

REFLECT NOW

1. Why is union with Christ at the foot of the Cross the best way to reverse the devastating personal and social effects of self-love?
2. How would you describe the meaning of your baptized state of "adoptive filiation" in the Trinity?
3. Have you experienced the truth that the surest sign of growth in contemplative prayer is the love that flows from it?

READ MORE

Jordan Aumann, *Christian Spirituality in the Catholic Tradition* (San Francisco: Ignatius Press, 1985).

On the Cosmic Mystery of Jesus Christ: Selected Writings from St. Maximus the Confessor, trans. Paul Blowers and Robert Louis Wilken (Crestwood, NY: St. Vladimir's Seminary Press, 2003).

St. Maximus the Confessor, trans. Polycarp Sherwood (Westminster, MD: Newman Press, 1955).

10

Acknowledge Your Need for Direction and Become More Compassionate

---

GREGORY THE GREAT ON PASTORAL CARE

No one ventures to teach any art unless he has learned it after deep thought. With what rashness, then, would the pastoral office be undertaken by the unfit, seeing that the government of souls is the art of arts!

—Gregory the Great, *Pastoral Care*, 21

Striking today is the number of people who express an interest in and a need for spiritual direction. St. Gregory the Great would have understood the urge to know whether or not we are living in God's will. Of a person as wise and learned and experienced as he was, we might want to ask, *Where have I come from on my journey in faith, where am I now, and where might God be leading me in the future?*

Gregory would have known from experience how to help us resolve the conflict in our heart between virtue and vice. How and why do bad dispositions often pose as good ones? In his masterpiece *Pastoral Care*, he describes many of the causes of pain in the human condition and explains how to cope with them in a compassionate way. He would have insisted that we show mercy to our own and others' wounded condition by living unselfishly and loving unconditionally.

MEET THE MASTER

St. Gregory the Great (540–604) was the son of a Roman senator, who saw to it that he had an education fitted to what would have been a lifetime career in politics but for the plan of God. By the age of thirty, Gregory had become prefect of the city of Rome. By the age of thirty-five, he recognized a higher calling in light of his Christian heritage. He abandoned his worldly ambitions, resigned from his secular appointments, and shifted his energy and talent to attending to God's affairs. He turned his palatial residence into what would become St. Andrew's monastery, where he lived as a monk in the tradition of St. Benedict. He became the abbot there and founded several other monasteries.

A mere fifteen years later, having been ordained to the deaconate and served as papal nuncio to the emperor of Constantinople, he saw his life take a drastic and, for him, unwanted turn. In 590, he was proclaimed the successor of Pope Pelagrius II and advanced from his quarters in the abbey as the superior of his monastic order to the papal states as the pope of the Roman Catholic Church.

Reluctant as he was to leave the solitude offered by the monastic life, Gregory accepted this high office and public appointment with humility and the hope that he would be of service to the Church. Building on both his familial and religious background, Gregory made a preeminent impression on the ecclesial and secular worlds at a time when the Roman Empire was crumbling from within. His goal was to oversee a republic modeled on the vision presented by St. Augustine in *The City of God*. He devoted himself to social concerns, care of the poor, and governance of the Church, making a special contribution to the liturgy by the introduction of Gregorian chant. In addition to his famous book on pastoral care, he wrote the *Dialogues*, where he devoted the whole of Book 2 to the life of St. Benedict and the astounding feats he performed.[1]

Prodigious a worker as he was, Gregory from his youth had a weak constitution; he accepted this condition of poor health as coming from the hand of God to teach him how to empathize with the sick of body, mind, and spirit. His compassionate outreach complemented his awareness of the need for inner renewal through continual compunction and unceasing prayer, ideals he derived from the desert tradition and especially from John Cassian.

His term as pope, in which he insisted that he be addressed as the "servant of the servants of God," was marked by numerous accomplishments. One of the most significant occurred in 597, when he oversaw the successful mission of St. Augustine of Canterbury to bring Christianity to England. On the home front, he weathered the onslaughts of civil war, famine, and plague, and saw to it that Church revenues would be used to aid the homeless and those suffering from starvation as the once-glorious Roman Empire fell into ruin. As the architect of the medieval papacy, he used his gifts for administrative excellence and theological reflection, writing rules for monastic and ecclesiastical offices, scriptural commentary, and a codification of the seven capital sins in dialogue with the presentation of Evagrius Ponticus on the eight evil thoughts. Thanks also to his seminal book on the care of souls, Gregory became one of the most read Latin Fathers of his own and all ages.[2]

Gregory spanned the distance between the patristic age and the monastic culture of the Middle Ages. In so doing, he left an indelible mark on the spiritual life of the Church.[3] According to Jean Leclercq, in the realm of theological analysis of the Christian experience, nothing essential has been added to Gregory: "His ideas and his expressions had passed into the doctrine and the language of countless spiritual writings generally after having lost any connection with their original context. Without knowing it, we are living in great measure, on his modes of expression and on his thoughts, and for that very reason, they no longer seem new to us."[4] History confirms that his *Pastoral Care* provided a pattern of conduct for secular clergy in the West, just as *The Rule of St. Benedict* had done for the monastic life.

Around 593, Gregory wrote his *Dialogues* to honor the memory of the saints of Italy, notably Benedict of Nursia, and to use their example of fidelity to Christ to instruct the readers of his day on the ways of God. He wanted them to remember, despite the wars, plagues, and famines they had undergone, that they were living in a land where "God chose what is weak in the world to shame the strong" (1 Cor 1:27). The purpose of the glowing picture he paints of St. Benedict in Book 2 was to show the worldly-minded that they can never gain mastery over the mysterious plan of God.[5] Gregory stresses in his depiction of the saint the centrality of childlike trust and the miraculous power of living in fidelity to Christ. He revealed what happens when injustice is met by forgiveness and when cold-hearted pride melts under the warmth of humility.

Being an astute observer of the human condition as well as a gifted storyteller, Gregory drew moral lessons from the mundane episodes of daily life. His answers reflect a characteristic combination of theological reflection and pastoral flexibility. In response to a question put to him regarding what to do with someone who robs a church, he concurs in respect for civil law that they must be taken into custody to determine what caused the crime and the extent of its severity and only then to assign the proper punishment. Was their motivation malice or poverty? Good judgment meant a consideration of the circumstances in which bad judgment occurred.

Another example of his way of applying to social matters sound spiritual direction concerned his handling of the question of whether an expectant mother could be baptized. His reply was, "It is no offense in the sight of Almighty God to bear children." He reminded the questioner that the woman who suffered an issue of blood touched the hem of the Lord's robe, adding, "Why may not one who suffers nature's courses be permitted to enter the Church of God?"[6] Venerable Bede (672–735) paid a well-deserved compliment to Pope Gregory: "While other popes devoted themselves to building churches and enriching them with costly ornaments, Gregory's sole concern was to save souls."[7]

Gregory's ability to integrate doctrinal theology with his respect for human anthropology may explain why his works were widely read by other "physicians of the heart" (*Care*, 1,1:21), as well as by new converts and the priests who instructed them in the faith. As a monk with years of experience and as a sought-after guide for hungry souls, Gregory had to balance his love for solitude with the solidarity demanded of him as head of the Church and guardian of its liturgical and sacramental life. Of great concern to him was the selection of men for ordination, both in monastic and diocesan settings. He did all he could to resolve the tension between the rigorous ideals of community life and the realism of everyday ministry in the world.[8]

Gregory wanted nothing more than to uphold the tradition he himself lived and to infuse priests serving the laity with the same spiritual depth he expected to find in his fellow monks. For this reason, he insisted on maintaining as unbreakable the bond between contemplation and action since without a life of prayer the goals of leadership, be they secular or sacred, can never be reached. We cannot be so eager to pursue contemplation that we decline to be of service to our neighbor, but neither can we be so bound to serve others that we disregard bowing in prayerful presence to the "Author of humility" (*Care*, 4:235).

SIX FOUNDATIONAL KEYS TO PASTORAL CARE

For Gregory, the contemplation-in-action style of pastoral care he lived led him to compare it to the art and discipline of medicine (see *Care*, 1,1:21–23). As the father of spiritual direction, he articulates in *Pastoral Care* six key assumptions that constitute the foundations of his spirituality. They can be summarized as follows:

1. Spiritual formation is the art of arts.
2. Christian caregivers are physicians who are adept at reading the hearts of those they have been instructed by the Holy Spirit to help.
3. The healing work they do represents a special vocation within the general call to follow Christ.
4. One skill spiritual caregivers must cultivate is to recognize that a virtue displayed by those under their care may conceal a corresponding vice. For example, greed may disguise itself as frugality; wastefulness as generosity; laziness as kindness; and wrath as zeal.
5. Penetration of hardness of heart, either by careful questioning or reasonable correction, is the doorway through which every interior thought is made visible. An examination of external symptoms can make known the stability of hidden thoughts.

6. Compassionate concern for human frailty enables people in need of inner healing to discover their illusory dependence on the satisfaction of their own needs rather than their real need to rely on God.

One diagnostic skill for which Gregory is renowned was his ability to detect the tension between virtue and vice. Some examples he offers are:

+   patient/impatient
+   respectful/envious
+   sincere/insincere
+   healthy/sick
+   taciturn/talkative
+   meek/choleric
+   humble/haughty
+   flexible/obstinate

Gregory illustrates the patient/impatient conflict we may feel by showing how vain it is to put indignation, clamor, and blasphemy away outwardly if interior malice, which is a mother of vices, continues to reign. Of what use is it to cut wickedness away from the outer branches of our life if it is retained in the root within? To people who appear patient but do not show love, Gregory asks: "*Why seest thou the mote that is in thy brother's eye, and seest not the beam that is in thy own eye?*" (*Care*, 3,9:111). The turbulence of impatience is the mote, says Gregory, but malice in the heart is the beam.

The empathy displayed by Gregory for sicknesses of body and soul can be traced to the great value he saw in human weakness insofar as it could be a catalyst to seek spiritual strength. As Jean Leclercq concludes, "Gregory's poor health is one of the great events in the history of spirituality, since to some degree it determines his doctrine."[9] Gregory wants us to live with the awareness of our own mortality, to see it as the surest sign that we must give up the prideful assumption that we are in control and remain mindful of our total dependence on God. We must be vigilant of heart to detect the first signs of agitation and disquiet triggered by puffed-up pride and block them with the contrasting virtues of patience and obedience. Gregory believes that compunction, or the commingling of sorrow for sin and joy for forgiveness, initiates the healing process that sutures the wounds of pride. Compunction (*penthos*) reminds us that we ought only to boast about our commitment to obey the commandment to love God with our whole heart and to love others as we love ourselves.

What occasions such compunction may be experiences ranging from the trials of life and its sufferings to the temptation to function on our own, independent from God, despite the gross unhappiness this choice brings. For example, Jesus could not reach the Samaritan woman until she experienced compunction; only then could she enter into the joy of conversion from self-ishness to self-giving love and move onward to fulfill the call to discipleship.

Compunction hollows out self-centeredness and increases our capacity for God. That is why Gregory insists on our adopting not one, but two faces of this virtue:

1. *Compunctio Timoris.* In this case, the suffering we experience results from the tendency to sin coupled with the desire for God. Though at times obscure and only glimpsed in a veiled way, this suffering prompts us to stand before God in fear and trembling.
2. *Compunctio Cordis.* In this instance, compunction awakens us to our need for God. This pricking of our heart is a sign that God initiates the purification of our intentions, humbles us, and offers us freedom from the demon of pride. Now we realize that all the good we do comes from God alone, who works in us by the mysterious action of his grace.

Our duty is to consent to this divine intervention and to develop anew our "spiritual senses," often symbolized in tears of repentance as well as in the weeping that signifies our longing for union with God.

GROWING IN VIRTUOUS LIVING

Complementing the spiritual nourishment we receive from compunction is Gregory's insistence that we cultivate the virtue of detachment. It elevates us beyond our customary modes of knowing and enables us to contemplate the beauty of the Creator in all that is. This adhesion of our human spirit to the Holy Spirit is not the result of our striving; it is a taste of God, a relishing of divine wisdom. Ours becomes a mode of contemplative understanding through love, which enriches our faith and increases our hope.

Amid a host of self-inflicted and demonic temptations, we strive to preserve our desire for God. It may be stronger than we previously experienced due to our having tasted and savored a deeper state of humility born of the knowledge of God and effecting our growth in virtuous living. Life is no longer a question of what we *have* but of who we *are*. As a result, we perceive what in ourselves is contrary to the self we want to be in God.

To help us follow the divine directives God sends our way and to show us by example how to grow in virtuous living are essential elements of pastoral care. To illustrate his point, Gregory says that "every preacher should make himself heard rather by deeds than by words, and that by his righteous way of life should imprint footsteps for men to tread in, rather than show them by word the way to go" (*Care*, 3,40:232).

Since the governance of souls is the art of arts, pastors must be both physicians and teachers. To be fit for this office, they must place themselves under the tutorship of humility and draw in their preaching upon what they have learned from life experience. They fix their attention on the central meanings of their office: to lead others to Christ; to prevent dissipation in a show of distracting preoccupations; and to be sensitive to the rhythm that must be maintained between contemplation and action.

Obstacles to this office include coveting preeminence and the praise of others, worldly gain, and the performance of good works rooted in the desire for reward and the craving for power. Aids that facilitate this office are death to the passions of the flesh by leading a spiritual life; putting aside the desire for worldly prosperity and welcoming the lessons for life granted by adversity; being moved by compassion to empathize with the frailty of others; shunning the capital vices; and avoiding encapsulation in earthly cares. In short, a pastor, like all spiritual directors, must be clean of heart and exemplary in conduct; discreet in keeping silence while being inspirational in speech; compassionate toward all; zealous for righteousness and stern toward evildoers; and adept at balancing care for external matters with solicitude for the interior life. Pastors have to be wary of every form of self-love and prudent in applying correction to others. Their office requires ongoing meditation on the Word of God to ensure that they will never depart from the occupation of sacred reading or from adherence to the teachings of the Church.

Gregory believes that one counsel does not fit all and that a "properly measured word . . . may not be wasted on a heart too limited in its capacity to hold it" (*Care*, 3,39:231). He says that the rule of thumb he follows in his care for souls is to help them to cast aside anxiety and to do what they can to improve themselves, always with humility. The goals of pastoral care span the ages: to help us follow the divine directives of God and to show us by example how to grow in virtuous living. Gregory adds, as if he were speaking of himself, "In restoring others to health by healing their wounds, [the pastor] must [be sure not] to develop tumors of pride" (*Care*, 4:234). Nothing then stands in the way of the practice of virtue, and vice loses its attraction.

The many illnesses he suffered opened St. Gregory to the reality of his finitude and enabled him to set his sights on the Infinite Light of God. Christ is the Physician who heals our deepest sicknesses of soul due to sin. He comes to us, often when we least expect it, to give us a glimpse of love that is unfading, of care that never ends. On the eve of his passing to eternity, Gregory concluded his book *Pastoral Care* with this heartfelt prayer: "In the shipwreck of this life, sustain me, I beseech you, with the plank of your prayers, so that, as my weight is sinking me down, you may uplift me with your meritorious hand" (*Care*, 4:237).

REFLECT NOW

1. Where do you feel the most tension in your life? Is it between patience and impatience, greed and generosity, pride and humility?
2. What do you do to resolve the conflict between virtue and vice?
3. Does acceptance of your own and others' faults and failings evoke compassion or condemnation? Why is mercy the chief quality of pastoral care?

READ MORE

Urban T. Holmes, *A History of Christian Spirituality* (New York: Seabury Press, 1980).

Bernard McGinn, *The Doctors of the Church: Thirty-Three Men and Women Who Shaped Christianity* (New York: Crossroad, 1999).

Thomas C. Oden, *Classical Pastoral Care*, 3 vols. (Ada, MI: Baker, 2000).

PART TWO

MEDIEVAL MASTERS

(1100–1600)

INTRODUCTION

MEDIEVAL MASTERS

Be vigilant. Guard your heart. These imperatives were watchwords of the ancient masters. Their discretionary powers are unrivaled. In one saying they could identify every expression of resistance to divine directives. They unmasked the lie that worldly fame and fortune alone can fulfill the deepest longing of the soul for God.

Throughout the rich treasury of medieval classics, we find traces of such perennial themes as detachment, docility, and discernment. We discover with convincing examples how to integrate contemplation and action; how to grow in poverty, chastity, and obedience; how to suffer with joy; and how to derive insights from holy scripture in the light of multiple levels of meaning. The *literal* prompts our search for connections with daily life; the *symbolic* points us in the direction of the "more than" and the surplus of meaning found in biblical words and images; the *moral* challenges us to find Christ-formed resolutions to ethical dilemmas; and the *spiritual* inspires prayer and personal practice. The intention of these writers is that we let the word move from our lips through our mind to the inmost chambers of our heart.

Medieval masters speak with one voice in their conviction that no human effort or sensible consolation, no virtuous accomplishment or spiritual exercise, can in and by itself grant us the grace of ongoing conversion to Christ and intimacy with the Trinity. The mystics and spiritual masters we meet alert us as well to the devious designs of the demonic that mar the beauty of spiritual friendship and block our commitment to follow the way of perfection. They direct us away from paths of perdition to the inroads of beatitude intended for us by God.

Though we roam in the land of unlikeness to the Sacred through sin, we can count on Divine Mercy to redirect us in repentance to the land of likeness that is our true destination. We learn by means of the spiritual disciplines of silence, formative reading, meditative reflection, and prayer how to integrate contemplation and action, wordless adoration and apostolic ministry. Returning to our adoptive state in the bosom of the Trinity restores our dignity and encourages our lifelong expression of care and concern for others.

Among the countless gifts we receive from the medieval masters are light, love, and learning: the *light* that pierces the veil sin puts over our eyes; the *love* that redeems us despite the doubts that assail us; and the *learning* that shuns arrogance and banishes pride for the sake of increasing awe and humility. The masters we meet challenge us to pursue a life of beatitude and to acknowledge with one voice, many though we are, that without God we can do nothing.

II

Walk in the Truth of Who You Are

BERNARD OF CLAIRVAUX ON LOVING GOD AND GROWING IN HUMILITY

You wish me to tell you why and how God should be loved. My answer is that God himself is the reason why he is to be loved. As for how he is to be loved, there is no limit to that love.

—Bernard of Clairvaux, *Treatises II*, "On Loving God," 93

We use the word "love" in so many contexts it risks losing its meaning. Love can be reduced to a valentine verse or equated with a warm puppy. So what does it really mean?

St. Bernard of Clairvaux assures us that the need to love and be loved must transcend every form of selfishness, envy, hatred, and revenge. True love, as exemplified by Jesus, is other-oriented, patient, compassionate, healing, and forgiving.

Defaced as our earthly condition may be by sin, we must never forget that God sent his only begotten Son to save us. Love means to abandon ourselves to his redeeming mystery and to trust that the measure of love is to love without measure.

MEET THE MASTER

"Last of the Fathers." This was the accolade bestowed on Bernard of Clairvaux (1090–1153). It signifies his fulfillment of a long tradition of teaching and preaching extending from Augustine in the West to Gregory of Nyssa in the East. For these saints and scholars, reason and faith fused together in a single act of seeking the truth with a loving will in harmony with the total obedience of the Son of God to the Father. For them, there was no separation between hearing the Word in contemplative silence and acting upon it in service, themes St. Bernard highlighted in his eighty-six sermons on the first four lines of the Song of Solomon, first delivered in 1135 and reworked until the end of his life.[1]

Abbot and founder of the Cistercian reform, Bernard was the dominant force in the revival of monastic spirituality in the twelfth century. Not only clergy and religious but also laypeople referred to him as the conscience of Europe, whether he was debating his contemporary Peter Abelard; obeying ecclesial commands to preach in support of the Second Crusade; or crafting an eloquent treatise on the works of love.[2]

After the failure of the Second Crusade, Bernard was led by the Spirit to a time of profound soul-searching. He realized that he had read into the hearts of fighters and foes alike, not his own integrity of motive but what turned out to be bloodthirsty fanaticism. As a confidant of the papacy and the conscience of kings, he settled a papal schism in 1130. As an opponent of the rationalistic influence of Peter Abelard, he denounced dialectical scholasticism and its attempt to exalt, in Bernard's opinion, the complexity of reason above the simplicity of faith central to mystical theology.[3]

Like St. Benedict, his father in faith, he would have preferred to stay within the confines of the monastery, but he accepted his duty to serve the Church as the zealous spokesperson and able administrator he was. Though his health was poor—he seems to have suffered from anemia, migraine headaches, hypertension, and an atrophied sense of taste—his holiness was evident to all who sought his counsel, from the aristocracy to the peasant classes.

In the reformed monastery of Clairvaux, the monks were led by their founder to live joyful, devout, and productive lives. Bernard taught them to face with unbending faith the misery of the human condition defaced by sin while still insisting on the nobility of the soul created in the image and likeness of God. In language at once didactic and inspirational, he showed religious and laity how to live with renewed fervor Benedictine obedience, humility, and ongoing conversion of heart.[4]

Bernard grew up in a family of five brothers and one sister, where he learned from experience what loving God and others really meant. Both of his parents were models of virtue, teaching him by example what he himself later observed: that love yields the highest form of knowledge. It would appear that his mother exerted an influence on him reminiscent of St. Monica's on her son Augustine. The year of her death, 1107, marked the beginning of his long road to lasting conversion. In 1112, he felt drawn by God to cease his quest for a literary education and, as a result, relinquish his chances for ecclesiastical and academic advancement. With the spontaneous display of zeal and abandonment to God for which he would become famous, he joined the monastery of Citeaux, founded by St. Robert of Molesme in 1098, to follow a stricter observance of the Rule of St. Benedict. So magnetic was Bernard's personality that he brought with him twenty-five family members, all of whom expressed a similar desire to pursue a life of self-renunciation and solitude.

Three years after he joined the community at Citeaux, Bernard, along with twelve other monks, founded the Abbey of Clairvaux to preserve the purity of the Cistercian reform. He witnessed the fruits of his efforts as the Cistercian order went from one to more than three hundred foundations in a single generation.

St. Bernard died in 1153 within the confines of the abbey, celebrated then and now as a saint and servant of God whose literary, political, and religious life impacted the whole of Western society and strengthened the foundations of Roman Catholic and orthodox Christianity. In letters, sermons, and treatises, in public and private discourses and disputations, Bernard's starting point was a mystical life of love and absorption in God flowing into the active shepherding of souls in need of salvation.[5] He was canonized in 1174, only twenty-one years after his death, and in 1830 he was named a Doctor of the Church.

FROM SELF-KNOWLEDGE TO LOVING KNOWLEDGE OF GOD

The greatest anguish Bernard experienced was due not to the daily humiliations caused by his poor health but to the agonizing sense of not yet possessing God in the full measure of his desire. For him, the possession of pure love is the prime condition for the possibility of gaining knowledge of God, self, and others.[6]

The call to mystical union with God is put into practice in the monastery, which is in essence a school of charity, regulated by prayer and penance and revealing that the only source of fulfillment for the longing soul is God. According to Bernard, our chief task on earth is to rid ourselves of all that conceals the beauty and dignity of our true self. To choose lesser goods over the greater good keeps us prisoners of the sin and suffering caused by unconformity to Christ.[7]

Bernard meditates on three dynamics leading to union with God in love and service. They are *caritas*, or charity; *ascesis*, or asceticism; and *excessus*, or an ecstatic reaching out to the Divine that culminates in the renunciation of our own will and complete conformity to the Love that reaches down to lift us up.

Caritas. Bernard turns to the first letter of John the evangelist to find and reflect on the meaning of caritas: "No one has ever seen God; if we love one another, God lives in us, and his love is perfected in us. By this we know that we abide in him and he in us, because he has given us of his Spirit" (1 Jn 4:12–13).

If God is love, then selfishness, vainglory, and sinful separation from him have no place in our life. Charity, the greatest of God's gifts, reverses this downward spin to self-destruction and draws us to generosity, obedience, humility, and nearness to the Lord. This transformation is only possible because God has loved us first. The bond of love that unites us to God is due not to any merit of our own but to God's action of mercy for us.

The fruit of love comes to full bloom as these inner-directed transformations move us outward in service of God and neighbor. What motivates us to do good is no longer the fear of punishment but the thought that we might fail to trust in God's unfailing love. Thanks to the grace of caritas, we move from knowledge of self as loved by God to intimacy with the Trinity:

What, then, is God? He (Father, Son, and Holy Spirit) is the purpose to which the Universe looks, the salvation of the elect. What he is to himself, only he knows. What is God? All-powerful will, benevolent virtue, eternal light, changeless reason, supreme blessedness. He creates minds to share in himself, gives them life, so that they may experience him, causes them to desire him, enlarges them to grasp him, justifies them so that they may deserve him, stirs them to zeal, ripens them to fruition, directs them to equity, forms them in benevolence, moderates them to make them wise, strengthens them to virtue, visits them to console, enlightens them with knowledge, sustains them to immortality, fills them with happiness, surrounds them with safety.[8]

Ascesis. The moral and ascetical foundations of the mystical life need to be strengthened by self-denial and time spent in silence, formative reading, meditation, prayer, and contemplation. The spiritual disciplines help us to live fully as disciples of our Master. The basic meaning of asceticism for St. Bernard rests in the renunciation of our own will through charity and conversion of heart. Letting go of our ego-self releases us from willfulness and the refusal to place ourselves under the higher authority invested in the Church by the Lord and seen, for Bernard, in the submission of a monk to his abbot. Submission is not a sign of weakness but a way to liberate our true self from too much self-love. It is no use attempting a study of what is holy if we are caught in the throes of seeking worldly glory and the entanglements it spawns. Bernard holds that the Holy Spirit cannot teach the truth to a person who lacks self-discipline and has not mastered the disturbances caused by the vices. *Ascesis* opens the path to virtue, letting us sing of the Lord's ways and rejoice in the hope of good things to come. As he says, "It is not a sound from the lips but a stirring of joy, not a harmony of voices but of wills. It is not heard outwardly, nor does it sound in public (Is 42:2). Only he who sings it hears it, and he to whom it is sung—the Bride and the Bridegroom. It is a wedding song indeed, expressing the embrace of chaste and joyful souls, the concord of their lives and the mutual exchange of their love" (*SW*, 215).

Excessus. We must not associate this word with such extraordinary phenomena as visions or locutions. What Bernard means by *excessus* is that all that is, was, and will be moves toward God as the Sovereign Lord who loves us beyond all understanding. This movement outward and upward to God is a fusion of the soul with its Source, which results in a reclaiming of our true transcendent identity. This discovery of who we are in the depths of our Christ-formed personhood strips us of the last remnants of egocentricity and in an infused experience of consuming love draws us wholly into God—not dissolving our uniqueness but confirming it in the perfection of eternal goodness, truth, and beauty.

For Bernard, *excessus* is the crowning point of a life lived charitably, thanks to the asceticism of self-renunciation. Now, by the grace of God, we can be united to his Divine Son and ordained to accomplish his will in the light of who we are and what he asks us to do. To be wise in these matters, we must strive always to "treat transitory things as passing, as necessary for the moment," while clinging to "eternal things with an enduring desire." In Sermon 50 of his eighty-six sermons on the *Song of Songs*, the master himself concludes in a state of near ecstasy:

> O Truth, fatherland of exiles, end of their exile! I see you, but imprisoned in flesh, I may not enter. Muddy with sins, I cannot be admitted. O Wisdom, stretching from end to end, establishing and ordering everything (Wis 8:1), and arranging all things sweetly by enhancing feeling and making it orderly, guide what we do as your everlasting truth requires, so that each of us may securely glory in you and say, "He ordained love in me" (Sg 2:4). For you are the strength of God and the Wisdom of God (1 Cor 1:24), Christ, the Bridegroom of the Church and our Lord, God blessed forever. (*SW*, 245).

LOVING GOD WITHOUT MEASURE

In one of his most powerful treatises on loving God, written in 1141, Bernard proves a truth often reiterated in his sermons—that God is to be loved without any limit because God loved us first (see 1 Jn 4:9–10). And even if we love God with our whole heart and soul, with our body, spirit, mind, and will, we will never be able to love God enough. There are many motives for why we love God, especially when we face life's hardships and realize how much we rely on God's help. This is a good but lesser motivation compared to our loving God solely for his own sake. From this depth of divine love proceeds pure charity, which places the good of our neighbor above our own needs.

Bernard's treatise on loving God culminates in his analysis of the four degrees of love, beginning with the experience of well-regulated self-love that is not imposed by a precept but planted in us by nature: "Who is there who hates his own flesh? Yet should love, as it happens, grow immoderate, and, like a savage current, burst the banks of necessity, flooding the fields of delight, the overflow is immediately stopped by the commandment which says: 'You shall love your neighbor as yourself.'"[9] From this first degree of love we learn that we cannot operate on our own; we need the help of others, for we cannot survive for long without their kindness. Thus carnal love under the impetus of God's grace becomes social love, which reflects our reliance on God's mercy mirrored in our compassion for others who, like ourselves, need to be pardoned from the tyranny of sin.

The second degree concerns our loving God for the benefits we receive, that is to say, for the gifts and consolations God offers to us so abundantly. As we learn to distinguish between the consolations of God and the God who consoles, we cannot fail to see how lovable a benefactor God is and how highly and undeservedly we are blessed.

Third, we love God for God's sake, for himself alone, and for his ultimate goodness. Bernard puts into words this ineffable experience, saying, "This love is pleasing because it is free. It is chaste because it does not consist of spoken words but of deed and truth. It is just because it renders what is received. Whoever loves this way, loves the way he is loved, seeking in turn not what is his but what belongs to Christ. . . . who confesses to the Lord . . . because the Lord is good, truly loves God for God's sake and not for his own benefit."[10]

Lastly, in the fourth degree of love, we love ourselves for the sake of God. We enjoy participative transformation in the life of the Trinity. Embraced by infinite Love, we become one in spirit with God. The charity that flows from us proceeds from a pure heart, a peaceful conscience, a mature faith:

> To experience something of this sort, so rare in life, even if it be but once and for the space of a moment. To lose yourself, as if you no longer existed, to cease completely to experience yourself, to reduce yourself to nothing is not a human sentiment but a divine experience. . . . The satisfaction of our wants, chance happiness, delights us less than to see his will done in us and for us . . . just as air on a sunny day seems transformed into sunshine instead of being lit up; so it is necessary for the saints that all human feelings melt in a mysterious way and flow into the will of God.[11]

Bernard says that granting this degree of love is God's prerogative. Such a gift leaves no room for lesser loves that close the door of our heart to visitations from the Beloved moment by moment.

Taken together, these four degrees of love produce in us a confidence that prompts us to aspire to divine union, to obey the Great Commandment, and to live in the spirit of charity, cooperating with grace and storming heaven with ardent love. Now we operate from the center of our humility as adopted children of the Trinity.

Opposing growth in this foundational virtue is pride, which prevents us from practicing the presence of God and may even lead us to defend our sins to look good in the eyes of our confessors. Lack of humility may result in a hypocritical confession, rooted in duplicitous deceit, especially when we are caught in wrongdoing. Fueled by a brazen insolence that refuses to obey any voice other than our own, we may excuse ourselves from sinning ensnared in a torrent of vice, and may violate humility at the highest degree by choosing to call evil good and good evil.

As Bernard concludes, there is no other way to learn the full truth of why we are here than by getting rid of the beam of pride that blocks the light from our eyes. Brought face-to-face with ourselves, we may blush at what we see, but the love of truth makes us hunger and thirst after the promise of justice, peace, and mercy made to us by the Lord: "Thus I warily enter on the narrow way, step by step safely ascend the steep ladder, and by a kind of miracle climb to the truth, behind the time perhaps and limping, but still with confidence."[12]

REFLECT NOW

1. How would you assess your capacity to hear the Word of God in contemplative silence and act upon it in service?
2. Why does loving God above all else yield the highest form of knowledge?
3. Do you see submission not as a sign of weakness but as a way to liberate your true self to serve the Lord?

READ MORE

James France, *Medieval Images of St. Bernard of Clairvaux* (Kalamazoo, MI: Cistercian Publications, 2007).

Jean Leclercq, *A Second Look at St. Bernard*, trans. Marie-Bernard Said (Kalamazoo, MI: Cistercian Publications, 1990).

John E. Thornton and Susan B. Varenne, eds., *Honey and Salt: Selected Spiritual Writings of St. Bernard of Clairvaux* (New York: Vintage Books, 2007).

12

BE FRIENDS OF GOD
AND THEN BEFRIEND
ONE ANOTHER

AELRED OF RIEVAULX ON
SPIRITUAL FRIENDSHIP

Thus rising from that holy love with which a friend embraces a friend to that with which a friend embraces Christ, one may take the spiritual fruit of friendship fully and joyfully into the mouth, while looking forward to all abundance in the life to come.

—Aelred of Rievaulx, *Spiritual Friendship*, 126

In a world dominated by social media, a person today may be inclined to boast, "I have a thousand friends," but is that possible? Not according to Aelred of Rievaulx. He was a follower of the Cistercian school begun by St. Bernard of Clairvaux. For him true spiritual friendship—lasting, loyal, and always loving—is a rare and beautiful gift; it goes far beyond short-lived pleasure seeking. Friendship between two people, with Christ at the center, lasts for a lifetime because it passes the test of selfless service and sacrifice.

Aelred reminds us that we can befriend others only if we are friends of Christ. Only then can our outreach be charitable enough to resolve misunderstandings and foster the virtue of forgiveness.

All too often, we enter into false friendships characterized by selfish sensuality, betrayal of trust, and fits of anger that have nothing to do with Jesus' commandment to "lay down one's life" (see Jn 15:13). Aelred respects the rarity of such friendships while assuring us that Christ can lead us to these harmonious bonds in time as a foretaste of eternity.

Spiritual friendship is never possessive. In Aelred's words, it is not a meeting of lips but a mingling of spirits. Such intimacy is a testimony to Gospel living. Aelred's familiarity with Cicero's dialogue *De Amicitia* ("On Friendship") inspired him to reinterpret and modify its pre-Christian descriptions in the light of Christ's love for us and his commandment that we love one another since "God is love" (1 Jn 4:8), leading him to make the bold proclamation that "God is friendship."

MEET THE MASTER

St. Aelred of Rievaulx (1110–1167) lived in the golden age of the Cistercian reform. Thanks to the prophetic vision and apostolic zeal of St. Bernard of Clairvaux, there were at least five hundred foundations of the order in Europe alone. Under the tutelage of this great reformer, Aelred founded the Abbey of Rievaulx and attracted over six hundred new members. An excellent orator and author, whose wisdom and holiness earned him the title "Bernard of the North," Aelred manifested a style of leadership that revealed his genius for combining gentleness and firmness, compassion and monastic discipline.

Before he became a monk, Aelred mingled with members of the Scottish court, but he soon discovered that worldly ambition failed to satisfy his soul's longings for God. Overcome with feelings of self-loathing and disgust over the superficial life he led, in 1134 he heard and heeded the call to become a Cistercian monk, and he spent the remaining thirty-three years of his life, including the twenty he served as abbot, at the Abbey of

Rievaulx. Henceforth contemplation would be the source and center of his commitment to Christian charity and its expression in spiritual friendship.

Integral to this disclosure and to Aelred's religious life was his personal gift for making lasting friendships in keeping with the high moral standards of Christian virtue. To be a saint does not mean that we must stay away from or be wary of human affections, though their expression must be in accord with our vocational calling to the celibate or the married life.

In his treatise titled *Spiritual Friendship*, Aelred details how beneficial being friends of God and then befriending one another is to life in community, in society, and in the Church.[1] Such friendships model the person-to-Person relationship of intimacy to which Jesus invites his followers. As we read in 1 John 4:12, only when we live in love is God's love "perfected in us." Aelred concurred that "whoever loves God must love their brothers and sisters also" (1 Jn 4:21). He expands this thought, saying that in the perfection of charity "we love very many who are a source of burden and grief to us, for whose interest we concern ourselves honorably, not with hypocrisy or dissimulation but sincerely and voluntarily but yet we do not admit these to the intimacy of our friendship."[2] He says that we must exercise caution before we make any mutual commitment in the Lord because the virtue of friendship is bound to be under attack by the vices of corruption, cupidity, and carnality.

Essential to authentic spiritual friendship is the counsel Aelred offers us in the first part of his treatise: "You and I are here, and I hope that Christ is between us as a third" (*SF*, 1:1, 55). This hope is the most profound reason why spiritual friendship is both a gift and a challenge. It is a response to what Christ himself asks and expects of us. Otherwise it must be unstitched—a caution Aelred lends to exclusive or particular friendships, which often manifest "you and I" but not Christ "in our midst."

DISTINGUISHING TRUE FROM FALSE FRIENDSHIPS

The inclusive orientation of spiritual friendship is seen by Aelred as the fruit of Christian charity. It is a foretaste of heaven since "the right kind of friendship between us, which should begin in Christ, [ought to] be maintained according to Christ, and have its end and value referred to Christ" (*SF*, 1:8, 57).

True friendship, faithful and detached from any semblance of carnal pleasure or possessiveness, lasts through the trials and tribulations of life. Motivated by charity, not childishness, it expels such character faults as self-seeking fits of anger, annoyance, betrayal, and impatience. It teaches us what it means to "lay down one's life for one's friends" (Jn 15:13); it is, therefore, "that virtue . . . through which by a covenant of sweetest love our very spirits are united, and *from many are made one*" (*SF*, 1:21, 59).

Following what Aelred learned from his master, St. Augustine, the one who seeks true knowledge of self and of God will come to see humankind as a "little Trinity" mirroring in faith, hope, and charity the Holy Trinity.[3] The divine image in the substance of our soul accounts for the restless yearning of our heart for God; it explains why nothing we know or acquire can fill the empty space in us reserved for God alone. Though disobedience plunged us into the wretchedness of sin and death, making us vulnerable to demonic seduction and loss of friendship with God, that was not the last chapter of our story. We can begin anew because God befriended us by sending his only begotten Son to save us. Although we must be on guard against our inclination to lose ourselves in the land of unlikeness due to sin, we need not despair. The *imago dei* etched on our soul invites us to return to the home of our Father and to the unwavering warmth of his affection for us.

Suffering the loss of likeness to God alerts us to our need for redemption. Christ is the Divine Friend who restores our rightful place in the Father's merciful design. He bridges the gap between our temporal struggles and our longed-for eternal bliss. As Aelred proclaims, "What statement about friendship can be more sublime, more true, more valuable than this: it has been proved that friendship must begin in Christ, continue with Christ, and be perfected by Christ?" (*SF*, 1:10, 57). Christ never withholds from us this gift of holy affection, but he does expect us to extend the same spiritual kiss to one another.

The first part of Aelred's book is a commentary on the origin of friendship; the second outlines its fruition and excellence; and the third addresses the conditions and characteristics of unbroken friendship. His style of writing emulates that of Ciceronian dialogue with carefully realized conversations between Aelred and his three friends, Ivo, Walter, and Gratian.

The question that intrigues Aelred at first concerns how spiritual friendship can be preserved and brought to a holy end. Its origin, citing Cicero, is *"agreement in things human and divine, with good will and charity"* (*SF*, 1:11, 57). To this classical definition, Aelred adds: "Hence even the philosophers of this world placed friendship not among the accidents of mortal life but among the virtues that are eternal. Solomon seems to agree with them in this verse from Proverbs: *'a friend loves always.'* So he obviously declares that friendship is eternal if it is true, but if it ceases to exist, then, although it seemed to exist, it was not true friendship" (*SF*, 1:21, 59).

By contrast, relationships that are carnal spring from mutual togetherness in behaviors lacking moral rectitude. Pseudo-friendships are often undertaken without deliberation and indulged in imprudently, with no concern for how they affect others and governed more by passion than reason. Such contacts may be more worldly than wise, enkindled by hope of gain rather than by non-possessive, inclusive love and other-centered service. Among spiritual friends, prudence directs; justice rules; fortitude guards; and temperance moderates.

Superficial relationships have the opposite effect. Idle chatter replaces honest conversation. What we agree upon one day may be forgotten the next. We prefer trifles and deceptions rather than the discernment true friendship demands. Relationships must be tested to be sure Christ is in our midst, helping us to grow beyond carnal friendship in mutual benevolence and charity, "by a likeness of lifestyles and interests" (*SF*, 1:38, 62).

Since friends like this are few and far between, Aelred cautions us not to rely on a felt affinity but to exercise caution and proceed in cooperation with grace. He believes that nature impressed upon the human soul a desire for trustworthy, honest friendships; experience increased that desire and Christ confirmed it. However, original sin corrupted the splendor of our friendship with God and, by extension, with one another, thereby introducing disordered conduct, contention, dishonest defensiveness, hatred, and suspicion. Is it any wonder that mere affection is not sufficient and that true friendship cannot flourish outside of a binding relation with the Lord? Any behaviors, desires, and ends not in keeping with his example ought to be rejected or submitted to reform. So, then, whom ought we to call friends? Aelred replies, "only those to whom we have no qualm about entrusting our heart and all its contents, while these friends are bound to us in turn by the same inviolable law of loyalty and trustworthiness" (*SF*, 1:32, 61).

FRUITS OF CHRIST-FORMED FRIENDSHIPS

Having distinguished fair-weather acquaintances from real friends, Aelred describes how friendship in Christ increases our capacity to assert virtue and assail vice, temper adversity and foster prosperity. Among the many excellent outcomes of friendship are overcoming self-centeredness and rejoicing in another's accomplishments without a trace of envy. In the presence of a true, Christ-formed friend, we can unburden our minds; make sure that petty annoyances do not threaten our trust; and, best of all, converse about the illuminating inspirations we receive.

According to Aelred, the "heavenly flavor" of exchanges such as these frees us from the hold of lesser loves that promise fulfillment but never deliver it, whereas the one who is the friend of another in Christ "becomes the friend of God" (*SF*, 2:14, 74). Holding these friends together is the purity of their intention and their mutual practice of restraint and moderation. For Aelred, a friend is medicine for the ills of life and a sure foundation for growth in virtue.

To be rejected are puerile relationships embedded in fickle sentiment rather than in reason and faith. Encounters that despoil friendship tend to be reward-oriented, overly loquacious, and all too often disloyal. To such types we would hardly choose to entrust the secrets of our soul. From a true friend we receive loyal silence and forgiveness for our mistakes. There is no gossip between friends, only a renewed pledge to abide in Christ and to foster the intimacy that accompanies Gospel living. Here we ascend from Christ's inspiring the love with which we love our friend to Christ's offering himself to us as the friend we both love. Joined together are honor and charm, truth and joy, sweetness and goodwill, affection and action (see *SF*, 2:20, 75). These are among the most lasting fruits of spiritual friendship, having had their beginning in Christ, having advanced through Christ, and having been perfected in Christ.

STAGES OF SPIRITUAL FRIENDSHIP

To advance to the summit of spiritual friendship requires at its first stage *selection*, accompanied by the vigilance that guards our heart from being weakened or overcome by the five vices Aelred depicts as particularly dangerous:

+ *Slander*, which injures reputations and extinguishes love.
+ *Reproaches* made against our neighbor.
+ *Displays of pride*, leaving little or no room for humble service.
+ *Revelations of hidden things*, combined with the thoughtless breaking of confidentiality and the betrayal of trust.
+ *Detraction* from another's goodness or goodwill, exacerbated by displays of envy and jealousy.

Troublesome as well are displays of excessive anger, irascible mood swings, consuming suspicion, and divisive instability:

> Although one who is rarely moved by these passions is not easily found, still many are found who are above them all. They overcome anger by patience, check levity by respect for gravity, and banish suspicion by focusing on love. In my view, because of their great experience in conquering vice by virtue, they should be especially welcomed into friendship and kept with greater assurance the more firmly they have been accustomed to counter the assaults of vice. (*SF*, 3:32, 95–96)

The second stage is *probation*. Aelred warns us not to form friendships too quickly. If an intimacy of soul into which we enter proves to be untrue, it should not be broken off or dissolved at once but "unstitched little by little." We are to continue the love while slowly withdrawing the friendship. The grounds for dissolving it include the revelation of secrets; the dispensation of hidden stings of detraction; envy of others whom we love equally; and misunderstandings caused by jealousy. With great sensitivity, Aelred adds, "If the person you love harms you, love him still. If he be such that your friendship should be withdrawn, still never let your love be withdrawn. As much as you can, consider his welfare, respect his reputation, and, even if he has betrayed the secrets of your friendship, never betray his" (*SF*, 3:44, 98).

Aelred says to his friend Walter, in fond memory of their friend Ivo, that there are four qualities that must be tested in a friend during this probationary period:

+ *Loyalty*, or sticking by us through thick and thin.
+ *Right intention*, or expecting nothing from the friendship except obedience to God's will and doing what is good versus the hope of gaining some mercenary advantage.
+ *Discretion*, or a prudent understanding of what is to be done on behalf of our friends, of what is to be sought, and what sufferings are to be endured for their sake. This virtue also includes openings for fraternal admonition and the manner, time, and place of its disclosure.
+ *Patience*, or not grieving when rebuked, neither being angry nor hateful toward the one inflicting the rebuke but seeking the grain of truth in every criticism and being willing to bear every adversity for the sake of our friend.

The third state is *admission* to a possibly true and faithful friendship that begins in time and is perfected in eternity. Its elements are:

+ *Love*, revealed in the rendering of services with benevolence.
+ *Affection*, which moves us inwardly and manifests itself outwardly.
+ *Security*, or the revelation of counsels and confidences without fear and suspicion.
+ *Happiness*, characterized by a pleasing and friendly sharing of all events that occur, whether joyful or sad.

Aelred pays tribute to the grace of admission in this touching experience he shares with Walter and Gratian:

> The day before yesterday, as I was walking around the monastery, with the brothers sitting in a most loving circle, I marveled at the leaves, blossoms and fruits of each single tree as if I were in the fragrant bowers of paradise. Finding not one soul whom I did not love and, I was sure, not one

> soul by whom I was not loved, I was filled with a joy that
> surpassed all the delights of the world. Indeed as I felt my
> spirit flowing into them all and the affection of all coursing
> through me, I could say with the prophet, *"See how good and*
> *how pleasant it is for brethren to live in unity."* (SF, 3:82, 108)

This experience draws Aelred to reflect on the fourth stage of spiritual
friendship, that of true love and *perfect harmony* in matters human and
divine. Such love is more than being able to converse and jest together, to
disagree with one another at one moment and learn something new the
next. While such exchanges and admonitions may not be dishonorable,
Aelred pursues a higher standard of holiness: a growth in prayer and piety,
in a zeal for things of the spirit so that "with affection purified, such friends
may mount to higher realms . . . because of a kind of likeness the ascent is
easier from human friendship to friendship with God himself" (SF, 3:87,
109). When friendship is perfect, constant, and pointing toward the Eternal,
envy does not corrupt it, nor suspicion diminish it, nor ambition dissolve it.
Reverence and respect dispel bitterness and condescension.

Since those who dwell in friendship dwell in God and God in them,
it is with the evidence of reason and the conviction of faith that Aelred
concludes:

> Was that not like the first fruits of bliss, *so to love and so to*
> *be loved*, to help and to be helped, and from the sweetness
> of brotherly love to fly aloft toward that higher place in the
> splendor of divine love, or from the ladder of charity now to
> soar to the embrace of Christ himself, or, now, descending
> to the love of one's neighbor, there sweetly to rest? Conse-
> quently, if in this our friendship, which I have introduced to
> you by way of example, you discover something to imitate,
> make it serve your own progress. (SF, 3:127, 124)

Spiritual friendship is that rare gift that fulfills the divine plan by which
God willed a loving and harmonious exchange between the rational creatures
he created and befriended, walking with them hand in hand. No separation
is strong enough to destroy this mysterious flow of love between us and the
Trinitarian mystery. Even then, a final favor awaits us: "With the beginning

of relief from care we shall rejoice in the supreme and eternal good, when the friendship to which on earth we admit but few will pour over all and flow back to God from all, for God will be *all in all*" (*SF*, 3:134, 126).

REFLECT NOW

1. Do you agree that virtuous living in intimacy with the Lord is an essential ingredient of spiritual friendship?
2. In what way are the spiritual friendships you enjoy a response to Christ's command to love one another as he has loved us?
3. How does your primary friendship with Christ help you to overcome self-centeredness and become more charitable to others?

READ MORE

Christopher Kiesling, *Celibacy, Prayer, and Friendship: A Making-Sense-Out-of-Life Approach* (New York: Alba House, 1978).
Kenneth Leech, *Soul Friend: A Study of Spirituality* (London: Sheldon Press, 1977).
C. S. Lewis, *The Four Loves* (New York: Harcourt, Brace & Co., 1988).

13

DEPEND ON GOD
FOR EVERYTHING

FRANCIS AND CLARE OF ASSISI
ON THE PRIMACY OF POVERTY

Where there is poverty with joy, there is neither covetous-
ness nor avarice.

—Francis of Assisi, *The Complete Works*, 35

It was the vocation of Francis of Assisi (1181–1226) to imitate Christ in
every possible way—at one moment delighting in the abundance of creation
and in the next practicing the most rigorous self-denying mortifications.[1]
Countless tales reveal the humorous and humble way he pursued his mission. Once, it was said, he overheard a friar complaining of hunger. Rather
than making him feel ashamed, Francis accompanied him to a local vineyard,
where the two of them feasted on grapes to their heart's content, counting on
the mercy and generosity of the proprietor to protect them from any liability.

Francis approached life with a disposition of foolhardy abandonment to
the mystery of Divine Mercy. He was never dour or predictable. One year
when Christmas fell on a Friday, a friar asked if they should fast. Legend
avows Francis to have replied that on the birthday of Jesus even the walls
of the house should eat! In a crucial meeting with the pope and his cardinals, when he was at a loss for words to explain his life, he danced. This

wildly spontaneous act won the pope over; he was probably tired of being surrounded by sane and stuffy diplomats. He recognized the work of the Holy Spirit in Francis's holy foolishness and felt in it a surge of new hope for the Church.

Meet the Masters

Francis was the son of a wealthy silk merchant, Pietro di Bernardone, who loathed the fact that his heir would never carry on his ambitious projects. Francis would instead become the legendary repairer of God's Church, the recipient of the stigmata, and the founder of a worldwide religious family. Rather than be corrupted by power, pleasure, and possessions, Francis wedded himself to Lady Poverty, seeking to conform in body and soul to his crucified and risen Lord.

Until the year 1206, Francis surrounded himself with the worldly comforts due to a young gentleman of his social standing. These trappings dropped from him the day he drifted into the broken-down chapel of San Damiano to pray, to seek the meaning of his life, and to convince himself that he had heard with the ears of his heart Christ speaking to him from a relic of a cross. Answering the Lord without hesitation, he prayed that God would enlighten his heart and give him the faith, hope, and charity he needed to carry out every commandment he received.[2] With childlike trust, Francis took it upon himself to relay the bricks and seal the mortar of the ruined Church. Everyone thought he was crazy, including his father, who would soon disown him and declare him insane. Christ's call only intensified and, contrary to his entire upbringing, Francis obeyed it and began to live on alms. He disrobed in the public square and threw himself on the mercy of the bishop. He had nowhere to go but the open road and a few caves and hovels to shield him from the elements.

By 1209 Francis discovered that his mission was not to take up arms to defend Assisi or to seek any kind of political or ecclesiastical favor. It was to reinstate in the Church the essence of Christ's message by preaching repentance; by living a life of poverty, chastity, and obedience; and by letting the Christ in him meet with mercy and forgiveness the Christ in every true believer and sincere seeker he would thenceforth encounter.

Francis soon attracted twelve companions who, inspired by his witness, accepted a life of radical discipleship. By 1219, their numbers had expanded beyond all expectations. Three years before his death, Francis received the stigmata, the gift of the five wounds of Jesus, marking the intensity of his union with Christ and his uncanny ability to preach the Gospel without saying a word. Being as in tune as he was with the earth and all creatures upon it, men and beasts alike, drew Francis in ecstasy and awe to their Divine Source. In his "Canticle of Brother Sun," he praises sun, moon, and stars, day and night, life and death.[3]

Everything he saw, everyone he met, from lepers in rags to knights in armor, evoked in him the praise and glory of God. What motivated Francis's attraction to material poverty was not a penchant for heroism but an interior movement of total dependence on God. Knowing his own profile of sinfulness prompted him to relinquish all claims to ownership and to rely on his Lord and Savior to meet his needs. His friend Thomas of Celano, to whom history owes a great deal for the biographical information we have about Francis, recorded that poor as he was physically, he acted with undaunted spiritual boldness. From his travels to Rome to receive a papal blessing on his new order to his pilgrimage as a peacemaker to the Middle East, Francis refused to call attention to himself. He spoke with the authority invested in him as a disciple of the Lord, who took upon himself the burden of sin we carry. Though not a scholar of the law, he felt compelled to speak the truth to the most learned and with equal care to give the living Gospel to the illiterate.

Though Christ is the victor, Francis showed that we must go through fire to follow him. The self-stripping he chose was not an end in itself but a sign of his selfless identification with the Cross. For him, privations were causes for perfect joy devoid of any complaint. The elation he exuded in word and song convinced those with ears to hear of the primacy of poverty and the torrent of repentance it released that alone could restore the Church.

Though Francis enjoyed unexpected popularity in his time—he would be canonized two years after his death—he was not necessarily understood by his peers. Controversy swirled around him regarding the nature of poverty and the place of learning, but Francis died in peace in the blessed assurance that his identification with Christ crucified was complete. Lying nearly naked on the bare earth, he welcomed Sister Death, having nothing and wanting nothing but his Lord. To the brothers and sisters mourning him, he offered this poignant reminder, "Let us begin, brothers, to serve the Lord our God for up to now we have made little or no progress" (FC, 3). Before earthly death transitioned him to heavenly life, he whispered this testament to his friars: "Since because of my weakness and the pain of my sickness I am not strong enough to speak, I make known my will to my brothers briefly in these three phrases, namely: as a sign that they remember my blessing and my testament, let them always love one another, let them always love and be faithful to our Lady Holy Poverty, and let them always be faithful and subject to the prelates and all clerics of Holy Mother Church" (FC, 164).

LIVING IN CONFORMITY TO THE CROSS

The seedbed of Franciscan spirituality is the belief that in all circumstances of life the Love that embraces us is reason enough to radiate joyful optimism and sacrificial generosity. These virtues align our intellect, memory, and will with the Word of God just as self-denial and docility direct our thoughts, feelings, and desires to Christ. For Francis, pain was as nothing compared to the pleasure of sharing life with the Crucified. Conformity to the Cross in harsh and happy times frees us from the bondage of sin and identifies us as the adopted children of God.

Though Francis's writings are few, they offer an itinerary for how to match Christ-centered contemplation with a life of service to people abandoned physically and spiritually. Francis derived strength for his apostolate from reception of the sacraments and participation in the liturgy that for him renewed and manifested the whole history of salvation. He insisted that we show reverence and respect for the Church and its hierarchy. The main features of his spirituality were devotion to the Mystical Body of Christ in communion with the triumphant in heaven, the militant on earth, and the suffering in purgatory and reliance on the protection of Mary, Mother of God and mediatrix for all God's children. Francis directs us to conform to the truth of the Beatitude that the kingdom of heaven belongs to the poor in spirit. These ideals appear in the first chapter of the primitive *Rule of the Friars Minor* (1210):

> The rule and life of these brothers is this: to live in obedience, in chastity, and without anything of their own, and to follow the teaching and the footprints of our Lord Jesus Christ, Who says: *If you wish to be perfect, go* (Mt 19:21) and *sell* everything (cf. Lk 18:22) *you have and give it to the poor, and you will have treasure in heaven; and come, follow me* (Mt 19:21). (FC, 109)

While Francis never reduced conformity to Christ to acts of bodily mortification, he knew he had to subdue the impulses of his nature in response to the guidance of grace. The fact that this illumination looked excessive to others may explain why Francis offered an end-of-life apology to "Brother Ass," his body, for any mistreatment he may have done to it. He wanted his legacy to be a stripping of self-love, because it disfigured the Christ-form of his soul. He taught that our human nature is a gift given to us by God so that our whole being may be an embodiment of Christ's infinite love for souls. Francis lived from his center in Christ and insisted that his followers do the same. The more they imitated the hidden life of Jesus of Nazareth, the happier they would be. Men of all ages were so attracted to his spirituality that they dropped what they were doing and followed him. So did one special woman.

The table Francis set would have been incomplete had not Clare of Assisi (1193–1253), foundress of the Poor Clares, put into practice the teachings he lived. Clare saw herself as a little plant in the great greenhouse of Francis's mission to rebuild and revitalize the Church. In reality she was both a pillar of strength and a prophetic voice. Despite her poor health, she fulfilled every duty asked of her by her nuns. She showed them that it was possible to be a lover of solitude and a servant of the community at one and the same time. Her reforming efforts have a special place in the history of the Church, contributing as they did to the renewal of the contemplative as well as the apostolic life.[4]

Clare knew from the moment she met Francis that she could no longer be satisfied with a mere worldly existence, no more than he had been. She, too, wanted to be as perfect a reflection of Christ as possible. Though hidden in him, Clare's life would be visible to all. She was silent, yet her words and witness were destined to be known throughout the world (see *FC*, 178).

SHARING IN POVERTY THE WEALTH OF GOD'S LOVE

Of noble birth and reputed beauty, Clare of Assisi could have elected a life of ease, until this young man of Assisi, who chose to be a beggar and follow Lady Poverty, touched her heart and changed her life. Other people mocked him as a misguided fool, but not her. After Clare heard Francis preach at a Lenten retreat in 1212, she stole away to meet him and to ask how she, too, might live the Gospel to the full. Francis accepted the genuineness of her vocation and blessed her espousal to Christ. On the night of Palm Sunday, she left her home to join him and for the next forty years lived in a convent attached to the Church of San Damiano.

To the young women who joined her in the first family of Poor Clares, she wrote in her testament:

> In the Lord Jesus Christ, I admonish and exhort all my sisters, both those present and those to come, to strive always to imitate the way of holy simplicity, humility, and poverty and [to preserve] the integrity of [our] holy manner of life, as we were taught by our blessed Father Francis from the beginning of our conversion to Christ.... Loving one another with the charity of Christ, let the love you have in your hearts be shown outwardly in your deeds so that, compelled by such an example, the sisters may always grow in love of God and in charity for one another. (*FC*, 231)

Clare lived long enough to oversee the remarkable growth of her cloistered community of women under Francis's tutelage. She had already witnessed what a harvester of souls Francis was, so it did not surprise her when her community flourished. Shunning offers of patronage, as he had done, she, too, embraced Lady Poverty with rigor and love. It was she who urged Francis to go into the world teaching and preaching while she devoted her life to contemplative prayer. One of her greatest joys was to learn two days before her death that Pope Innocent IV approved the rule she had written for her sisters and with it the life of radical poverty they had chosen with joy to lead. As she told her sisters, "Always be lovers of God and your souls and the souls of your Sisters, and always be eager to observe what you have promised the Lord" (FC, 234).

Clare epitomizes the Franciscan ideal of faithfulness to Christ in poverty of spirit and purity of heart. Her love for the cloister complemented his zeal for the salvation of souls. Together these two disciples became one epiphany of the mystery of redemption. If Francis was fire, it was Clare who struck the match. If Francis was oil, it was Clare who lit the lamp. She, who had fallen as madly in love with God as Francis had, had no choice but to sing:

> Happy, indeed is she to whom it is given
> to share this sacred banquet,
> to cling with all her heart to [Jesus]
> whose beauty all the heavenly hosts admire unceasingly,
> whose love inflames our love,
> whose contemplation is our refreshment,
> whose gentleness fills us to overflowing,
> whose remembrance brings a gentle light,
> whose fragrance will revive the dead,
> whose glorious vision will be the happiness
> of all the citizens in the heavenly Jerusalem. (FC, 204)

These exquisite lines were written in 1253, the year of Clare's death. In some way, their exultant expression reveals Clare's last words. They represent her mature voice. There is nothing in them of the girlishness of courtly romance or the unbalanced extremes of excessive asceticism. They serve as pointers to the foundational, faith-filled spirituality available, through the power of grace, to all baptized persons. In them we catch a glimpse of the spirit of faith, hope, and love that flowed through this cloistered nun like an eternal spring, inviting everyone trapped in the bondage of sin to turn for help to the Divine Liberator, to whom she dedicated her life.

The vowed state of obedience, poverty, and chastity, of letting go of inordinate attachments and of loving others as God has loved us, prompted Clare from the confines of her convent in San Damiano to pray for the whole world. She found continual refreshment for her vocation at the eucharistic table. Reception of the Body and Blood of Christ drew her whole being to a posture of listening to the inspirations of the Holy Spirit and following them as Francis did.

LIVING THE PASCHAL MYSTERY WITH JOY

By clinging to Jesus with all her heart, Clare found the confidence she needed to be faithful to her mission and the courage it took to withstand suffering for Christ's sake and to learn to depend on God for everything. As a result, Clare withheld nothing of herself from the immolating fire that quenches every trace of narcissism. Her living the Paschal Mystery with joy expressed itself in three ways:

Bodily, she chose the charism of virginity, knowing that her love for the Lord must be and remain chaste, respectful, and pure—an acceptable offering to the Most High. Her counsel to Bl. Agnes of Prague came from what she herself had experienced: "When you have loved [him], you shall be chaste; when you have touched [him], you shall become pure; when you have accepted [him], you shall be a virgin" (FC, 191).

Mentally, as well as emotionally and functionally, Clare's life of inner purity, or "inviolable virginity," had to be revealed in holy service to others and charity to all. For Clare, Christian love must be put to the test of self-sacrificing service. Having witnessed the work of Francis, she knew that to preach love without practicing charity would constitute the height of hypocrisy. As Francis had shown her and his community, if Christ appears to us in the guise of a leper, we must follow the prompting of grace, overcome our natural revulsion, and give him a kiss.[5]

The call to follow Christ and the command to wash others' feet were for Clare one and the same. Thus she tells Agnes, "Be strengthened in the holy service which you have undertaken out of an ardent desire for the Poor Crucified" (FC, 191). Ardent charity is an unmistakable sign that we are walking in the footprints of the Master. As Clare wrote in her testament, "Loving one another with the charity of Christ, let the love you have in your hearts be shown outwardly in your deeds so that, compelled by such an example, the sisters may always grow in love of God and in charity for one another" (*FC*, 231).

Spiritually, on the highest level of transcendent transformation, the love of God, self, and others became a continuous, lasting disposition of Clare's heart. If chastity, charity, and communion with Christ are each a tributary flowing from the side of Christ, then contemplation is the great river into which they pour. The chaste bride of the Most High King is the one whose sole refreshment is unceasing prayer. Clare's prescription for progress in contemplation can be found in her second letter to Bl. Agnes. There she suggests that a true lover of God must gaze upon Christ with awe-filled attention and abiding adoration; she must, above all, contemplate him with the intention of imitating his love for humankind. For Clare, presence to the Mystery becomes the only wellspring from which a Christ-centered ministry can flow.

With the passion that accompanies contemplation, Clare says that such prayer makes us sigh with desire for the Beloved. The love in our heart swells to magnanimous proportions. We are compelled to cry out, as Clare did, with the bride in the Song of Songs: "Draw me after you! . . . O heavenly spouse! I will run and not tire" (*FC*, 205).

Witness Clare's docility to Francis, her compassion for the poor, her dedication to daily prayer. All that she received, she wanted to give away. As with Francis, nothing was seen as her possession. The words *I*, *me*, and *mine* were not permitted by either of them. All is to be shared as part of the common life. Both saints acknowledged that every good and perfect gift comes to us from the Giver of grace (see Jas 1:17).

Never would Clare or her sisters be captivated by the illusory promises of happiness pulsating through the society of their time, nor be disturbed by the clamor connected to worldly power, which passes like a shadow: "How many kings and queens of this world let themselves be deceived! For, even though their pride may reach the skies and their heads [pierce] through the clouds, in the end they are as forgotten as a dung-heap!" (*FC*, 201).

Clare advises Agnes, as Francis had reminded her, to be so conscious of the origins of her call that she will hold on to it unswervingly, receiving from God the impetus she needs "to go forward securely, joyfully, and swiftly, on the path of prudent happiness, believing nothing, agreeing with nothing which would dissuade you from this resolution or which *would place a stumbling block* for you on the way, so that you may offer *your vows to the Most High* in the pursuit of that perfection to which the Spirit of the Lord has called you" (*FC*, 196).

The papal bull of canonization summarizes the paradoxical reality of her life and why from its inception God had called her to follow him through Francis: "She was hidden yet her way . . . was open. Clare kept silent, but her fame cried out. She was concealed in a cell, but she was taught in the cities. It is no wonder that so bright and glowing a light could not be hidden, but must shine forth and give clear light in the Lord's house."[6]

REFLECT NOW

1. What can you do to help others adopt the disposition of being a caretaker of creation and fostering insofar as possible ecological sensitivity?
2. Do you try to associate the virtue of poverty of spirit with the practice of total dependence on God?
3. What must you do to be and become another Christ in this world?

READ MORE

Ian Morgan Cron, *Chasing Francis: A Pilgrim's Tale* (Grand Rapids, MI: Zondervan, 2013).

John V. Fleming, *An Introduction to the Franciscan Literature of the Middle Ages* (Chicago: Franciscan Herald Press, 1977).

Jon Sweeney, *The Enthusiast: How the Best Friend of Francis of Assisi Almost Destroyed What He Started* (Notre Dame, IN: Ave Maria Press, 2016).

14

SEE IN EVERY ENDING
A NEW BEGINNING

BONAVENTURE ON THE
SOUL'S JOURNEY INTO GOD

When, therefore, the soul considers itself, it rises through itself as through a mirror to behold the blessed Trinity of the Father, the Word and Love: three persons, coeternal, coequal, and consubstantial. Thus each one dwells in each of the others; nevertheless one is not the other but the three are one God.
　　　　　　　—Bonaventure, *The Soul's Journey into God*, 84

Life as a journey is a metaphor familiar to all of us. From birth to death, we move from where we were, through a myriad of expected and unexpected events, to the unknown land that lies beyond the places and people we know and love.

St. Bonaventure speaks of our journey as one into ever greater knowledge of God. We move forward with humble awareness, knowing how much we will never know because of the limits of the human condition. Awe overtakes us as we access under the saint's watchful eye the resources of both faith and reason. In every ending we find, as he does, a new beginning. We need not fear what lies ahead, provided we trust that the Risen Lord is with us, ready to reveal what lies behind the finite door we must pass through to reach the infinite corridors of paradise.

MEET THE MASTER

Called upon by the General Chapter of the Friars Minor to be the official biographer of his spiritual father, St. Francis of Assisi, St. Bonaventure of Bagnoregio (1217–1274) was a humble servant of the Lord as well as a brilliant theologian and a mystical poet. In the year 1257, he was elected minister general of the Franciscan order, becoming, so to speak, its second founder and the chief architect of its enduring spirituality.

By 1263 he had completed his biography of Francis, focusing on his original ways of living the Gospel to perfection.[1] Bonaventure attributes his own miraculous cure from a youthful sickness that could have claimed his life to the intercession of St. Francis. In him he saw what it means to adhere to God's will and never deviate from the demands of conformity to the crucified Christ.[2]

Committed as he was to the pursuit of truth, Bonaventure studied theology at the University of Paris, receiving his professorship in 1253. One of his finest accomplishments was to integrate his orientation to the mystery of the Trinity with his devotion to the humanity of Christ. Both elements are present in his book *The Soul's Journey into God*, where he depicts the convergence of the contemplative and the active life.[3]

For Bonaventure, action is contemplation incarnated, and contemplation is action purified and at rest. This truth, validated in his own life, led Bonaventure to view the entirety of our journey as a quest to know, love, and serve God. Its hallmarks are poverty, or detachment from excessive material or spiritual acquisitions; chastity, or reverential respect for creation in its myriad human and nonhuman forms; and obedience, or listening so deeply to God's Word that it comes to fruition in zealous prayer and service to others. Living these virtues to the full results in the spiritual stamina that allows us to cultivate other Christlike attributes. These include reciprocal compassion, heartfelt repentance, and watchful waiting upon the Lord, in whose light our journey proceeds from birth to death.

In the prologue of his masterwork, Bonaventure invokes Christ to enlighten the eyes of our soul and to guide our feet to the repose of peace, the splendor of truth, and the sweetness of love (see *Soul's Journey*, 53). Faithful to the spirit of his father Francis, he dwelt on the truth of revelation as a means to increase our humility in the face of the incomprehensible mystery of the Trinity. The Supreme Cause of all things enlightens our human intelligence so that we may return to God by means of natural reason and the light of faith. Thus Bonaventure advises that in the pursuit of truth we read with unction; speculate with devotion; investigate with wonder; observe with joy; work with piety; gain knowledge through love and understanding through humility; and do what we do with the awareness that all is grace (see *Soul's Journey*, 55–56).

The wellspring of Bonaventure's work is holy scripture.[4] He hardly writes a sentence without a quote from the Bible. As a scholastic theologian he, like his contemporary St. Thomas Aquinas (1224–1274), knew both Platonic and Aristotelian philosophy and therefore respected the two wings of truth, reason and faith. He also drew upon the philosophical reflections of Augustine of Hippo and consulted *The Mystical Theology* of Pseudo-Dionysius, a book that inspired his presentation of the triple way of purgation, illumination, and union.[5] Bonaventure also summarizes and sheds fresh light on such traditional avenues to attaining Christian perfection as meditation, prayer, and contemplation.

St. Bonaventure, representing the Franciscans, and St. Thomas Aquinas, representing the Dominicans, carried the tradition of the love of learning and the desire for God to its fullest measure. As scholars seeking rational insight, they studied philosophy and theology to come to a better understanding of what they believed while striving to model in their personhood that purity of spirit whereby God lets us taste and see what we know from experience to be true. Their writings offer the Church a legacy of spiritual inspiration and doctrinal depth that is as foundational as it is practical.

Man of God that he was, Bonaventure ministered to believers and sincere seekers whose piety aroused his compassionate care. He appreciated the fact that their motives for living the faith relied not so much on speculative insight into its content as on the imitation of Christ. The Seraphic Doctor passed to the eternity he had depicted so eloquently on July 15, 1274. He was canonized in 1482 and named a Doctor of the Church in 1587.

JOURNEYING TO GOD OVER A LIFETIME

The moment we embark on the journey to God, we realize that we are not alone. Beneath the complexity of rational analysis resides the simplicity of childlike faith in Jesus Christ, who is the way, the truth, and the life. To follow him from Bethlehem to the beatific vision implies that we cooperate with the action of grace, expel sin, and find rest for our weary souls at the wellspring of divine forgiveness.

As we journey onward, we let the action of grace supersede all personal effort, resulting in purer forms of prayer that clarify the truth of who we are; clear the channels of divine union obscured by sin; and enable us to embrace the Cross that sets us free. What follows is a mystical knowing in love by which we respond to God's leading, savor the sweetness of charity, and adore the beauty of the Divine that is beyond all telling.

In the opening lines of *The Soul's Journey into God*, Bonaventure depicts the path to Christian perfection that committed disciples must follow. He derives his inspiration from the text of the prophet Isaiah (6:2), which focuses on the six wings of the seraph. He interprets this symbol as a pointer to six levels of illumination by which the soul can pass over to the place promised by Jesus "through ecstatic elevations of Christian wisdom" (*Soul's Journey*, 54).

Bonaventure describes our ascent to God, starting with a meditation on the first revelation in creation and ending with contemplation of the mystery that holds in being all that is. The last stage leads us in body, mind, and spirit to the goal of union with Christ crucified and glorified. In summary, these are the ways by which the soul journeys into God:

1. *Through God's vestiges in the universe.* When we meditate on the physical-sensible world, we glimpse God's traces or footprints everywhere we look; we experience, as St. Francis did, the beautiful order and abundance of nature. These vestiges reflect the power, wisdom, and goodness of their Divine Source. Behind them all, we behold in faith the outflow of Trinitarian love in universe and history. In Bonaventure's view, the Father is the fountain

of fullness, who generates every facet of initial and ongoing creation. The Son is the perfect image and Eternal Word of the Father. The Spirit, who proceeds from the Father and the Son, manifests their mutual love. He is the Paraclete through whom all good gifts are given to us.

2. *Through God's vestiges in the sense world.* The whole created world is a mirror through which we may pass over to God, the supreme Craftsman of all that is. As we read in the book of Wisdom:

> If through delight in the beauty of these things people assumed
>   them to be gods,
> let them know how much better than these is their Lord,
> for the author of beauty created them.
> And if people were amazed at their power and working,
> let them perceive from them how much more powerful is the one
>   who formed them. (Ws 13:3–4)

What, then, must we do to enhance this capacity to see God in all that surrounds us? Bonaventure advises us to contemplate, for example, the weight, number, and measure of things. We ought to pay attention to their order, substance, power, and operation. Such in-depth seeing requires that we believe in their origin and end in accordance with the revelation and the power and providence of God. We ought also to investigate things as they are, discerning in them their divine source.

3. *Through God's image stamped on our natural powers.* By these powers, Bonaventure means memory, intellect, and will. Slowly but surely, we begin to reflect on the outer world as a window through which we learn more about the inner dynamics of our ascent to God. We remember in hope; we understand in faith; and we will in love God's will for us.

4. *Through God's image in us reformed by the gifts of grace.* These gifts are the three theological virtues of faith, hope, and charity bestowed on us in Baptism. By these supernatural powers, we are redeemed from the fallenness of the human condition and made ready by grace to imitate Christ. Prideful disobedience begins to be overcome by means of Christ's perfect obedience. This reformation is an affective experience, not merely a product of rational analysis. We cease sinning because we love God in the fullness of devotion as

opposed to the fear of punishment. Ours is a superabundance of exultation and a prelude to union.

5. *Through contemplating the Divine Unity in its being.* The omniscient, omnipresent God whom we adore is utterly simple (one Lord, one God) and all-powerful, the Alpha and Omega, the "efficient, exemplary and final cause of all things" (*Soul's Journey*, 98). And yet this immense and perfect God revealed himself to us in the Incarnate Word, who speaks to our heart and draws us to himself. No proof of this stage of the itinerary is more convincing to Bonaventure than the reception by St. Francis of the stigmata on Mount Alverna. This sign of total union with Christ readied him for his *transitus* to eternity. The experience of perfect conversion to God and obedience to lawful authority are among the Franciscan ideals Bonaventure sets forth in his depiction of the tree of life. There we meet Jesus in the humility of his hiddenness, in the loftiness of his power, in the plentitude of his piety, in the mystery of his Passion, and in the sublimity of his Resurrection and Ascension.

6. *Through contemplating the Most Holy Trinity in its goodness.* Now the soul rises above itself and its inherent divisions to behold the Divine Unity of one God in Three Persons. Our lives at every moment are to be lived in the name of the Father, the Son, and the Holy Spirit. Purged, illumined, and perfected in response to grace, we can witness to the essential truth of our faith that God is one in three, unified in "essence, form, dignity, eternity, existence, and unlimitedness" (*Soul's Journey*, 106). We ascend in childlike trust and intimacy to a contemplation of the Trinity beyond words and concepts.

7. *In spiritual and mystical ecstasy.* In this seventh stage, our affections pass over entirely into God and on to Sabbath rest. All intellectual activity ceases, only to be replaced by an outpouring of wisdom revealed to us by the Holy Spirit. In the light of these once-hidden secrets of contemplation, our efforts are of little or no worth. There is in us less inquiry and more unction, fewer words and more inner joy. What matters on this highest plane of reality is grace, not instruction; desire, not understanding; the groaning of contemplative prayer, not discursive meditation. The Holy Spirit gifts us with the awareness that Christ alone is our guide and our teacher. He is the God-man whom we adore in the darkness of pure faith; he returns us to our essence in the Trinity that preceded our existence in time. Now we

enter into the fire and light of love that inflames our soul and carries us to our journey's end: conformity to Christ.

REUNITING WITH GOD THROUGH PRAYER AND PARTICIPATION

The practices that follow upon these stages of our journey into God are detachment from excessive materialism, reverential respect for creation, and zeal for a life of prayer and participation through preaching, healing, and teaching.

Though curved in upon ourselves due to the original fallenness of the human condition, we have been given a second chance to reunite with God. Thanks to the grace of redemption, we have the potential, in Bonaventure's view, to stand upright before God by means of the gifts of right seeing in faith and right listening in obedience. These gifts prompt our attempts to cooperate with grace and to incarnate God's truth in this world, leading to the right use of things in poverty of spirit and their distribution in charitable service.

As Bonaventure explains, the more passionately we long to ascend to God, the more we will eliminate nature-deforming sin and move toward the reforming and transforming pursuit of the truth that sets us free (see Jn 8:32) and turns our reason toward the light (see Mt 5:14). True doctrine can then be drawn out and multiplied by prayer, devotion, meditation, and the kind of preaching, by word and wordless witness, perfected by St. Francis.

The nourishing spiritual food Bonaventure offers for our instruction proceeds first of all from self-knowledge. We must be willing to enter into the hidden recesses of our conscience to explore and appraise our faults and their deforming effects on our dispositions, affections, and deeds. Knowledge of our misery evokes humility accompanied by the awareness of God's mercy. For Bonaventure and his mentor St. Francis, to humble ourselves as Christ did is the foundation of virtue since it leads to contemplation of God as the origin of all that is good; remembrance of Christ as our Savior; and ongoing attentiveness to the guiding power of the Holy Spirit, who prompts us to persevere in prayer and the grateful acceptance of our having been created, forgiven, and saved by God.

Having made this journey of the soul into God under the guidance of St. Bonaventure, we realize that in pursuit of Christian maturity we must never mistake the baby steps of initial conversion for the end stages of contemplative prayer. Through the spiritual disciplines of silence, formative reading, and meditative reflection, we learn to taste and savor the goodness of the Lord (see Ps 34:8). Surprisingly, what aids this ascent is aridity. It reminds us that nothing short of the possession of God can ever satisfy the longing in our heart. In due time, we may sense the peace of Christ invading our soul and bringing us to a place of grace where the tempests of evil have no access. Restored is our trust in God as the source of our delight and the motivating force of our pursuit of the good.

SIX DISPOSITIONS FOR MATURING IN CHRIST

As Bonaventure writes in *The Triple Way:* "Thus, in the intimacy of our loving soul, let us always say to the Lord: It is you I seek, in you I hope, for you I long, to you I rise, you I receive, in you I exult, and to you I finally cling."[6] In his meditation titled "The Six Wings of the Seraph," Bonaventure presents six counsels for maturing in Christ.[7] He explains how to clear the debris of spiritual complacency from our interiority and open ourselves to the acquisition of six lasting dispositions of the interior life. By living them, we move with grace from lukewarm modes of following Christ to lasting expressions of Christian maturity. They are zealousness, compassion, patience, virtuous living, discretion, and devotion to God.

Being zealous. On the lowest level of zeal for righteousness, says the saint, are those who do no evil yet who do not devote themselves with particular sincerity to doing good. They strive to be socially acceptable but are careful not to disturb the status quo. Next in line are those who refrain from evil and devote themselves to the performance of the good deeds required of them but no more than that. There is in them no burning desire for holiness. They are content with a minimum of prayer, seeking stillness, if at all, more as a duty than as a joy. Above them are those who detest wrongdoing. They pray fervently and desire to acquire a more intimate knowledge of God, yet they tend to hold themselves in reserve, with the intent of preserving their own peace at any price. Beyond these still rather self-centered orientations,

Bonaventure describes those on fire with zeal for holiness and the salvation of souls. They avoid wrongdoing and practice virtue; they receive little comfort from their own progress unless it also leads others to God.

Being compassionate. Compassion for brothers and sisters suffering ailments of the spirit, mind, and body wells up as we recognize in others our own spiritual, mental, and physical vulnerability. Whether we are physically enfeebled or spiritually weak due to lapses in morality, other-centered, egoless care and concern must prevail in imitation of Christ, who said, "Those who are well have no need of a physician, but those who are sick. Go and learn what this means, 'I desire mercy, not sacrifice.' For I have come to call not the righteous but sinners" (Mt 9:12–13).

Being patient. Responsibility for the bodily and spiritual welfare of others cannot be accomplished in a rush. Patience is necessary in any kind of ministry since instant results are seldom, if ever, forthcoming. When our ego has been quieted by contemplative prayer, we can address others more modestly and maturely. We avoid impetuous actions in favor of peacemaking. Instead of desiring vengeance, we make an effort to heal those responsible for perpetrating the offense. As we practice patience, our holiness increases because of the good we do and the evil we suffer, at times unjustly, through no fault of our own.

Being virtuous. To be an example of virtuous living is to match the teaching we receive from scripture to the deeds that flow from it. As St. Bonaventure reminds us, if the shepherd deserts the flock, he exposes the sheep to the wolves. Those who feel called to lead others to the Lord never act whimsically. They conduct themselves with candor, courage, and cautious deliberation. They do not indulge in sarcastic humor. They are affectionate but not overly so. They do not play favorites or arbitrarily change their plans. In short, they exercise good judgment and maximum discretion. They try to form those in their charge according to the pattern of Christ, leading them to imitate the Lord in all that they say and do.

Being discreet. Those living virtuous lives strive to become masters in the art and discipline of good judgment or discretion. An area of discernment that requires special attention is to ascertain if our life mirrors our knowledge of God's Word. Other goals include taking care of business and administrative matters while providing for our own and others' spiritual needs and finding the middle way between strictness and laxity.

Being devoted. Devotion to God gives us the strength to persevere to such a degree that, according to St. Bonaventure, demons flee from us and angels become our companions. To be avoided at all costs is mere devotionalism and the false piety a holier-than-thou attitude evokes. He concludes by reminding us that prayer is the portal to finding and following God's plan for our life.

On the sea of change that challenges the navigational skills of anyone in pursuit of spiritual maturity, St. Bonaventure's advice is well founded. We need to ask God to restore in us fervent zeal, compassion for others, patience in adversity, exemplary behavior toward those we lead, prudence in regard to daily decisions and actions, and devout praise of the Lord. St. Bonaventure realistically concludes, "Not everyone in charge of souls can possess all these virtues with equal perfection; all, however, must have them at least to some degree, in order both to edify their subjects and to promote their own salvation."[8]

Through trial and error, sin and forgiveness, setbacks and new starts, trust in the providence of God quiets our fears and illumines our understanding of the significance of every event we experience. All the forces that have formed our life so far—beauty and ugliness, joy and sorrow, laughter and sadness—unfold under the loving gaze of God.

The readiness to accept as providential whatever God sends our way and to see in every ending a new beginning purges the illusion that we can subject life at will to our preferred agenda. These dispositions prevent us from falling into the trap of believing that life is a useless passion or that God rains suffering arbitrarily upon the innocent. All such negative thoughts are cast out the more we trust in the providence of God and treat every obstacle as a formation opportunity.

REFLECT NOW

1. Have you begun to view the entirety of your life as a quest to know, love, and serve God and to link this mystical longing to your sense of mission?

2. In the complexity of the modern world, how do you cultivate the simplicity of childlike faith in Jesus?
3. In what way does the quality of your devotion to God enhance your compassion for others?

READ MORE

Rosaline B. Brooke, *Early Franciscan Government: Elias to Bonaventure* (New York: Cambridge University Press, 1959).

Joseph Ratzinger, *The Theology of History in St. Bonaventure*, trans. Zachary Hayes (Chicago: Franciscan Herald Press, 1971).

Richard Rohr, *Eager to Love: The Alternative Way of Francis of Assisi* (Cincinnati: Franciscan Media, 2014).

15

LET GO AND
LET GOD LEAD YOU

JAN VAN RUYSBROECK ON THE
GIFT OF SPIRITUAL ESPOUSAL

Now God beholds the abode and place of rest which he has
made with us and in us, namely, our unity with him and our
likeness to him. He wishes ceaselessly to visit the unity with
new comings of his sublime birth and with a rich outflux
of his fathomless love, for he desires to live in bliss within
the loving spirit.
 —Jan van Ruysbroeck, *The Spiritual Espousals*, 121

Were the mystical life a magnet, it would attract to itself without hesitation
the writings of Bl. Jan van Ruysbroeck. He tells us from the depth of his own
experience what it means to be espoused to Christ and how our Bridegroom
comes to greet us. He shows us how to unclutter our interior life to such
a degree that we can go forth amid the mundane demands of the day and
meet Christ, who longs to encounter us and reveal to us a glimpse of the
sublime nature of God. Ruysbroeck wants us to enter into the "God-seeing
life," in which beholding the Beloved is not a rare event but a normal part of
our day. There we discover from personal experience that those who dwell
in love dwell in God and God in them (see Jn 15:4–11).

MEET THE MASTER

Born in Brussels, Jan van Ruysbroeck (1293–1381) was a pious youth whose call to follow Christ by becoming a priest was apparent to all who knew him.[1] At the age of eleven, he was apprenticed to his uncle, John Hinckaert, canon of the Church of St. Gudula. There he received all the benefits of a medieval education, complemented by the religious formation that stirred his heart and drew him to dedicate his life to the Lord.

In 1317, he fulfilled his desire to be a priest. Once ordained, he executed with zeal the tasks demanded of him by parish life, but at a significant cost to his contemplative orientation. Finally, in 1343, he took a decisive step to follow his true calling. Along with another devout priest, Francis van Coudenberg, he sought and found a place of solitude, a wooded valley named Groenendal. Seven years later, all three men took the habit of the Canons Regular of St. Augustine.

As an Augustinian Canon, Ruysbroeck was inspired to explore Trinitarian mysticism both by St. Augustine and by the twelfth-century Cistercian reform of St. Bernard of Clairvaux. Ruysbroeck invites us into the inner circle of souls who pray ceaselessly and experience the joy of wordless adoration of the Trinity. He appeals to us to embody in worship and work the Gospel revelation that the Bridegroom is coming and we must go out to meet him (see Mt 25:6). He also adheres to the tradition of depicting the active life of beginners, the interior life of proficients, and the contemplative life of those perfected by grace.[2]

Among his distinguished visitors were Johannes Tauler (1300–1361) and the famous Dominican preacher and representative of German mysticism Gerard Groote (1340–1384), prior of a neighboring charterhouse and founder of the movement known as *devotio moderna*. This movement numbered among its adherents Thomas à Kempis (1380–1471), author of *The Imitation of Christ*, a Christian classic that rivaled the Bible in its popularity among laity, clergy, and religious. Ruysbroeck was much appreciated by his contemporary the Flemish mystic Hadewijch of Antwerp (d. 1282), as by the later writer Denis the Carthusian (1402–1471), for whom he was a "divine teacher." Jacques-Bénigne Bossuet (1627–1704), a luminary of the French school of spirituality, regarded Ruysbroeck as the most renowned master of mysticism of his own or any age. In part, his popularity may be due to the fact that he wrote in the Brabant dialect of the Flemish language, which made his work as accessible to a broad audience as to theologians and teachers. In the chaos of fourteenth-century Europe (the Hundred Years' War, the Black Death, peasant uprisings, and the papacy in Avignon), out of the depths of solitude Ruysbroeck wrote a *summa* of the mystical life.

There he confirms the doctrinal truth that our essence in God precedes our existence in time. He invites us to contemplate the ground of our being as the source from whence shines the resplendence of the Divine in daily life. At one and the same time, we remain distinct from God and yet we are capable, by virtue of our creation, of entering into the blissful state of the enjoyment of God, an experience so intense that it becomes the basis for all our activity. As Ruysbroeck concludes, "This [blessed meeting] is constantly renewed in the bond of love, for just as the Father ceaselessly sees all things anew in the birth of the Son, so too are all things loved anew by the Father and the Son in the flowing forth of the Holy Spirit. This is the active meeting of the Father and the Son, in which we are lovingly embraced by means of the Holy Spirit in eternal love."[3]

For the remaining years of his life—he died at the age of eighty-eight— Ruysbroeck sought to be united with God while engaging in pastoral work and dictating to a lay brother who accompanied him the thoughts and inspirations that best communicated his personal holiness and his profound understanding of mystical theology (see *SE*, 70).

EXPERIENCING ESPOUSAL TO THE LORD

In the first book of *The Spiritual Espousals* on the active life, Ruysbroeck teaches us how to see and obey the command to behold the coming of the Lord, who wants to become flesh in us. This is the time to lead a virtuous life, humble of heart and ardent in charity, and to engage in good works.

In pursuit of this active beholding, Ruysbroeck beseeches us to draw upon God's prevenient grace. God goes before us, beckoning us to follow his Son. He wants us to see the divine essence of creation in our own being and in the splendor of the life that surrounds us. The Bridegroom is coming—indeed, he is already here—and it would be dreadful to miss him because too many distractions clutter our mind.

We must be willing at every moment to go out to meet the Lord by living honorably and by advancing God's reign on earth. As we go out to meet Christ, Christ comes to meet us. He strips our spirit, heart, mind, and will of deformative images and attachments; he teaches us the art and discipline of prudent discretion; and he attracts us to the Father in loving surrender, preparing us to receive the graces of mystical union.

In the second book of *The Spiritual Espousals* on the interior life, Ruysbroeck compares this "second coming" of the Lord to a living spring with three streams. The first one affects our memory by delivering it from distracting expressions and drawing us to a state of simplicity and purity of intention. The second stream enlightens our understanding and sheds light on many truths of the faith that previously eluded us. He says that we "see and behold in a creaturely way the sublime nature of God and the fathomless attributes which are in God" (*SE*, 100). The third stream enflames our will in love, igniting it in response to grace and enriching every facet of the life of prayer from petition to paying attention to the promptings of the Holy Spirit in consolation and desolation.

The effect of our living in the ebb and flow of the Bridegroom coming to meet us and our running to greet him is an increase of devotion. Sorrow for sin and a contrite spirit urge us to beg for forgiveness and for the grace of partnering with the Lord to help those who need healing as much as we do.

Ruysbroeck summarizes this maturing of our interior life by confirming that this meeting between us and Christ occurs in privileged moments "without intermediary," that is, by means of a direct or immediate experience of God, described in mystical literature as our being "wounded by love." The more common way is the meeting between us and Christ "with intermediary," that is to say, through the seven gifts of the Holy Spirit, including fear of the Lord (submission to his will), kindness (gratitude for his generosity), and knowledge (of the truth of the revelation).

The next two gifts of the Spirit, fortitude and counsel, help us to respond to the coming of Christ in our life in the sweetness of sensible and spiritual delight and in the desert of aridity. The sixth gift, understanding, effects in us simplicity, enlightenment, and the will to love. The seventh gift, wisdom, enables us to see God with the eyes of faith, devoid of self-seeking and savoring God in a life of sanctity and service. Ruysbroeck assures us that "in this way, we will flow forth and flow back again in true charity and will be firmly established so as to abide in simple peace and likeness to God . . . with this we will possess a truly interior life in all its perfection" (*SE*, 144).

In the third book of this masterpiece on the contemplative life, Ruysbroeck focuses on the soul's entrance to the superessential or God-seeing life, the unitive way. Here we are unhindered by willfulness and immersed in the abyss of ineffable love, characterized by a well-ordered exterior and interior life. No longer do we seek consoling signs of progress; we are content to stay in the "darkness of delectation."

We experience the perfection of the fourfold path traced by Ruysbroeck in the first two books of *The Spiritual Espousals:*

1. *Behold.* The Beloved requires of us a perfect ordering of the virtues of Christian discipleship, the inner freedom to pursue them, and an inward cleaving to God, freed of self-centeredness and open to the cleansing power of grace.

2. *The Bridegroom comes.* Here Ruysbroeck describes the new birth by which God elevates the temporal nobility of our spirit, enlightens our understanding, and leads us to the loving path of Christian perfection. He compares our progress to three rills. The first rill raises the powers of the soul above all multiplicity and grants us the grace of simplicity of spirit, freed from the complexity of distracting thoughts and images. The second rill represents the gift of discerning God's will with alacrity and perceiving in a more profound way the light of the revelation. The third rill is like the fire that burns but does not consume. It invites us to obey the Lord in every facet of our life.

3. *Go ye out.* The transformation we have undergone so far may lead us where we would rather not have gone, but there is no turning back. Our life is in God's hands. His Son is the way and the truth, and there is no other we would follow: "By means of this love we have died to ourselves and through a loving immersion of ourselves have gone out into a state of darkness devoid of particular form. There the spirit is caught up in the embrace of the Holy Trinity and eternally abides within the superessential Unity in a state of rest and blissful enjoyment" (*SE*, 148).

4. *To meet him.* At last our encounter with the Beloved comes to fruition. It is a meeting like no other, characterized by a loving embrace, a passing over or sinking into "essential nakedness" and an eternal resting in and flowing out of love, which culminates in a union of "mutual inhabitation" and "a blissful embrace of loving immersion" (*SE*, 152).

At this culminating point of unity with the Trinity, Ruysbroeck speaks of our becoming one in being with God while retaining our uniqueness as sons and daughters of God. In this state of bliss, we both rest in God and restlessly desire to know, love, and serve God in every way that accords with his will. Since we never lose the humble awareness of our difference and distance from God, our going out to meet him is a lifelong quest.

LETTING GOD LEAD US

When we become children of God, we put our life of sinful selfishness behind us and strive after virtue. We do not wish to remain hirelings; we want to become faithful followers, detached from wanton pursuits of power, pleasure, and possessions, and living in trust of God. We rely on God's grace to obey the commandments and to purge ourselves of all traces of self-centeredness.

God calls us to enter into new depths of interior faith, hope, and love. He introduces us to the wealth of wisdom represented by the hidden life of Jesus of Nazareth and shares with us the secret joys that accompany the bond of friendship, the highest of which is loving adherence to the will of God and a concern for the common good of humankind.

Letting God lead us enhances our discovery of supreme truth, not in theory but from personal experience. We are captivated by God, intoxicated by love, and fastened to the Beloved in a bond of intimacy that can never be broken. At rest and at work, we are one with God, knowing that "just as the branch cannot bear fruit by itself unless it abides in the vine, neither can [we] unless [we] abide in [the Lord]" (Jn 15:4).

In his catechetical teaching titled *A Mirror of Eternal Blessedness*, Ruysbroeck links the interior life to living the Beatitudes and worthily receiving the Eucharist, for it is here that our desire to mature in Christ is tested daily.[4] He wrote this book for the Poor Clares in Brussels with the intention of helping them to grow in likeness to Christ in the solitude of the cloister and through their prayers for the Church as a whole. In it he details his eucharistic doctrine, stressing that worthy reception of the sacrament leads to the death of our self-will to such a degree that we desire nothing other than to obey God's will for us. In the Eucharist, "we receive the living food which gives us life and strengthens us in all our suffering, allowing us to win the victory over all our foes and over everything which stands in our way" (*SE Mirror*, 201).

Ruysbroeck also describes in his catechesis eight different kinds of persons who receive the Blessed Sacrament, offering in the process a detailed view of what the greatest marks of Christian maturity are (see *SE Mirror*, 219–34). In brief, the first group, the weakhearted, respond in ways that focus more on the satisfaction of their desires than on the sacrifice in which they participate.

The second group are more inclined to focus on their works and the results of their prayer, often resulting in too much attachment to consolations. The third group, though more advanced in recollection, are prone to pay attention to their transgressions and failings rather than to God's mercy. They may be governed more by reason than by faith in the eternal love of God and the peace that surpasses all understanding. The other danger they face is that of turning "inward in contemplation without turning outward in works of charity" (*SE Mirror*, 227).

The fourth group are persons of goodwill, who orient themselves to God's glory but may still fall into "spiritual disorder by doing too much or too little, so that their conscience accuses them of sin" (*SE Mirror*, 227). The best solution for them is frequent confession and reception of Holy Communion in accordance with their state of life.

Ruysbroeck describes the fifth group as tempted to behave in a holier-than-thou manner, proud of their progress in the spiritual life and lacking in humility. Those in the sixth group approach the sacrament to strengthen their faith and save them from losing their way. The seventh identifies with Jesus vilified and rejected but submissive to the Father's will and in dying bringing us to eternal life. They could not imagine receiving the sacrament in a state of sin, and they remain aware of their need for redemption. The eighth group follows the dictates of the Church, relies on God's mercy, and begs to receive the sacrament worthily by confessing their sins and striving, with the help of grace, to amend their lives: "If we live in this way, we may receive our Lord in the Sacrament as often as we wish, or may do so spiritually through love" (*SE Mirror*, 234).

REACHING HEAVENLY HEIGHTS

A central motif of Ruysbroeck's life and work is our desire to move from earthly attachments to heavenly heights in a rhythm of moving back and forth between ingoing and outflowing, between the deepest interiority and the practice of everyday virtue. In *The Little Book of Clarification*, he reflects on three modes of union with God already alluded to in *The Spiritual Espousals*: with an intermediary, without an intermediary, and without difference or distinction.

The intermediary to which he refers is God's grace, together with the sacraments of the Church, and the virtues of faith, hope, and love by which we live an upright life in accordance with God's commandments: "To these," he adds, "there is joined a dying to sin, to the world, and to all the inordinate desires of our nature."[5]

The experience of being united with God without intermediary is a relatively rare one, a pure gift bestowed by the initiative of God. The effect of this state of union is that the loving spirit "responds docilely to God's grace and movements in the practice of every virtue and interior exercise . . . so that he yields himself up with all his powers and undergoes the transformation wrought by the incomprehensible truth which is God himself" (*SE Little Book*, 257).

Though the union between the loving spirit and God is without intermediary, there is a difference, "for the creature does not become God nor does God become the creature" (*SE Little Book*, 260). Words almost fail Ruysbroeck in his attempt to describe union within the Godhead. He says it is a feeling of "our superessential beatitude"—a blessed encounter in the stillness that allows us, for however brief a duration, to lose ourselves in a "maelstrom of essential love" (*SE Little Book*, 262).

Without difference or distinction, God remains God and we God's children, but we experience in wordless wonder "an ever-new sense of contentment accompanied by a new outflow of love in a new embrace in Unity" (*SE Little Book*, 263). Here mystics feel present to Father, Son, and Holy Spirit in an eternal now, lost in that cloud of unknowing that is the ground of all true knowing: "There all light is turned into darkness and the Three Persons give way before the essential Unity, where without distraction they enjoy eternal bliss" (*SE Little Book*, 267).

At the end of his clarification of the meaning of contemplation, Ruysbroeck turns to the time Christ prayed that all those he loved might be made one, even as he is one with the Father (see Jn 17:22). He concludes by describing those who are united with God: "If we are willing to walk with God along the lofty ways of love, we will rest in him eternally and without end. In this way we will eternally approach God and enter into him and rest in him" (*SE Little Book*, 268).

REFLECT NOW

1. Can you describe experientially your understanding of the threefold path of purgation, illumination, and union?
2. What changes for the better might occur in your life were you aware at every moment of the invitation to go out to meet the Lord?
3. How might you go about helping others to live a God-seeing life?

READ MORE

Louis Dupré, *The Common Life: The Origins of Trinitarian Mysticism and Its Development by Jan Ruusbroec* (New York: Crossroad, 1984).

Hadewijch: The Complete Works, trans. Mother Columba Hart (New York: Paulist Press, 1980).

Paul Mommaers, *The Land Within: The Process of Possessing and Being Possessed by God according to the Mystic Jan van Ruysbroeck* (Chicago: Franciscan Herald Press, 1975).

16

Always Say "Yes, Father" with Jesus

CATHERINE OF SIENA ON TRUE OBEDIENCE

Obedience has a wet nurse, true humility, and the soul is as obedient as she is humble, and as humble as she is obedient. ... But disobedience comes from pride, which in turn comes from selfish love for oneself and deprives one of humility. Selfish love gives disobedience impatience as a sister and pride as a wet nurse. And in the darkness of infidelity she runs along the darksome way that leads to eternal death. ... Your entire faith is founded on obedience, for it is by obedience that you show your fidelity.
—Catherine of Siena, *The Dialogue*, 328–29

Few mystics have enjoyed as much direct dialogue with God as did St. Catherine of Siena. This future Doctor of the Church, from an early age, was God's familiar. All too often, we create an artificial distance between ourselves and God. Catherine teaches us how to cross it by always saying "Yes, Father" with Jesus.

The cell of self-knowledge she advises us to enter is that place of grace where we come to know who we are and who God is. Though Catherine's fame as a spiritual guide grew in lay and ecclesiastical circles, she remained the soul of humility—so radiant with the light of Christ that to see her, it was said, was to seek conversion.

Central to her teaching was her commitment to uphold the Christian dogma of the divinity and humanity of Jesus Christ. She begged us to bow before him in awe and to embrace him as loving parents would cradle their child.

St. Catherine strove to reform the Church in her day by helping those entrusted to her care to see Christ as the bridge by which we cross over the chasm created by sin and return to our redeemed self in God.

Meet the Master

Catherine Benincasa (1347–1380), the twenty-fourth child of a prosperous merchant, was born in Siena on March 25, 1347. A Doctor of the Church and the patron saint of Italy, she is one of the greatest Christocentric mystics of the fourteenth century.

Her new life in Christ began in 1354 when she vowed her virginity to God. When she was fifteen, she cut off her hair, thus putting a stop to her parents' plan that she enter into an arranged marriage. At the age of eighteen she joined the Mantellate, a group of laywomen affiliated with the Dominican order. She withdrew from the world, lived in seclusion in her own home, and served her family from her "cell of self-knowledge," where she learned how to read.

In 1368, she reported, to the consternation of her family, that the Lord himself appeared to her and asked her to consecrate herself totally to him. She obeyed this miracle of "mystical espousal" without hesitation, setting the pattern of obedience that would characterize the rest of her life. Then, at the Lord's command, she left her seclusion to reach out and help the needy of Siena—the prisoners, the sick, and the poor. As Jesus told her:

> It is your duty to love your neighbors as your own self. In love you ought to help them spiritually with prayer and counsel, and assist them spiritually and materially in their need—at least with your good will if you have nothing else.

If you do not love me you do not love your neighbors, nor will you help those you do not love. But it is yourself you harm most, because you deprive yourself of grace. And you harm your neighbors by depriving them of the prayer and loving desires you should be offering to me on their behalf. Every help you give them ought to come from the affection you bear them for love of me.[1]

By 1370, her world expanded to a more extensive ministry to people in all walks of life. Guided by her lifelong confessor and spiritual director, Bl. Raymond of Capua, O.P., she responded to an ever-widening circle of supporters, who drew upon her gifts as a peacemaker, a healer, and a spokesperson for the Lord. Her diplomatic skills were put to the test in 1375 when she journeyed from Siena to Pisa to dissuade a cohort of politicians from joining what was fast becoming an antipapal league. A year later she traveled to Avignon to meet Pope Gregory XI and encourage him to return to his papal residence in Rome, which he did in 1377. In 1380, shortly before her death, with the help of friends and scribes, she composed her masterpiece, *The Dialogue*, and penned more than four hundred letters, including many sent to leaders of both Church and state.

The guiding theme of *The Dialogue* is God's truth about which the soul seeks understanding through faith enlightened by reason and radical obedience to the Word of God. The entire book can be read as the fruit of Catherine's listening to a series of mystical locutions concerning Christian formation as both interior and relational. From the time she spent in prayer and solitude came her growth in charity and her ability to minister to others. In *The Dialogue*, she offers an extended meditation on the Incarnate Word as the Way to the Father; as the Truth that led her to the heart of the Trinitarian mystery; and as the Life renewing his Body, the Church, and lifting his Bride from the devastation of disobedience to the glory of restored fidelity.[2]

Upon the death of Gregory XI, Catherine gave her full support to Urban VI, but the schismatic cardinals elected another antipope, Clement VII. Amid this papal turmoil, Catherine obeyed Urban's request to support his succession and threw herself into the work of ecclesial reform. Against this backdrop of external schism and internal uprisings, she succumbed to a severe illness, unable to eat or drink but making the journey anyway to St.

Peter's to receive Communion daily and intercede for Church unity. She died on April 29, 1380, surrounded by her family and friends. Her body, which showed visible signs of the stigmata she had received invisibly in Pisa in 1375, was laid to rest in Santa Maria Sopra Minerva Basilica in Rome, where it remains today.[3]

THREE STEPS TO ONENESS WITH THE TRINITY

Catherine identifies three steps in the process of our being drawn to intimacy with the Trinity, utilizing the imagery of Christ's feet, heart, and mouth. The image of Christ's wounded feet suggests to her that all too often the motivation for our obedience is fear of punishment—a reason to obey she considers both imperfect and mercenary.

The symbol of Christ's wounded heart or open side reminds her that we are to follow him out of love, not fear. Unfortunately, our love is still mingled with selfishness because we lack sufficient understanding of what Christ has done for us. Progress is being made insofar as we are no longer fearful slaves but faithful servants.

If the first step sparks our desire for God and the second enlightens our mind, then the third leads to a transformation of heart, imaged by Catherine as the mouth of Christ. He himself claims us with a mystical kiss and instills in us, as a permanent disposition of heart, the grace of filial love. We are now truly children of God.

Catherine adds to this description a fourth stage, symbolized by the fire of charity toward our neighbor. She establishes as a foundation of Christian spirituality the obligation not only to hear the Word of God in our heart but also to proclaim it to the world. The culmination of this journey from human love to Love Divine is none other than presence to the Trinity in the eternal face-to-face of the beatific vision.

Complementing this description of Christ's feet, heart, and mouth is Catherine's teaching on the three powers of the soul. She identifies them as the means by which we avoid falling into the abyss of selfish sensuality. These gifts of memory, intellect, and will are the dowry given to us by Christ.

The function of memory is not to catalog faults and failings but to remember God's faithfulness to us, his giving and forgiving love. Deformed memory wallows in its own misery and forgets that creation abounds with God's mercy. Christ intends that we use our intellect to perceive and live in the Truth, know that we are wholly dependent on God, and attain the humility necessary for transformation of heart. Being drawn by God into the furnace of charity enables us to minister to others freed from every remnant of self-willed love.

Just as self-love is the source of every deviation from divine grace, so saying yes to the Father and willing the good guarantee our conversion to Christ and prevent us from living in self-deception. As the eternal Truth tells his daughter:

> One comes to knowledge of the Truth through self-knowl-
> edge. But self-knowledge alone is not enough. It must be
> seasoned by and joined with knowledge of me within you.
> This is how you found humility and contempt for yourself
> along with the fire of my charity, and so came to love and
> affection for your neighbors and gave them the service of
> your teaching and your holy and honorable living. (*Dialogue*,
> 158)

LIVING IN THE LIGHT

For Catherine, truthful growth in self-knowledge leads to knowledge of Christ as the light of truth. His disciples share in three degrees of this light: ordinary, more perfect, and glorious. The first or ordinary light refers to those who walk in the light of reason, complemented by the light of faith received in Baptism: "In baptism, through the power of my only-begotten Son's blood, you received the form of faith. If you exercise this faith and virtue with the light of reason, reason will in turn be enlightened by faith, and such faith will give you life and lead you in the way of truth. With this light you will reach me, the true light; without it you would come to darkness" (*Dialogue*, 185).

This first light bears fruit in those whose charity is ordinary, but to it Christ would add two other lights, bestowed on those who are seeking a fuller life of union and communion with him. The "more perfect" light enables us to sense the transitory nature of persons, events, and things in this world, thus invigorating our desire for God and encouraging us to live a disciplined life, engaging in mortification for the sake of mastering our willful selfishness.

Glorious light is equated with the wisdom achieved by those who recognize the will of God and conform to it, regardless of what God asks of them. Such persons live in intimacy with the Trinity, in a spirit of Christlike surrender, and in a "sea of peace":

> When the soul . . . has come to taste this light after so delightfully seeing and knowing it, she runs to the table of holy desire, in love as she is and eager with a lover's restlessness. She has no eyes for herself, for seeking her own spiritual or material comfort. Rather, as one who has completely drowned her own will in this light and knowledge, she shuns no burden, from whatever source it may come. She even endures the pain of shame and vexations from the devil and other people's grumbling, feasting at the table of the most holy cross of honor for me, God eternal, and salvation for others. (*Dialogue*, 188–89)

Three directives help us to reach this always nourishing goal. We must be united with God in loving affection, bearing in our memory the blessings we have received from him. With the eye of our understanding, we must behold how unconditionally he loves us and draws us to union. Then, if we consider God's will before our own, we can quell our secretly self-centered intentions and approach others in an attitude of selfless service.

Catherine is adamant on this point. She says that we must never pass judgment in human terms on anyone we serve or on anything we see. In our relations with others we must refrain from judging, for no one can see the hidden heart but God. Our stance is to be one of mercy and compassion. This way of relating is essential because as the Lord tells Catherine, "You would think you were judging rightly when in fact you were judging wrongly by following what you saw, for often the devil would make you see too much of the truth in order to lead you into falsehood. He would do this to make you set yourself up as judge of other people's spirits and intentions, something of which, as I told you, I alone am judge" (*Dialogue*, 193).

RESPONDING TO DIVINE DIRECTION WITH SORROW AND JOY

Showing what a superb directress of souls she was, Catherine explains how judgment should be qualified. We are not to confront others with specific sins but to correct their bad habits in a general way—for instance, by balancing the vices we detect in them by the virtues we cultivate in ourselves. The general rule is gentleness, though there are times when we must add admonition to admiration, correction to kindness. In short, we must not focus on the faults and foibles we see in others but hold fast to the sight and knowledge of ourselves as the beneficiaries of God's generosity. Our place is to exercise compassion and leave judgment to God.

Of the many insights Catherine offers in her quest to live in the light of Truth, her doctrine of tears is as original as it is insightful. She says that tears come from the heart of the one who feels sorrow for sin. Some weep because they fear punishment for their offenses against God. These are tears of slavish fear. Others, who have begun to rise up from sin and taste the goodness of God, weep joyfully and long passionately to serve him. These tears diminish fear and manifest hope in God's mercy. For souls close to perfection in their love for God and neighbor, tears of burning affection may create ridges on their cheeks. These are, in Catherine's analysis, tears of sweetness, unitive tears shed with great tenderness. So happy is the soul that now patterns her life after Christ's that she weeps tears of fire, knowing that her desire for union with God can never be satisfied in this life.[4]

While such tears can be consoling, Catherine herself is distrustful of any inclination to pay more attention to the gift than to the Giver. People desirous of spiritual consolations may miss the chance to help a neighbor in need. To test the depth of our faith, Catherine says that God may withdraw his consolations for a time with the intention that these dry periods humble us and help us to identify with Christ crucified. Without this time of testing, we might play into the hands of the devil, who uses inordinate attachments to consolations to fill us with delusions of grandeur:

> He does this in different ways: now as an angel, now under the guise of my Truth, now as one or the other of my saints. And this he does to catch the soul with the hook of that

very spiritual pleasure she has sought in visions and spiritual delight. And unless she rouses herself with true humility, scorning all pleasure, she will be caught on this hook in the devil's hands. But let her humbly disdain pleasure and cling to love not for the gift but for me, the giver. For the Devil for all his pride cannot tolerate a humble spirit. (*Dialogue*, 133)

Underlying the dialogue between Catherine and the Lord is total trust in his providential care from the beginning to the end of time. God's all-encompassing love is a mystery never to be comprehended by us. Yet in its light Catherine sees the meaning behind all that she experienced. The Lord assures her that no matter where his faithful daughters and sons turn, no matter how far away from him his servants and friends roam, they will find his burning charity and nothing but the greatest, gentlest, truest, most perfect providence, nothing but the boundlessness of his mercy, surrounding them.

God wakes up worldly souls with a pricking of conscience or by the weariness they feel in their hearts. He rewards the virtuous by making them fall more deeply in love with his mystery. He encourages those on the way to him to bring their disordered memory, understanding, and will into consonance with his revelation, orchestrating their spiritual unfolding as a conductor draws forth all the beauty of a symphony. The farther we progress, the more we learn to walk along the way of Christ's gentle but firm teaching. All of this leads to harmony between the inner and outer life, between praising God's name and serving our neighbor. Each of us needs other people, and all of us need God:

> Thus you will see the artisan turn to the worker and the worker to the artisan: Each has need of the other because neither knows how to do what the other does. So also the cleric and religious have need of the layperson, and the layperson of the religious; neither can get along without the other. And so with everything else. Could I not have given everyone everything? Of course. But in my providence I wanted to make each of you dependent on the others, so

that you would be forced to exercise charity in action and will at once. (*Dialogue*, 365)

From start to finish, Catherine's dialogue with the Father, the Son, and the Holy Spirit can be read as a powerful prayer for self-understanding, for the Church, for the whole world, and for God's providential care. She reiterates the necessity of retiring to the cell of self-knowledge where we can be alone with God and attend to his Word before venturing into the world as his followers. We seek the inspiration that will make our actions effective and our witness edifying. We behold the wretchedness of human perdition, but this sober reality serves to increase our petition for God's mercy. We pray that no decision or deed of ours will mar the beauty of the Mystic Body of the Church, pictured by Catherine as a bride ever in need of being cleansed by the sacrificial blood flowing from the side of Christ on the Cross.

MINISTRY ROOTED IN TRANSFORMING LOVE

God confirms Catherine's conviction that nothing is more necessary for the revitalization of the Church than good ministers of the sacraments, who instruct the faithful in doctrinal and moral truths. By the same token, nothing is more detrimental to reform than unfaithful ministers, who pursue their own ambitions and forfeit their obligation to form the people of God. Catherine was disedified by religious superiors who failed in their duty to "keep their eyes on their subjects," resulting in the treachery that "they become the devil's arms, and they throw their venomous filth both within and without: without among seculars and within in the religious community. They are bereft of fraternal love. Everyone wants to be the greatest and everyone wants possessions. So they transgress both the commandments and the vows they have made" (*Dialogue*, 241–42).

Such confused ministers provide for their own needs first and neglect the poor, scandalize the laity by parading with their mistresses and children, shun just admonitions from superiors, jeer at those who obey the Rule, and choose gluttony and lust in place of fraternal love. Their neglect, the Lord told her, did not render the sacraments less valid, and for this reason Catherine felt some of her sadness lifted, while she continued to beseech him to reform the guardians of his truth. She prays that they will recall their high dignity and the duty placed upon them by God "to be merciful to the world and make holy Church blossom again with the fragrant flowers of good holy shepherds whose perfume will dispel the stench of the putrid evil flowers" (*Dialogue*, 276).

In the face of such disobedience and ignorance of Divine Providence, Catherine asks the Lord if anything can be done. His answer to her offers a glimpse into how ministry must be rooted in the mystery of transforming love: "My daughter, let your respite be in glorifying and praising my name, in offering me the incense of constant prayer for these poor wretches who have sunk so low and made themselves deserving of divine judgment for their sins. And let your place of refuge be my only-begotten Son, Christ crucified. Make your home and hiding place in the cavern of his open side. There, in his humanity, you will enjoy my divinity with loving affection" (*Dialogue*, 238–39).

The Lord reminds Catherine that there is no easy solution to the quest for Church reform except that of returning to the foundations of the faith and rooting our life in constant prayer. In due time, the virtues of obedience, humility, and purity of heart will once again prevail, provided we turn from selfish concerns to care for others. God sends us into the vineyard of life to play our part in the work of redemption. If we trust in God, he will not fail to hear our prayers.

In the prologue to the *Dialogue*, Catherine asked for four petitions: for herself, for the Church, for the whole world, and for Bl. Raymond. All of these prayers bore fruit.[5] She attained knowledge of herself and God, and God heard her plea for mercy for the Church and for the world as well as for her spiritual director.

The most fitting summary of *The Dialogue* can be found in Catherine's prayer to the Holy Trinity to grant her the grace of final consummation: "You, eternal Trinity, are the craftsman; and I your handiwork have come to know that you are in love with the beauty of what you have made, since you made of me a new creation in the blood of your Son. O abyss! O eternal Godhead! O deep sea! What more could you have given me than the gift of your very self?" (*Dialogue*, 306).

REFLECT NOW

1. What do you perceive as the chief demand of discipleship Christ asks of you?
2. How do the three powers of your soul—intellect, memory, and will—help you to come closer to Father, Son, and Holy Spirit?
3. What prevents you from entering the cell of self-knowledge that teaches you who you are and who God is, and what attracts you to this time of solitary reflection?

READ MORE

Selina O'Grady and John Wilkins, *Great Spirits, 1000–2000: The Fifty-Two Christians Who Most Influenced Their Millennium* (New York: Paulist Press, 2002).

Joseph Marie Perrin, *Catherine of Siena*, trans. Paul Barrett (Westminster, MD: Newman Press, 1965).

Sigrid Undset, *Catherine of Siena*, trans. Kate Austin-Lund (New York: Sheed and Ward, 1954).

17

BOW IN AWE
BEFORE THE MYSTERY

THE CLOUD OF UNKNOWING ON
THE WORK OF CONTEMPLATION

If you cannot understand what I say, lay it aside until God comes and teaches you. Do this, and keep out of harm's way. Be on your guard against pride, because it blasphemes God in his gifts and makes sinners arrogant. If you were truly humble, you would have the right feeling for this divine work, even as I say: That God gives it freely without any meriting.

—*The Cloud of Unknowing*, 184–85

The *via negativa*, or the way of unknowing, described by the author of this medieval masterpiece tempers the know-it-all attitude we may adopt in an informational age such as our own. Awe, not arrogance, places us in the presence of a mystery no mind can fathom. The author reminds us that thought knocks; only love enters. Visible as the Lord is in his humanity, we can never fully understand his invisible essence in the Divinity.

In the darkness of unknowing, we press under the "cloud of forgetting" whatever separates us from God. We stretch toward God with a "blind stirring of our will," with a "sharp dart of longing love" that keeps us humble and draws us to unceasing prayer.

There is no room in the author's world for pseudo-contemplation that calls more attention to the self than to God. He suggests that "head-knowledge" alone can hamper our progress unless it is complemented by the "heart-knowledge" that lets us enter the inner chambers of intimacy with the Trinity.

MEET THE MASTER

The identity of the author of this fourteenth-century text from the English school of spirituality remains a mystery. What we do know is that he lived in anything but a contemplative age. From 1305 to 1378, the French popes abandoned Rome for the comfort of Avignon, from whence the Great Schism engulfed the continent until 1420. The nations of France and Italy rallied behind two rival popes, each calling the other the anti-Christ. The Great Plague swept away the lives of paupers and princes. The seeds of the Protestant Reformation took root in northern Europe, and yet, amidst this turmoil, there arose in England some of the most outstanding Christian masters and mystics of this or any age in the history of the Church.[1] How was it possible to possess one's soul and live in peace in this raging sea of secular and ecclesial turmoil?

The consensus is that *The Cloud* may have been written by a priest, perhaps a Carthusian monk from the central East Midlands, who must have had the reputation of being an experienced director of souls. He honored the request of a young man of twenty-four who, after having spent time in the religious life, wanted to experience his vocation more fully and sought direction on how to do so. His need may account for the author's personal tone. Although he may have had a broader audience in mind, his message confirmed that mysticism is both a practical endeavor and a work dependent on the grace of God. More than a doctrine requiring analysis, it is a way of life that changes our hearts.[2] This is not to say that we discard intellectual pursuits. The point is to simplify thoughts, not to abolish them; to move from meditation to contemplation; and to "focus all our attention on this meek stirring of love in our will" (*Cloud*, 216). The author's main belief is that "love alone can reach God in this life, and not knowing" (*Cloud*, 139).

Though shrouded in mystery, the language of *The Cloud* is vigorous and eloquent, revealing the author as a forceful and original thinker whose masterpiece radiates enthusiasm, humor, and literary beauty. He directs us to turn to Jesus for the help we need to succeed in this contemplative work: "So love Jesus, and everything that he has is yours. By his Godhead he is the maker and giver of time. By his manhood he is the keeper of time. . . . Knit yourself . . . to him by love and by faith. And in virtue of that knowledge you shall be a regular partner with him and with all who are so well fastened to him by love" (*Cloud*, 125).

Inherent in this tradition is the conviction that contemplation must be built on obedience to Church teachings and fidelity to its liturgical and sacramental life. It is the culminating point of that sanctifying grace received at Baptism and restored through the sacrament of Penance. Thanks to these gratuitous gifts of God, contemplation is the climax of the normal way by which God leads his chosen ones to perfection, calling them from self-deceptive illusions rooted in pride to ways of knowing in unknowing rooted in humility.[3]

EXPERIENCING IN LOVE THE INFINITE BEING OF GOD

Despite the incomprehensibility of the divine mystery, God deigns to offer every disciple the possibility of being led to an experience of the Infinite Being of God. To accept in humility the darkness of unknowing does not plunge our soul into helpless obscurity; rather it raises us up to God in wordless wonder and the fervor of pure love. The insight thus attained bestows upon us a sense of knowing God rather than merely knowing about God. Far from disdaining the duty of the active life, we excel even more because what we do proceeds from the ground of who we are.

The first requirement of the contemplative is to press what interferes with this work under what the author identifies as the cloud of forgetting. He says, "Just as this cloud of unknowing is above you, between you and your God, in the same way you must put beneath you a cloud of forgetting, between you and all creatures that have ever been made" (*Cloud*, 128). Under this cloud we are to press sensual distractions, sins already forgiven, inordinate attachments to anything less than God, and whatever else prevents us from attending with the eyes of faith to God alone.

Above the cloud of forgetting is the cloud of unknowing that stands between us and God and that can be penetrated only by a "naked intent" or a "blind stirring of our will." This desire soars upward like a "sharp dart of longing love" (*Cloud*, 131) and grants the contemplative a glimpse of the mystery that even at this height remains hidden: "During this time be blind, and cut away all desire of knowing; for this will hinder you more than it will help you. It is enough for you that you feel moved in love by something, though you do not know what it is; so that in this affection, you have no thought of anything in particular under God, and that your reaching out is simply directed to God" (*Cloud*, 186).

By responding to grace in this way, we gain spiritual sight, knowing in unknowing the way to union with God.[4] We begin this work not with a vacant stare into space but with the Sign of the Cross, suggesting that the goal of contemplation is intimacy with the Trinity (see *Cloud*, 101). We anchor this hope in the Word made flesh, whose love for sinners in need of redemption shows that the fruit of contemplative prayer has to be seen in charitable service, not in busy activity severed from reliance on God: "The perfect worker . . . considers all men alike as his kinsmen, and no man a stranger to him. He considers all men his friends and none his foes" (*Cloud*, 170).

The outward comportment of contemplatives ought to be such that everyone they meet desires to have them as their friend. Contemplation teaches us how to pick off the rough shell of a life forgetful of God so we can find the sweet kernel of Christ's peace. At the end of *The Cloud*, the author offers definite signs by which to determine whether or not we are ready to engage in this work of contemplation.

The first is to discern if we have done all in our power to purify our conscience of deliberate sin according to the precepts of holy Church and the advice of our spiritual director.

The second is to ascertain if we are habitually attracted to this simple contemplative prayer more than to any other devotion.

The third is to admit that our conscience leaves us no peace in any exterior or interior work unless we make this secret love fixed upon the cloud of unknowing our principal concern. In the same vein, should we for some reason stop this work for a while, we feel our passion for it renewed with a fervor that is undeniable.

Having offered these counsels, the author ends his work by extending to his spiritual friend God's blessing, praying, "I beseech almighty God that true peace, sane counsel and spiritual comfort in God with abundance of grace, always be with you, and with all those who on earth love God. Amen" (*Cloud*, 266).

REMOVING OBSTACLES BETWEEN US AND GOD

The work of contemplation described in *The Cloud* and the nourishing spiritual food it offers entail experiential knowledge of God as he is in himself. This knowing in unknowing is supraconceptual, sanctified by grace and experienced in the mutual embrace of the soul and God. "Therefore," says the author, "it is my wish to leave everything that I can think of and choose for my love the thing I cannot think. Because [God] can certainly be loved, but not thought. He can be taken and held by love but not by thought" (*Cloud*, 130).

To proceed beyond sensible experiences and intellectual analyses requires the removal of as many inner and outer hindrances to loving union as possible. The author directs us to eliminate distractions, obey God's will, yield to the divine initiative, and acknowledge our nothingness. Only then may we begin to pierce the cloud and be drawn by love into union with God. We need to "leave him to act alone. [Our] part is to keep the windows and the doors against the inroads of flies and enemies. And if [we] are willing to do this, all that is required of [us] is to woo him humbly in prayer, and at once he will help [us]. . . . He is always most willing, and is only waiting for [us]" (*Cloud*, 119).

One way to prepare our heart for this gift of supreme intimacy is, as the author recommends, to repeat a monosyllable such as "God" or "Love" or "Help" (*Cloud*, 134). Another way is that of "blind beholding" by which the soul abides in this darkness in childlike trust, knowing that little can be said or done with a blabbering tongue, for this is a work God alone can initiate and bring to fulfillment.

The disciple's effort is a progressive abstraction from sense and sensible things and from the intensity of discursive thought. Meditation is necessary, but not now. The thrust of grace is to urge the soul to dwell on God in his pure being, to forget all that it knows and, by that dart of longing love, to pierce through "head-knowledge" to loving "heart-knowledge." This piercing attains what mere human comprehensibility is forbidden to behold.

The most treacherous obstacle to progress is pride, which elevates self-knowledge to a higher place than knowledge of God. It makes us vulnerable to diabolic temptations and standards of worldly living that cause us to "desert the common teaching and counsel of holy Church" (*Cloud*, 89).

Next in line comes a search for consolations that violates the dispensation of God's grace. Self-initiated activity may destroy equanimity, also in the face of desolation and the aridity that enables us to face the reality of sin. It is seen by the author as a "lump" (*Cloud*, 254) that inflicts disunity in our soul and weakens our God-given powers of intellect, memory, and will. We need to pray that God will soften this lump and let it disappear altogether so that we can live again in humble presence to the Divine Presence. Leave it, the author says, at the door of the confessional and do not torture yourself with scrupulous thoughts, lest the lump reappear. Though the roots of sin run deep in our soul and though they may not be uprooted totally in this life, we must not despair. The "witness of our conscience" (*Cloud*, 152) will leap up in our heart and once again render us restless until we rest in God. The power of sin can be checked and its influence weakened by repentance, vigilance of heart, and, above all, contemplative prayer.

FOLLOWING A COURSE OF CONTEMPLATION

Outlined in a series of imperatives in chapter 3 of *The Cloud* is a course of contemplation every lover of God can follow. It can be summarized in several texts written with authority by a spiritual director who wants us to make these marks of Christian maturity our own. They begin with the counsel "Lift up your heart to God with a humble impulse of love; and have himself as your aim, not any of his goods" (*Cloud*, 119). This counsel reminds us that we must be willing to set our sights on God alone and to remain constantly vigilant lest secondary goals interfere with the goal of meeting God in love and humility.

Next, says the author, "take care that you avoid thinking of anything but himself, so that there is nothing for your reason or your will to work on, except himself" (*Cloud*, 119–20). If God is to be our All in all, we must refuse to make worldly ambitions ultimate since our longing for God is the sole motivation behind who we are and what we do.

Third, we are told to try "to forget all the creatures God ever made, and their works, so that neither [our] thought nor our desire be directed or extended to any of them, neither in general nor in particular" (*Cloud*, 120). This directive must be read not as life-denying but as a reminder that nothing but God ought to take precedence in our lives. This discipline of leaving creatures alone and refusing to allow them to occupy the center of our attention is the work, according to the author, "that pleases God most" (*Cloud*, 120).

Being in the world without being of the world does not succeed at once, but it is worth the effort to center our thoughts on God and to place any interference with this intention under the cloud of forgetting, confident that the saints and angels will rush to our aid and drive away the devils that want to sidetrack and destroy this work of contemplation. Never must we doubt the help we receive from God's grace, which implanted this desire for union in us from the start of our ascent to God.

Now we are told, "Set yourself to rest in this darkness as long as you can, always crying out after him whom you love" (*Cloud*, 121). This love veers away from pious thoughts that lack perseverance. Their power decreases every time we exercise that naked intent toward God in the depths of our being. With or without consoling feelings, we know that we are in God and that God is in us. Our task is not to try to understand the divine giftedness of this work of contemplation but to let it lead us into the cloud of unknowing with childlike faith.

Though conceptual thinking does not disappear, we ought never to snatch at grace like a "greedy greyhound" (*Cloud*, 209) as if we could force our way into the Father's embrace. The self-initiated illusion that we are without a doubt being drawn up to God can lead to pseudo-contemplative behaviors that make the devil's work easier and doom a soul to increasingly severe bouts of self-deception.

The author's description of these deluded souls, full of hypocrisy and bordering on heresy, is unforgettable: "The eyes of some of them are so set in their heads as though they were sheep suffering from the brain disease, and were near death's door. Some of them hold their heads on one side as though a worm were in their ears, some squeak instead of speaking normally, as though there were no breath in their bodies" (*Cloud*, 222).

To counter this backsliding to pseudo-contemplation, the author counsels us to abandon these imaginative stirrings with haste and allow ourselves to rest in the darkness of unknowing "as long as [we] can, always crying out after him whom [we] love. For if [we] are to experience him or to see him at all, insofar as it is possible here, it must always be in this cloud and in this darkness" (*Cloud*, 121). While there is no room in this inner chamber of intimacy with the Trinity for pride, presumption, and complacency, there is ample room for humility, repentance, and unassuming service of others.

This paradoxical infusion of dazzling light in the midst of darkness fills the soul with a "sovereign wisdom" (*Cloud*, 156) that reveals the awesome truth of the dying and rising of our Lord. This knowledge of revelation allows the soul to proceed to a knowledge in love that casts out fear and leads to abandonment to God.

For the author there are two kinds of love we must cultivate as contemplatives. One is *ordinary love* that irrigates like a gentle stream what we already know of God through our senses and our adoration of God's first revelation in creation. The second is *supernatural love* that wells up from the core of our being. This love moves us beyond what our senses can tell us to the mystery that transcends us. Now meditation and the use of our faculties of intellect, memory, and will recede, to be superseded by the loving stillness of naked faith. Love, having abandoned reliance on analytical knowledge, enters into a higher level of knowing infused by God himself. Reason continues to do its work of discerning the origin of these gifts and of protecting the soul from entrapment in pride that is ever present on this mystical path. Its stubborn tentacles manifest themselves in the seven capital sins that taint our soul when we least expect it. What weakens their influence most is the blind stirring of contemplative love. Its flame burns out the roots of sin insofar as possible in this life, aligning our character and personhood with Christ's presence in the core of our being.

Reflect Now

1. How do you relate to the impenetrable mystery of the Godhead, to the truth that thought knocks but only love enters?
2. How do you balance the need to attend to "sense and sensible things," like Martha, and the desire to dwell in the presence of God, like Mary who sat at the feet of Jesus?
3. What is the best way you have found to align your character with Christ's presence in the core of your being?

Read More

Louis Dupré and James A. Wiseman, eds., *Light from Light: An Anthology of Christian Mysticism* (New York: Paulist Press, 1988).

William Johnston, *The Mysticism of "The Cloud of Unknowing"* (New York: Desclee, 1967).

Philip Sheldrake, *Spirituality and Theology: Christian Living and the Doctrine of God* (Maryknoll, NY: Orbis Books, 1998).

18

TRUST IN DIVINE PROVIDENCE

JULIAN OF NORWICH ON SUFFERING AND JOY

God gives joy freely as it pleases him, and sometimes he allows us to be in sorrow, and both come from his love. For it is God's will that we do all in our power to preserve our consolation, for bliss lasts forevermore, and pain is passing and will be reduced to nothing.

—Julian of Norwich, *Showings*, 140

Reality can be so harsh at times that we find it difficult to believe the bold claim of the English anchorite Julian of Norwich that "all shall be well." Can we say these words with conviction when we witness the suffering of the innocent, the devastation caused by natural disasters, and the upsurge of disrespect for life at its most vulnerable?

Despite the difficulties of life, Julian remains adamant in her conviction that God made us, God loves us, and God keeps us in being. No sooner does a window close than a door opens. She concludes without hesitation that we can and must trust in Divine Providence.

Julian beheld on her bed of sickness the fatherly and motherly goodness of God. Despite the gravity of the illness she describes in her book *Showings*, it did not obscure the delectable sight of the Lord. We have to expect, as she did, that the devil will try to destroy our allegiance to the Divine, but we must take heart. When we think God is absent from us, that is when God is most near.

The good Lord intends to make all things well for us and the whole world. Our task is to accept his help and to care for self and others as he cares for us.

MEET THE MASTER

An extraordinarily gifted fourteenth-century English mystic and solitary anchoress, Julian of Norwich (1342–ca. 1423) remains a mystery whose story continues to unfold.[1] We search her *Showings* for particulars about her parentage, home, friends, interests, and education, but they are few and far between. Prior to entering her anchorage in Norwich, England, she may have managed a household or a business, and perhaps have been a mother. A single historical reference to her life is found in the written history of Norwich: "In 1393 Lady Julian, the anchoress, was a strict recluse here and had two servants to attend her in her old age. This woman was in these days esteemed one of great holiness."[2]

An anchorhold, anchorage, or hermitage might have been a hut in the woods, a cave on the moors, or a hovel in the fields, but for Julian it was a cell adjacent to the Church of St. Julian that remains open today. Outlines of the ruins of her anchorage may still be traced. Her chamber probably had two windows: one looking into the church to enable her to take part in religious services, like the Divine Office and Holy Mass, and the other (the parlor window) giving her a view to the outer world. The inner two or three rooms were for herself and a serving maid, who protected her from intrusion and took care of her physical needs. The outside window was a gathering place for people who sought her spiritual direction. In time her reputation for holiness may have become an object of pilgrimage. On the day she began her new life as an anchoress, she enjoyed the privilege of a solemn dedication conducted by the bishop. Once she entered her cell, regular relationships were severed due to her now being recognized as the solitary spouse of Christ. Hers was seen not as a "living death" but as a "dying to life."

Julian seems to have imbibed the essence of Benedictine spirituality from the nuns in the adjoining convent of Carrow, but it was from her anchorage that she shared the fruits of her disciplined inquiry into suffering and joy. Though she described herself in modest terms, she became a central figure in the English school of spirituality. Her comprehension of the life of the spirit owes much to the Cistercian writings of William of St. Thierry and Bernard of Clairvaux, both of whom might have influenced her meditations on the motherhood of God. Texts from the Franciscan tradition (see chapter 13 herein), focusing on popular devotion to the Passion of Christ, would also have touched her in thought and prayer. She herself became part of the now-famous retinue of English mystical writers, including Richard Rolle, Margery Kempe, the anonymous author of *The Cloud of Unknowing*, and Walter Hilton.

Though little may be known of Julian's personal history, it is certain that she wrote her famous *Showings*, also called *Revelations of Divine Love*, in a turbulent era riddled with death and destruction. To this catastrophic backdrop, Julian adds few historical references and supplies instead a wealth of detailed descriptions of her physical, mental, and spiritual condition on the occasion of her visions; she withdraws the veil from her inner life and gives us a glimpse of the secrets of her soul. For the rest of her life, Julian pondered the meaning of what God revealed to her, first in the *Short Text*, written soon after the "showings," or visions, began on May 13, 1373, and then in the *Long Text*, composed after they ended in 1393. Through her ever-deepening communion with Christ, Julian came to a clearer knowledge of their "misty" teaching and of what had really happened to her.

Although women were largely unrecognized in intellectual circles, Julian's contributions were received with honor because her cloistered life commanded respect. Her incredible optimism in the face of overwhelming suffering contributed to her reputation as one of the holiest and wisest of spiritual guides. Her gift for homey expression would make her writings not only devotional masterpieces but also original contributions to English literature, mirroring the lasting dispositions of humility and joy that made hers a heart centered in God.

The waning of bodily powers, described in *Showings*, released her capacity for visionary reflections and allowed her to see in the agony of crucifixion the ecstasy of resurrection. In her infirmity, Julian found an opportunity to share in Christ's Passion and to prove for herself the truth told by the apostle Paul: "Therefore I am content with weaknesses, insults, hardships, persecutions, and calamities for the sake of Christ; for whenever I am weak, then I am strong" (2 Cor 12:10).

Many threads contribute to the tapestry of our trying to understand the connection between suffering and joy woven by Julian of Norwich: spiritual poverty grants us the grace of depending on God for everything, and misery attracts God's mercy. Though she introduces herself to us as a simple, unlettered woman—a tribute to her maidenly modesty—Julian walks us through a labyrinth of metaphysical thought: *Who are we most deeply? What is the meaning of life and death? How can we proclaim God's glory amid seemingly endless pain?* Even at the turning point between life and death, she teaches us to laugh heartily. Her genius, combined with a rare gift for literary expression, carries her to the highest summits of contemplation while enabling her to show courteous care for her fellow Christians.

SHOWING TRUST IN PROVIDENCE

In her thirtieth year, Julian experienced a series of sixteen revelations of divine love, which constitute the distinctive quality of her spirituality. Though she does not describe the exact nature of what she suffered, we can assume that her affliction resembled the Black Plague that gripped England at this time. Sick as she was, she sought to discover the meaning of her sickness in the light of God's fatherly and motherly goodness. For three days and nights she was so ill that those gathered around her were sure she would die. On the fourth night she received the last rites of the Church since it did not appear that she could live until daylight. She was not afraid to die, but she longed for more time to love and serve God.[3]

Unexpectedly, her malaise left her, and she began to feel well again. Having attributed this cure to the grace of God, she asked her Savior for the favor of understanding what had happened to her. She sought to identify with Christ's Passion in the deepest way possible. Then her visions or showings began: fifteen of them, one after the other, starting in the early morning and continuing until evening.

The sixteenth revelation, which was to mark their completion, took place the following night, after Julian had suffered a serious relapse. Her bodily sickness returned with its former violence and the spiritual comforts of this final revelation fled. Yet she describes it as a delectable sight in which the Lord assured her that he was the author of the previous revelations.[4] After this she was conscious of a deep peace—but not for long. The devil made one more attempt to shake her trust and allegiance to God, occupying her all that night and morning with dreadful distractions until the new day dawned. Julian resisted his assaults, giving herself over, in the silence and solitude of her cell, to prayerful investigations of their contents.

In the *Showings*, we find a synthesis of mystical experience and theological reflection, ranging from "bodily visions" of the Passion of Christ to "intellectual visions" of the Trinity; from reflections on creation and Divine Providence to intuitions penetrating the innermost secrets of redemption, mercy, and forgiveness.

Before receiving these visions, Julian asked God to grant her three gifts:

1. *The mind of Christ's Passion*, by which she might suffer with him and with the women at the foot of the Cross.
2. *The endurance of an illness* of such severity that it would procure for her the detachment proper to death so that she might be entirely purified and afterwards live for God alone.
3. *The bestowal of three wounds*: one of contrition, or sorrow for sin; one of compassion for the sufferings of Christ; and one of steadfast longing for God, accompanied by an absolute and unconditional will to love.[5]

It might be puzzling, even troubling, to us that Julian asks God for the "gift" of sickness. However, this gift is sought not for its own sake but as a means of grace, to purge her of her sinfulness and attune her to the redemptive mercy of God. This desire came to fulfillment through a divine intervention, thereby dismissing as its cause any pathological condition or permanent deficiency.

Julian was ready to believe that her visions were the ravings of delirium, but when she spoke of them to a religious person who visited her and was edified by what she told him, she felt ashamed of her own doubts and failures of faith. She lay in bed until nightfall, trusting in God's mercy. When she went to sleep, she had a frightful nightmare, but throughout her account she is careful to stress the difference between dreamlike visitations and divinely illumined revelations.

Julian contemplated her showings in full possession of her memory, intellect, and will. She considered, as a mystical theologian would, the immediate and permanent effects of these showings on her moral and religious life. She did not rule out the possibility that her sickness itself was of divine origin, but throughout the ordeal she grew more humble, seeing herself as no better than the simplest believer.

Far from being in a trance, Julian was conscious of what was happening to her; she was able to appraise each occurrence reasonably, drawing upon her lifelong habits of mental control and prudent judgment. She exhibited none of the chaotic, unorganized, rambling, and digressive traits of a hysterical temperament. On the contrary, she saw her showings as means to the attainment of deeper spiritual graces, beginning and ending in the Paschal Mystery of Christ's dying and rising. Even when she was convinced that she was dying, she remained in peace, ready to do God's bidding. Her stamina, as well as the natural forces of her mind and will, far from being diminished during her ordeal, were improved and strengthened. The aim of her prayer—to be purged of every remnant of self-will so as to live in pure worship of God—had been answered.

DISCOVERING WHO WE ARE IN GOD

In her reflections on the goodness of creation, the friendship of Christ, and the tender solicitude of the Trinity, Julian arrived at three significant insights that touched upon the nature of God and the relationship God desires to have with us:

1. *God as Mother.* Julian knew with the certitude of one who has seen for herself that her Redeemer lives and that he wants to be united with saints and sinners, in both their sufferings and their joys. So convinced was Julian of his solicitude that she dares to express the truth that God is our Mother and that in Christ this motherhood means mercy, as she prays, "My kind Mother, my gracious Mother, my beloved Mother, have mercy on me" (*Long Text*, 301). She adds, "And though our earthly mother may suffer her child to

perish, our heavenly Mother, Jesus may never suffer us who are his children to perish, for he is almighty, all wisdom and all love, and so is none but he, blessed may he be" (*Long Text*, 301).

Julian believed that, like all good mothers, Jesus is not content only to save us with much travail; he also wants to guide us to a new life of bliss, feeding us with the bread of life and the wine of salvation, as a mother suckles her child until he can be weaned. Jesus does so tenderly, with every intention of nurturing us as much in time as in eternity. He knows what is for our good, guiding us with such loving and wise care that we mature in faith. In celebrating the tenderness of Christ's humanity and the saving grace of his divinity, Julian posits that love, not sin, is the ultimate foundation of our existence.

2. *The Familiar Love of God.* In the familiarity of everyday life, Julian beheld the presence of God and welcomed the familiar love and goodness she received:

> Our good Lord showed a spiritual sight of his familiar love. I saw that he is to us everything which is good and comforting for our help. He is our clothing, who wraps and enfolds us for love, embraces us and shelters us, surrounds us for his love, which is so tender that he may never desert us. And so in this sight I saw that he is everything which is good, as I understand. And in this he showed me something small, no bigger than a hazelnut, lying in the palm of my hand, as it seemed to me, and it was as round as a ball. I looked at it with the eye of my understanding and thought: What can this be? I was amazed that it could last, for I thought that because of its littleness it would suddenly have fallen into nothing. And I was answered in my understanding: it lasts and always will, because God loves it: and thus everything has being through the love of God.[6]

When Julian held this tiny bit of creation in the palm of her hand, she saw in it something of the nature of God, our Creator, our Protector, our Lover. It convinced her that we can treat God as our familiar and pray with the faith of a child. And so he teaches us "to have firm trust that we shall have what we pray for, because everything which is done would be done, even though we had never prayed for it. But God's love is so great that he regards us as partners in his good work; and so he moves us to pray for what it pleases him to do, for whatever prayer or good desire comes to us by his gift he will repay us for, and give us eternal reward" (*Short Text*, 158).

3. *Doctrine of Wellness.* Thanks to the courteous care she received from the motherly love of her Lord, Julian counsels us to see each period of pain or purgation in our lives as a movement toward transfiguration. If we immerse ourselves in the Paschal Mystery, we will proceed as graciously as possible through life to death to eternal life. To see suffering and even the prospect of death from the perspective of transfiguration is what Julian refers to as "naughting," a disposition to view everything that happens to us with the eyes of love and to see nothing in this life as beyond redemption, although our final rest comes only when we rest in God, whose promise never wavers: "I will make all things well, I shall make all things well, I may make all things well and I can make all things well; and you will see that yourself, that all things will be well" (*Short Text*, 151).

Julian clearly distinguished between the extraordinary or accidental elements of the spiritual life, such as sickness and private revelations, and its essential and fruit-bearing components, such as contrition, compassion, and longing for God.

She insisted that her revelations do not communicate any truths not contained in the revelation entrusted to believers by the Church. Her attitude was that of a humble child of God, always ready to reject what she conceived to be a light if it were not in full accord with the teachings of the Church. Her revelations culminated in the simple yet profound message, "You will not be overcome" (*Long Text*, 315).

Though Julian considered her showings to be favors of God, she did not view them as of essential importance for a life of mystical union with God. She insisted that they were gratuitous gifts that did not make her better by the mere fact that they were given to her. She emphasized that they are not necessary for a life of union and communion with God.

The condition of those who seek God in pure faith, without the help of these extraordinary favors, is as good as that of those who are granted the grace of beholding God in special showings. These favors must not be asked for to satisfy curiosity or our natural desire for knowledge. Their aim is to facilitate our perception of spiritual truths since it is the love with which they are received that matters, not the sights themselves.

Although Julian acknowledged her showings with gratitude and humility, she does all that she can to convince us that they are not the only, or even the best, means to advance in our love for God. Rather they are channels of insight given to her by God to be used with prudence in full accord with the will of the One who granted them and with the authority of the Church that protected her life and work from error.

REFLECT NOW

1. Do you trust God equally in times of joy and suffering, and do you believe that all will be well?
2. How important in your spiritual life are the gifts of contrition, compassion, and longing for God?
3. Do you find evidence of God's care in something as small as a hazelnut?

READ MORE

Amy Frykholm, *Julian: A Contemplative Biography* (Brewster, MA: Paraclete Press, 2010).

J. Janda, *Julian: A Play Based on the Life of Julian of Norwich* (New York: Seabury Press, 1984).

Grace Tantzen, *Julian of Norwich: Mystic and Theologian* (New York: Paulist Press, 2000).

19

LIVE IN HUMILITY, DETACHMENT, AND FRATERNAL CHARITY

I don't say that if a person doesn't have the determination of which I shall speak here, he should stop trying; for the Lord will continue perfecting him, and if that person should do no more than take one step, the step will contain in itself so much power that he will not have to fear losing it, nor will he fail to be very well paid.
  —Teresa of Avila, *The Way of Perfection*, 115

Tempting as it might be to put Teresa of Avila on a pedestal of extraordinary mystical phenomena, that is exactly what she would not want us to do. As she reveals in her autobiography, she is a woman of common sense who experiences an uncommon passion for God. She wants who she is and what she does to be an expression of God's love working in, with, and through her. Without such humility, she affirms, we are and can do nothing.

She also teaches that freedom of spirit depends on our willingness to be detached from anything or anyone to whom we cling instead of giving priority to God. She invites us to examine the lesser gods we have made into our God and the subtle deceptions that allow us to reach this disastrous conclusion. Lacking detachment, she tells us, it is impossible to behave with charity. We can even become so attached to modes of piety that we overlook the needs of others and think of ourselves as holier than they.

St. Teresa was as tireless a teacher of prayer as she was a relentless worker dedicated to bringing God's reign to earth. She wanted her sisters, and us along with them, to be both Mary resting at the feet of Jesus and Martha in the kitchen cooking his supper.

The way Teresa followed had been trod by many saints and reformers who went before her. Like her, they adhered to and passed on the tradition that no one can come to the Father other than by the love-gift of their life to the Lord. What she gained in freedom correlated with what she renounced of worldly fame and fortune for his sake.

MEET THE MASTER

Were we to seek an ideal spiritual directress, it would be Teresa of Avila (1515–1582). Her youth was anything but peaceful. In her teens, she lost her mother and allowed herself to be enchanted by a frivolous cousin. Instead of cultivating the devotion she desired, she succumbed to vain and worldly ways. To tame her to some degree, her father sent her to a convent school under the watchful eyes of the Augustinian nuns. There her religious fervor reawakened, and she reached the decision to pursue a vocation—against her father's wishes—at the Carmelite Monastery of the Incarnation in her hometown of Avila, Spain.

When Teresa professed her vows in 1537, she did so without the joy she expected to feel. A short while later, she became seriously ill with a form of paralysis, mandating that she spend most of her time in the convent's infirmary. A year later she received the grace of a profound religious experience that led to the renewal of her interior life. What touched her heart was her rediscovery of the primitive rule of the Carmelite order with its emphasis on silence, poverty, and contemplative prayer—all of which had been mitigated at the Monastery of the Incarnation.[1] What was she to do?

In 1542, as she writes in *The Book of Her Life*, St. Joseph, to whom she had an avid devotion, enabled her to walk again. Though she resumed some of her old ways, the seeds of reform began to blossom in her. During Lent of 1554, while meditating before a statue depicting the scourging of Jesus at the pillar, God gave her the gift of a radical conversion—not unlike that of St. Augustine, whose *Confessions* made her dissolve in tears of compunction. As she recalls, "When I came to the passage where he speaks about his conversion and read how he heard that voice in the garden, it only seemed to me, according to what I felt in my heart, that it was I the Lord called" (*BL*, 9:8, 103).

In 1560, the year Teresa began to compose her autobiography, she made the move that would change her life—to return to the original rule of Mount Carmel and to initiate the Discalced ("without shoes") Carmelite reform that she began in utter poverty at the Convent of St. Joseph in Avila. Several sisters followed their spiritual mother, whose instructions to them were the basis of her didactic masterpiece, *The Way of Perfection*.[2]

In that book as well as in *The Book of Her Life*, Teresa shares the secret of how not to lose hope under trial and how to rejoice in the smallest success. It is never to stray from the sacred humanity and divinity of Jesus. He is the "living book" (*BL*, 26:5, 226), the Director of directors, who taught her the meaning of redemptive suffering. In the intimate conversation with the Lord that was the heart of her life of prayer, she said to her Friend, "You make things so possible that You manifest clearly there's no need for anything more than truly to love You and truly to leave all for You, so that You, my Lord, may make everything easy. . . . They who really love You, my Good, walk safely on a broad and royal road" (*BL*, 35:13–14, 308). For the next several years, from 1567 to shortly before her death, she founded new convents throughout Spain, travels she detailed in the *Book of Her Foundations*.[3] In 1579, she wrote her finest book on the mystical life, *The Interior Castle*.[4]

To the already fertile roots of traditional Christian spirituality, St. Teresa adds four distinctive strengthening agents. The first is her ability to write for everyday women and men who, like herself, do their best to cross the threshold of sainthood. The second is her uncanny capacity to stay in touch with daily reality by recommending moderation, not excessive mortification, as the best way to reform faults and failings. As legend has it, she knew when it was time for penance and when it was time for partridge! Third, she gives down-to-earth, practical advice to her sisters, using images such as watering a garden to convey precise insights about the life of prayer. And, finally, she makes explicit the connection between contemplation and action, insisting that we follow the traditional mentors who aided her, including Francis of Assisi; Bernard of Clairvaux, who "found delight in [Christ's] humanity"; Catherine of Siena; and "many others about whom your Reverence [a Dominican priest] knows more than I" (*BL*, 22:7, 194).

St. Teresa met the Lord she so loved and served on October 4, 1582. Her canonization by Pope Gregory XV took place in 1622, followed centuries later by an honor she could never have anticipated. On September 27, 1970, Pope Paul VI proclaimed her a Doctor of the Church, validating not only her life of heroic virtue but also her legacy to the people of God. On the eve of her death, St. Teresa prayed these prophetic words: "Lord, either to die or to suffer; I don't ask anything else for myself. I am consoled to hear the clock strike, for at the passing away of that hour of life it seems to me I am drawing a little closer to the vision of God" (*BL*, 40:20, 361).

FROM VIRTUOUS LIVING TO UNION WITH GOD

In her first Discalced Carmelite foundation at St. Joseph's in 1562, Teresa expressed her intention to establish a new way of living the cloistered life for "thirteen poor little women" consecrated to prayer. The problem she encountered was that most of the books on prayer available at the time were on the Index of Forbidden Books. The solution she found was typically Teresian. The sisters needed instruction from their trusted directress. Therefore, she would write an instructional manual herself, submit it for scrutiny to the proper authority, and then arrange for its distribution.

She completed *The Way of Perfection* in 1566. In it she captures the heart of Carmelite spirituality: its commitment to live in strict conformity to the Gospel of Jesus Christ and the rules and constitutions that upheld the sisters' vocation. Her approach was always two-pronged: the asceticism of virtuous living and the mysticism of union with God. In addition to adhering to the evangelical counsels of poverty, chastity, and obedience, Teresa grounds the spirituality of Carmel in three virtues in which she and her sisters must excel:

Do not think, my friends and daughters, that I shall burden you with many things; please God, we shall do what our holy fathers established and observed, for by walking this path they themselves established, they merited this title we give them. It would be wrong to seek another way or try to learn about this path from anyone else. I shall enlarge on only three things which are from our own constitutions, for it is very important that we understand how much the practice of these three things helps us to possess inwardly and outwardly the peace our Lord recommended so highly to us. The first of these is love for one another; the second is detachment from all created things; the third is true humility, which even though I speak of it last, is the main practice and embraces all the others. (*WP*, 4:4, 54)

To love one another is only possible because God has first loved us (see 1 Jn 4:10). To live in detachment is to be led from the bondage of pride to the freedom of the children of God, who lay aside their former way of life and acquire a fresh, spiritual way of thinking (see Eph 4:22–23). To be humble is to imitate Christ, who humbled himself for our sakes, becoming one of us in all things but sin (see Phil 2:6–7). From him, we learn the most valuable lesson of all: selfless love. We detach ourselves from narcissistic needs and cultivate compassion for community with Christ at the center. We give up our foolish striving for self-salvation and find the path to Christian perfection by listening to God's will in the details of the common life.

As eloquent as she is accurate, Teresa offers the sisters a timeless yet timely treatment of what is essential to preserve their life together and to render them true daughters of the Church, strong soldiers able to win the battle with evil and fortify the whole world by means of their unceasing prayer.

LOVING OTHERS WITH DETACHMENT AND HUMILITY

Teresa begins her teaching on fraternal charity by showing what can go wrong in our attempts to love one another. We err because our love is either excessive or defective. We love too much or too little, too possessively or too indifferently. The problem of possessive love is especially treacherous in the close confines of a contemplative community, where it may flourish under the guise of virtue and piety. However, such love, directed toward anyone but God, becomes a detriment to the soul that ought to be occupied in loving him. Instead of cultivating one special friendship over another, Teresa says that in a house where no more than thirteen women live, all must be friends; all must be loved, held dear, and helped. The Lord does not play favorites, and neither must the sisters.

1. *The call to love purely.* To clarify her concern for faulty ways of loving, she makes a distinction between love that is purely spiritual or unselfish and that which is mixed with sensuality or selfishness. The first love takes into account our inclination to despoil the way we ought to love by overly affective or controlling behavior. She reminds the sisters that compared to the greater love of God that draws every fiber of our being to him, lesser loves for gratification and possessiveness seem like shadows. They weary the soul compared to the endless refreshment granted by our love of God above all others. We do what we can and must do for them, but we avoid becoming preoccupied with their lives to the point of becoming forgetful of God.

Perfect lovers trample underfoot the comfort the world has to offer since they cannot tolerate being apart from God. No affliction is too great for such a love, no sacrifice too much to ask. Such lovers are more inclined to give than to receive, for theirs is a "precise love that imitates the Commander-in-chief of love, Jesus our Good!" (*WP*, 6:9, 65). This love is happiest when it sees others progressing beyond the manipulative, seductive modes of relating that trap us in nets of selfish sensuality.

Teresa cautions her sisters to avoid this lesser way of loving at all costs. If they keep Christ as their model, they will replace condemnation with compassion and respond with care to each one's needs. They will cultivate truly spiritual friendships, enjoy their times of togetherness at recreation, and observe the rule of chastity, not as a duty but as a delight. Words of endearment such as "my life," "my soul," and "my only good" will be kept only for their Spouse.

2. *The call to be detached.* In regard to the second directive, to be detached from all created things, Teresa casts this rather negative sounding disposition in a positive light. She says that detachment "if . . . practiced with perfection, includes everything . . . because if we embrace the Creator and care not at all for the whole of creation, his Majesty will infuse the virtues" (*WP*, 8:1, 11). Teresa never advocates a posture of despisal or disparagement of creation. She herself was a lover of beauty and nature. What she does advise is an inner attitude of carefreeness from the vicissitudes of ownership. All possessions come and go; all relationships are here for a while and then pass away. If we become absorbed in anything or anyone as ultimate, we lose our freedom and can no longer soar without shackles to God.

The solution is not to despise creation but to adore the Creator. In this way we come to see persons, events, and things in their proper order and relationship. All that is has to be seen as but a pointer to the Divine Mystery in whom and by whom everything exists. Withdrawal from ownership is a condition for the possibility of being united with God and through him gaining the happiness we seek. Any erosion of this inner stance of reliance on the providential plan of God makes us victims of worldly ambitions devoid of poverty of spirit. Letting go of external possessions is not enough; we must relinquish any excessive interior attachments, no matter how pious they may seem.

Teresa tells her sisters not to fool themselves. It is only when they have left the world and gone into the desert of Carmel that the real work of detachment begins: disentangling themselves from bodily comforts that lead to disobedience of the rule, avoiding heroic penances that lack discretion and increase vanity, practicing silence, and ceasing to complain about slight sicknesses not requiring medical attention that may aid their practice of interior mortification.

3. *The call to be humble.* Teresa insists that humility is the cornerstone of the edifice built by charity (love of others) and detachment (diminished seeking of self-satisfaction). It is the source of our strength to resist demonic plays on human pride. Progress in holiness occurs when we resist vain reasonings and defensive postures; take on lowly tasks; avoid the privileges of

rank and power; disengage ourselves from excesses of praise or blame; and bear with dishonor, ridicule, and misunderstanding. We need to use such occasions to imitate the humility of Jesus and Mary, not wavering from this intention by choosing subtly or overtly what connotes a need for worldly honor.

In one of her most memorable comparisons, Teresa places humility within the framework of a game of chess. She says:

> The queen is the piece that can carry on the best battle in this game, and all the other pieces help. There's no queen like humility for making the King surrender. Humility drew the King from heaven to the womb of the Virgin, and with it, by one hair we will draw him to our souls. And realize that the one who has more humility will be the one who possesses him more; and the one who has less will possess him less. For I cannot understand how there could be humility without love or love without humility; nor are these two virtues possible without detachment from all creatures. (*WP*, 16:2, 94)

With symbolic virtuosity, Teresa concludes that these three pillars of the virtuous life are both a preparation for and a consequence of the practice of vocal, mental, and contemplative prayer. Nothing erodes this practice more than failing to make the effort to grow more deeply in these three virtues. Teresa herself admits that for many years she was unable to pray without the help of a book; and yet it was this deprivation of delight that enabled her to walk with humility, waiting upon the Lord's will and being content with whatever he asked of her as his servant and friend.

PRAYING AS JESUS TAUGHT US

The Way of Perfection confirms that "it is a great thing to have experienced the friendship and favor [our Lord] shows toward those who journey on this road and how he takes care of almost all the expenses" (*WP*, 23:5, 127). On this charming, practical note, Teresa proclaims that there is nothing parsimonious about the generosity of God. More is given than we asked to receive or that we thought we deserved. Perfected in Christ, we become perfectly pleasing to the Father.

Teresa then proceeds to integrate the Church's teaching on the Lord's Prayer with the here-and-now needs of her sisters. In the process of commenting line by line on the Our Father, she answers their questions about the highest state of mystical marriage and the difference between true and false humility, petitionary prayers and recollection, and simple union and consummate communion. From her experience of living in a reformed convent, she knows what it means to walk from the Calvary of undiluted obedience to Christ crucified to the glory of Easter morn.

Every reiteration of the Lord's Prayer only proves the point that it is a synopsis of the whole Gospel, a distillation of the substance of the revelation that becomes richer with every repetition. While books of exegetical analysis may be beyond our mental prowess to absorb, the contents of the Lord's Prayer are etched on every believer's heart. We can turn to the words Jesus taught us in any circumstance. What a wonder it is that "the entire spiritual way [is] contained in it, from the beginning stages until God engulfs the soul and gives it to drink abundantly from the fount of living water, which he said was to be found at the end of the way" (*WP*, 42:5, 203).

Teresa sketches a map of prayer showing us how to move from methods of discursive meditation to mental prayer. We are not to mouth the words of the Lord's Prayer only with our lips but to meditate on what we say, keeping in mind our journey's end: union with God. Through stillness and listening, in recollection and prayerful receptivity, we may feel ourselves being drawn day after day into intimacy with the Trinity. The peace of Christ expands our hearts and penetrates our minds. We learn from experience that the quickest remedy for scattered thought is to become more mindful of the Divine Companion with whom we converse: "I want you to understand that it is good for you, if you are to recite the Our Father well, to remain at the side of the Master who taught this prayer to you" (*WP*, 2:5, 130).

Teresa ponders the petitions of the prayer Jesus taught us. One by one, she finds in them four progressively higher degrees of prayer. They are:

1. The initial stages of moving from vocal to mental prayer.
2. Active recollection whereby we acquire an ability to center our faculties on one particular truth, such as "Our Father who art in heaven."

3. Prayer of quiet, as in "hallowed be thy name." Here the soul is content to make peaceful acts of love, striving only to magnify the Lord's name.
4. Actual union with God, as in "Thy will be done on earth as in heaven."

This fourth degree connotes a supernatural state of infused contemplation, acquired not by our own efforts but by the grace of God—a movement parallel to her own experience of being drawn by the Holy Spirit from being wooed by God in spiritual courtship, to espousal, and to the consummation of spiritual marriage, descriptions of which she will reserve for *The Interior Castle.*

To stay true to our calling in Christ, we must never judge ourselves or others too harshly. In every activity we ought to exude as much affability and understanding as possible, "in such a way that everyone you talk to will love your conversation and desire your manner of living and acting, and not be frightened and intimidated by virtue" (*WP*, 41:7, 199).

Teresa concludes that the more we identify with the Lord's life, which ended in death out of love for us, the freer we are. His self-emptying in love was the sole force strong enough to combat the life-denying plan of evil unleashed. Never must we forget the truth that it is the Lord alone who can and does deliver us from evil—from the smallest venial sin to the gravest mortal fault. His torment released a torrential rain of grace, freeing us from the sting of death. For us pilgrims to walk in the truth of who we are, we must not be afraid to say with St. Teresa:

> I am not speaking about the saints—they can do everything in Christ, as St. Paul said—but sinners like myself. I see myself closed in by weakness, lukewarmness, and a lack of mortification, and many other things. I see that it behooves me to ask the Lord for a remedy.... I do not find this remedy while living, and so I ask the Lord to deliver me from all evil forever. (*WP*, 42:2, 201)

Now our sole longing is to let God's will be done, a desire we reiterate every time we pray the prayer Jesus taught us, since it frees "us from these dangers forever and [draws] us at last away from every evil" (*WP*, 42:4, 202).

REFLECT NOW

1. Have you begun to cultivate a habitual desire to imitate Christ in humility, detachment, and fraternal charity?
2. Why do you think that the asceticism of the virtuous life is the only sure foundation for the experience of mystical union with God?
3. What petitions of the Lord's Prayer mean the most to you personally and communally?

READ MORE

Tessa Bielecki, *Teresa of Avila: Ecstasy and Common Sense* (Boston, MA: Shambhala, 1996).

Keith J. Egan, ed., *Carmelite Prayer: A Tradition for the 21st Century* (New York: Paulist Press, 2003).

Steven Payne and Phyllis Zagano, eds., *The Carmelite Tradition: Spirituality in History* (Collegeville, MN: Liturgical Press, 2011).

20

BEAR YOUR CROSS AND SEEK INTIMACY WITH THE TRINITY

JOHN OF THE CROSS ON THE MOVEMENT FROM PURGATION TO UNION WITH GOD

This narrow gate is the dark night of sense, in which the soul is despoiled and denuded—in order to enter it—and grounded in faith, which is foreign to all sense, that it may be capable of walking along the constricted road, which is the night of the spirit. The soul enters this second night so that it may journey to God in pure faith, for pure faith is the means whereby it is united with God.
—John of the Cross, *The Collected Works*, 385

John of the Cross may have been small in stature, but he was a giant of insight into our fallen and redeemed condition. We may squirm a bit under his penetrating gaze, but we do not want to turn away. He teaches us to flee from all that is not of God so that we can experience with newfound freedom how to bear our cross and seek intimacy with the Trinity.

In the classical literature of Christian spirituality, we can trace the movement St. John followed from purgation to union in the writings of St. Augustine, Pseudo-Dionysius, and St. Bonaventure. Undergirding the way of purgation is the dynamic of detachment, central in St. John's body of work. To pray for a clean heart suggests that the inordinate attachments to which we cling curtail progress to union with God and must be washed clean (Ps 51:2) since they are contrary to God's will. Illuminated by the fruits of freedom from self-centeredness, we find our center in Christ and lift our thoughts and affections to him. We welcome undeserved touches of union and attend with joy to Christ's saying to us: "Listen! I am standing at the door, knocking; if you hear my voice and open the door, I will come in to you and eat with you, and you with me" (Rv 3:20). As St. John says:

> Before the divine fire is introduced into the substance of the soul and united with it through perfect and complete purgation and purity, its flame, which is the Holy Spirit, wounds the soul by destroying and consuming the imperfections of its bad habits. And this is the work of the Holy Spirit, in which he disposes it for divine union and transformation in God through love.[1]

MEET THE MASTER

John of the Cross (1542–1591), a saint canonized in 1726 and named a Doctor of the Church in 1926, began his life in obscurity in the small town of Fontiveros, Spain. His father, Gonzalo, came from a family of silk merchants, but they disowned him when he fell in love with Catalina Alvarez, the daughter of a poor weaver, and married her in 1529. God blessed them with three boys, John being the youngest. When he was only three years old, his father passed away after a long illness, leaving Catalina a widow to fend for herself and her children. Their second son, Luis, died, possibly of malnourishment, a few years later. In desperation, Catalina moved to Medina del Campo, begging assistance from her husband's family but not receiving it. Francisco, their eldest son, was sent to live with relatives, leaving John and his mother to find sustenance on their own.

To make ends meet in their new hometown, Catalina continued working as a weaver while John pursued his studies at a school for poor children comparable to an orphanage. He also assisted in a hospital for the destitute, where compassion became etched into his character. The Jesuit priest who directed his school was so impressed with John that he offered him the opportunity to learn humble trades like carpentry as well as to exercise his mind by studying grammar and rhetoric, along with Latin and Greek classics.

When John finished his studies, his mentor, Don Alonso, offered him the security of pursuing ordination to the Jesuits. Instead, at the age of twenty-one, in 1563, his contemplative spirit and his devotion to the Blessed Mother led him to enter the Carmelite order as a novice. A year earlier, in 1562, Teresa of Avila founded the first reformed Discalced Carmelite cloister, St. Joseph's in Avila. In due time, in accordance with God's plan, their paths would cross. In the meantime, John made his profession in the Order of Carmel and was sent to study at the University of Salamanca, where he majored in philosophy and theology. After his ordination in 1567, he returned to Medina del Campo to say his first Mass. This town was the site of St. Teresa's second foundation, and it was there that they met.

So taken was John by Teresa's vision of returning to the original rule of Mount Carmel that he questioned his suitability for teaching and preaching in accordance with the charism of his order and agreed to explore the discalced reform she had begun. Teresa saw in him exceptional gifts for spiritual direction and for helping her to fulfill her dream of establishing new foundations of friars seeking silence, solitude, and a life of contemplative prayer. John concurred with her request to establish on the site of an old farm in Duruelo, midway between Avila and Salamanca, the first monastery of the discalced friars. Like Teresa, he "wanted everyone to find comfort in the thought that however severe it may be, purification is still the work of God's gentle hand, clearing away the debris of attachment and making room for divine light."[2]

In 1571, John helped Teresa open another foundation at Alba de Tormes. A year later he became vicar and confessor at the Monastery of the Incarnation in Avila, remaining there until 1577. Needless to say, being recognized as the first master and spiritual director of the Discalced Carmelites did not endear John to his order. The reformers felt the hostility of the traditionalists from the start, as the original order had allowed many mitigations to slip into their way of living the rule. The wheels were set in motion, politically and ecclesially, to squelch the reform. On December 2, 1577, John was abducted in Avila, brought to Toledo, and thrust into what would be the darkest period of his life.[3] Kidnapped and imprisoned, he endured severe physical deprivation, the starkest solitary confinement, and cruel punishments at the hands of his own brothers. Yet it was in this prison that he found his poetic voice, composing there the first of his great lyrics, *The Spiritual Canticle* with its haunting opening stanza:

> Where have you hidden,
> Beloved, and left me moaning?
> You fled like the stag
> after wounding me:
> I went out calling you, but you were gone.
> (*CW, SC,* 1:1, 478)

Miraculously, nine torturous months later, John managed to escape from his prison cell. Having been led to safety, he sought refuge with the Carmelite sisters, who hid him from his captors, renourished him, and encouraged him to put on paper his prison poems and their haunting renditions of the dark night of his soul.

Much as John longed for peace and tried to resolve the conflicts in the order, the battle between its two branches went on until June of 1580, when Pope Gregory XII signed the documents declaring that the Discalced Carmelites were a separate province within the order. In 1585, John was elected one of their provincial counselors. At the same time, he continued to counsel the sisters and help Teresa with her new foundations. In addition to poems inspired by his experience of God while he was in prison, over the next few years he wrote his commentary on them.

The four books that resulted—*The Ascent of Mount Carmel, The Dark Night, The Spiritual Canticle,* and *The Living Flame of Love*—comprise an unprecedented compendium of ascetical-mystical theology. John wrote these masterpieces during the final fourteen years of his life when his intellectual and spiritual gifts had come to full flowering. He had passed through the nights of sense and spirit with the afflictive force of their purgative fires. He had experienced in this darkness the illumination of his intellect, memory, and will by faith, hope, and love and the grace of union between the lover and the Beloved.

Though he was at peace inwardly, he could not escape the shadows of unrest and suspicion that plagued the Discalced Carmelites. In the last year of his life, he was sent to the "desert" of La Peñuela and that summer suffered both physically, from an infected ulcer in his foot, and emotionally, from a persistent campaign to discredit him. St. John died as he had lived on December 14, 1591, happy to have drunk from the cup of Christ's suffering and thereby, in his words, to have penetrated "deep into the thicket" (*CW, SC*, 36:10–11, 613) of the "delectable wisdom of God."[4]

FROM RENUNCIATION TO LIBERATION

Woven by St. John into the tapestry of his work and validated by his life is his insistence that only when we are reduced to nothing, to the highest degree of humility, can the spiritual union between our souls and God be accomplished. As he says, "This union is the most noble and sublime state attainable in this life. The journey, then, does not consist in consolations, delights, and spiritual feelings, but in the living death of the cross, sensory and spiritual, exterior and interior" (*CW, A*, 2, 7:11, 172).

In the first book of *The Dark Night*, St. John identifies the inordinate attachments, passions, and appetites that impede our progress to union and must be purged.[5] He begins with the greatest obstacle of all, *spiritual pride*, or complacency in our accomplishments. It leads to our becoming overly attached to disciplines like fasting or to particular devotions as ends in themselves. Such vainglory cancels docility or the desire to be directed by God and to shun any boastful claim to self-sufficiency. It closes our heart to the healing power of humility.

Spiritual avarice leads to possessiveness of tangible things as ends in themselves and to keeping our mind fixed on such nontangible possessions as images and ideas rather than on their Divine Giver. What prevents us from engaging with God may be as thin as a thread or as heavy as a chain. Greed in either case curtails generosity and must be purged by poverty of spirit and the grace of interior detachment. Eroding the possibility of self-giving, spiritual avarice is the vice of being possessed by our possessions.

Spiritual lust tends to reduce transcendent longings to the senses of seeing, hearing, touching, tasting, and smelling rather than lifting these senses chastely and respectfully to God. It opens us to demonic seductions that arouse impure images, fantasies, memories, and expectations that erode our love for God and our need for a deeper life of prayer. This obstacle may lead to such remorse of conscience that it blocks our hope in God's mercy.

Purgation may take the form of sensory dryness, of spiritual aridity and distaste for lustful inclinations that have left us feeling sad and empty. What may happen with the grace of God is a calming of the urge for instant gratification, resulting in a new way of loving wholly reformed in the dark nights of sense and spirit: "Love, derived from sensuality terminates in sensuality; and the love that is of the spirit terminates in the spirit of God, and brings it increase. . . . When the soul enters the dark night, all these loves are placed in reasonable order. This night strengthens and purifies the love that is of God, and takes away and destroys the other" (*CW, DN*, 1, 4:7–8, 370).

Spiritual anger makes us ready to pounce when the least irritating person, event, or thing crosses our path. Accompanying this peevish penchant may be indiscreet zeal for putting our own plans first or feeling angry with ourselves when we fail to advance quickly or break our own perfectionistic resolutions. Anger of this sort breeds impatience as well as evoking temper tantrums and seething rage. Accompanying this outburst of irritability may be a sullen mood or an uncontrollable desire to place blame on others for our problems. The purging of this imperfection demands the cultivation of the fruits of the Spirit: "love, joy, peace, patience, kindness, generosity, faithfulness, gentleness, and self-control" (Gal 5:22–23).

Spiritual gluttony makes us focus on the delights we may initially experience in spiritual exercises; we strive for "spiritual savor" more than for "spiritual purity and discretion." We may also be inclined to go from one extreme to another, wavering between too much pleasure and too much deprivation, while opening ourselves to demonic temptations to gratify our own will. This obstacle leads to loss of devotion and repugnance for the cross; it blocks patient perseverance, makes us feel averse to any form of self-denial, and keeps us from making progress in compassion. It militates against the virtue and value of practicing moderation.

Spiritual envy arouses feelings of sadness in the face of the gifts and talents of others, whom we do not want to hear praised. It causes us to feel annoyed when another person receives a compliment we think ought to have been addressed to us. When others seem to move ahead of us on the spiritual path, envy arouses in us an almost automatic need to gossip about or undo altogether the good deeds they perform.

Spiritual sloth makes us weary of the disciplines and practices associated with faith deepening, especially when prayer does not produce the sensory satisfactions we crave. This obstacle blocks obedience to God's call and leads to the avoidance of any task that is difficult and unpleasant. Sloth is scandalized by the cross and repelled by the "narrow gate" that leads to life (Mt 7:13). The main cause of this listless response is our chronic need for excitement to shake us loose from laziness. Worse than this, we begin to begrudge serving God and others by performing pedestrian tasks. Of slothful types, St. John says, "Because of their sloth, they subordinate the way of perfection (which requires denying one's own will and satisfaction for God) to the pleasure and delight of their own will" (*CW, DN,* 1, 7:2, 374).

PURGATIVE, ILLUMINATIVE, AND UNITIVE POWER OF THE DARK NIGHTS

The *sensory night,* as St. John explains, is the first and most necessary arena of purgation. Our five senses (seeing, hearing, touching, tasting, and smelling) must undergo reformation to align with the spiritual dimension of our life. The purpose of this night is to liberate us from the seven capital sins he so accurately describes. This night accommodates the senses to the spirit. The *spiritual night* brings this purgative restructuring of our interiority to its unitive climax. The powers of intellect, memory, and will are redirected by the theological virtues of faith, hope, and love. In this way our conformity *to* God draws us into the intimacy of communion *with* God.

What we are to *do* in this phase of the dark night is basically nothing. This counsel is difficult to accept because it feels as if God has ceased to send us blessings, as if we must do something to earn or re-earn God's favor. Yet all we can do, according to St. John, is to accept what is happening to us as God's work. No matter how dry we feel, we must continue to pray for patience and trust in God. We must not feel that our inability to meditate in the usual way signals lack of devotion. Rather we are to be content with a *loving and peaceful attentiveness to God* without the concern or effort to feel something. For, as John says, "contemplation is nothing else than a secret and peaceful and loving inflow of God, which, if not hampered, fires the soul in the spirit of love" (*DN*, 1, 10:6, 382).

The dark nights of sense and spirit release us from the bondage of excessive attachments to "lesser gods" and cleanse us of lingering imperfections and inordinate attachments. They must be uprooted like the dead roots retarding the growth of an otherwise healthy tree. Traces of our old, dull, forgetful self, weakened by sin, need to be reformed by sensory purgation. Through the action of grace, we begin to overcome distractions and inattentiveness and to become recollected in God.

One subtle imperfection is to rely too much on such extraordinary spiritual apprehensions as visions, locutions, or other ecstatic sensations. Of special concern to St. John is the way the demonic can beguile us into believing that we are already in a state of union. Such a conclusion is seductive. That is why we must renounce it as quickly as possible and let ourselves be led by God into the spiritual night of pure faith, hope, and love. The aim of the spiritual night is to make us wholly receptive to God. This can only happen if our senses and spiritual faculties are disconnected from their dependency on such admittedly delightful touches and if the soul walks by pure faith, not by sight—for faith is the only proper and adequate means to union with God (see *CW, DN*, 1, 11:4, 385).

The God-guided initiative for purgation entails what St. John calls divestment—God leaving the intellect in darkness. It no longer understands by means of its natural light but by means of the divine wisdom to which it is now oriented. The memory is in emptiness. It no longer wishes to dwell on the past but to remember the promises fulfilled by God's providence with their presentiments of eternal bliss. The will is in aridity. It no longer loves with its natural strength but with the purity of the Holy Spirit. The object of its longing is now nothing but God.

Terrible as these afflictions can be, St. John says that this night darkens to give light; it gladdens the soul because it draws us closer to the Beloved. At times we feel with certitude that the light does shine in the darkness.

We experience in a serene way the self-communications of God, imparting mystical knowledge to the intellect, although the will in its affective dimension may still feel dry. The infusions of divine light are delicate and ineffable, transcending all knowledge.

At other times this "dark contemplation" affects both the intellect and the will at once, sublimely and tenderly enkindling love. What St. John has found is that the warmth of loving intimacy with God moves the very substance of the mind and purges the heart so much that the will becomes captivated by the force of love. That is why for him the *sad* night is a *glad* night, a night darkened by self-stripping but full of light. God conducts the soul by means of solitary and secret contemplation, outside of sensual attachments, so that no-thing (*nada*) can detain it on the road to union.

The dark night obscures the intellect's habitual way of understanding, annihilating it and preparing it for knowledge that is both divine and human. It strips the soul of its memory of consolations in the past and leaves it feeling empty, leading it to that hope-filled peace that passes understanding. It purges the will of all its inordinately attached affections and feelings, readying the soul for touches of divine union.

The flame of love that burns in our heart for the Beloved enables the soul to soar to God in ways known only to God. Even without many interior lights or exterior guides, the soul proceeds in peace along the unknown path to oneness with God. Engaged though we may be in daily chores, life through this "substantial transformation" (*CW, LFL,* 3:78, 706) has become one act of love. We long to do for God the exact measure of what God has done for us. This union, partially attained in this life, reaches its full promise in the life to come.

Love this mature conveys, beyond gratification or satisfaction, immense gratitude and lasting joy. This mystical relationship is the divine destiny God wills for us "according to the mode of the soul" (*CW, LFL,* 3:25, 683). Christ lights the flame of love that draws us from purgation to union, bathing "the soul in glory and [refreshing] it with the quality of divine life" (*CW, LFL,* 1:3, 611).[6]

REFLECT NOW

1. Do you ask God for the gift of "naked faith" in the midnight moments of your life, or are you still prone to rely too much on yourself?
2. Why is death to self the narrow gate to new life in Christ?
3. Why is purgation the only sure pathway to union with God?

READ MORE

Ruth Burrows, *Ascent to Love: The Spiritual Teaching of St. John of the Cross* (London: Darton, Longman and Todd, 1987).

Ross Collings, *John of the Cross* (Collegeville, MN: Liturgical Press, 1990).

Iain Matthew, *The Impact of God: Soundings from St. John of the Cross* (London: Hodder & Stroughton, 1995).

Part Three

Modern Masters

(1600—2000)

INTRODUCTION

MODERN MASTERS

The path to spiritual maturity represented by the modern masters is a continuation of the pathway upon which their ancient and medieval counterparts have already trod. Managing self and others without reference to the Spirit of the living God who sustains and embraces us renders life meaningless. We fail to see that every facet of reality is shot through with the light of eternity.

One of the most meaningful times of my life was the period when I chose to study post-Reformation spiritual writers from John Milton (1608–1674) to T. S. Eliot (1888–1965) as part of the requirements for receiving my PhD in English literature. Thanks to the pioneering work of Fr. Adrian van Kaam in the field of formative spirituality, I had come to see, as he did, the necessity of ecumenical sensitivity. Whatever our faith grouping might be, we were obliged to return to the foundations of our shared love for scripture and the classical masters of our Christian formation tradition.

My awakening to the riches of my own pre-Reformation tradition happened in great measure due to the works of the four post-Reformation writers featured in this section (John Wesley, Evelyn Underhill, Thomas R. Kelly, and Dietrich Bonhoeffer). They reintroduced me to Catholic writers whose works I rediscovered when I began to access the formation wisdom of our two-thousand-year faith tradition. Wesley found insights pertaining to the pursuit of Christian perfection in the desert literature of the undivided Church and in the Eastern father Gregory of Nyssa. Underhill was inspired in her pursuit of the meaning of mysticism by, among others, Jan van Ruysbroeck. Kelly, like many other Quakers, was drawn to the practice of the presence of God by Brother Lawrence of the Resurrection, and Bonhoeffer revealed to me a marked affinity to John of the Cross.

These masters remind us that the greatest mistake we can make, spiritually speaking, is to remain distant from God, exercising routine religiosity as a matter of moral duty rather than falling passionately in love with God. We pretend to be about the infinite business of God while still being absorbed in our own finite enterprises.

The modern masters know that a divided heart cannot be the dwelling place of God. Until we are ready to risk plunging into the divine abyss where God's love enkindles purifying fire and takes possession of our intellect, memory, and will, we cannot grow in spiritual maturity, nor can we become active-contemplatives and contemplatives-in-action.

The truth articulated by the spiritual masters, from the earliest ages to our own era, arises from a strong faith that stands firm in the face of both inner battles and outer attacks, often from secular and even anti-Christian forces. Such faith can never be satisfied with pop spirituality divorced from the wisdom of tradition.

Reading these timeless and timely texts grants us the grace of imbibing the gourmet food of in-depth spiritual formation. Instead of our thinking only about how to find fulfillment in worldly success, we listen to pre- and post-Reformation masters, who cut through the illusions of functionalism and rouse us from the slumber of self-deception. They move us beyond the limited horizons of a measurement mentality to disclosures of meanings that, century after century, inspire those who love God selflessly and extend this love to the service of others.

21

Relish the Richness
of the Ordinary

FRANCIS DE SALES ON
THE DEVOUT LIFE

Charity is spiritual fire and when it bursts into flames, it is called devotion. Hence devotion adds nothing to the fire of charity except the flame that makes charity prompt, active, and diligent not only to observe God's commandments but also to fulfill his heavenly counsels and inspirations.
    —Francis de Sales, *Introduction to the Devout Life*, 41

According to St. Francis de Sales, the chances of finding a good spiritual director are one in a thousand. Actually, he corrects himself to say it is more like one in ten thousand! For those who have yet to find such a guide, his book *Introduction to the Devout Life* offers a trustworthy path to the pursuit of a Christ-centered life attentive to the richness of the ordinary. According to Francis, the three most trustworthy signs of living in God's will are the humble admission that without him we can do nothing; "holy equanimity," or living in tranquility; and the refusal to allow either consolation or desolation to disrupt our search for the direction we seek. The demands made upon us may change from day to day, but what remains constant is our wholehearted desire to cultivate a listening heart that wells up with joy when we decrease that Christ may increase. Whatever our vocation may be—from active ministry to monastic hiddenness—we must turn to the Director of all directors, the Holy Spirit, to guide us in respect for our unique communal calling in Christ. The "little virtues" of trust, constancy, and deference to God's good pleasure are signs that we are on the way to living the devout life.

MEET THE MASTER

A native of Savoy in France, Francis de Sales (1567–1622) was the eldest son of an aristocratic family. Though they were Christian by commitment, they counted on their son's pursuit of a worldly career in law or education. The path carved out for him by God revealed that none of these expectations would be fulfilled. Francis would turn his attention instead to the study of theology at the University of Padua, where he received his doctorate in 1591. Upon his return to Savoy, he renounced his rights as a nobleman. In 1593, he answered the call to the priesthood.

In preparation for his ordination, he studied the writings of Thomas Aquinas and Augustine and read as well the mystical theology of Pseudo-Dionysius and the works of Bernard of Clairvaux and Bonaventure. He quotes these masters in his books and letters, for they adhered, as he did, to the truth that the human and divine are inextricably linked in us by virtue of our urge to imitate Christ and our hunger for union with God.

Inspiration from the Holy Spirit and its incarnation in our familial, professional, social, and political life were as inseparable in his mind as was the connection between asceticism (daily sacrifice of self for God's sake) and mysticism (knowing God experientially in prayer and eucharistic communion). Devotion for Francis meant belonging to God amid the business of the day. Consecration to Christ required showing compassion for our neighbor. Liberty of spirit resulted when we refused God nothing of who we are and of what we do.

Francis also drew upon the desert tradition and its teaching of both mortification and moderation, of the necessity to maintain vigilance of heart, and of the need to win the battle between virtue and vice. Devotion in no way precluded fulfilling our duty in life since to "live Jesus," as the Desert Fathers and Mothers taught, was to listen to the command to embody charity in the Church, in short, to put prayer into practice in solitude and in community.

Torn by the pressing questions aroused in his post-Reformation age, such as theological debates over the meaning of predestination, Francis placed his doubts and fears pertaining to his own salvation before the Blessed Mother. He begged the Lord who had ordained him, through her intercession, to show him mercy and to be his hope and salvation. Kneeling before a statue of the Black Madonna in the Church of St. Etienne in Paris, the spiritual crisis that had tempted him to despair came to an end. He received the grace of knowing that Christ was not the Damning One but the Saving One.

To study Salesian spirituality is to come to know Jesus of Nazareth in a lasting and loving way and to appreciate what a superb master of Catholic–Protestant dialogue Francis was. In the sixteenth century, religious warfare and unrest ravaged Europe. On one side were the reformers, Luther, Calvin, and Zwingli; on the other were the earlier works of such counterreformers as Teresa of Avila, John of the Cross, and Ignatius of Loyola, who sought to bring about renewal within the Catholic Church in keeping with the teachings promulgated at the Council of Trent (1562).

Francis spent time as a missionary in a district of France that had converted to Protestantism, serving with such fidelity as a confessor and preacher that by 1602 many people who heard him and sought his help returned to the Catholic faith. In the same year, he was consecrated bishop of Geneva, where he began work on two classics, *Introduction to the Devout Life* (1608) and *Treatise on the Love of God* (1616).[1] Both books mandate the pursuit of holiness for people in all walks of life, from manual laborers to officials at court. Salesian spirituality alerts us to the myriad ways by which we can live the Gospel with fidelity and simplicity—a theme traceable in writers representing the French school of spirituality, such as Cardinal Pierre de Bérulle, and culminating in St. Thérèse of Lisieux's doctrine of the little way of spiritual childhood.

Francis became a sought-after spiritual director. He offered guidance to the widow Jane de Chantal (1572–1641), with whom he founded the Order of the Visitation of Holy Mary, whose motto is, "Live Jesus!"[2] His spiritual friendship with Jane shows how much Francis appreciated the complementary role women played in the Church. He offered direction not only to her but also to many mothers, sisters, and daughters who at that time were deemed inferior in society and often, sadly, in the Church. Francis recognized the strengths women exhibited at home and in the marketplace. He encouraged members of the Order of the Visitation to exude the goodness of God moment by moment, become beacons of hope, and, in the chaos of changing times, witness to the calm that comes when we place our trust in God alone.

Francis died at Lyon on December 28, 1622, shortly after his last interview with Jane, who continued the mission that was the fruit of their partnership in the mystery of redemption until her death in 1641.[3] Pope Alexander VII declared Francis a saint in 1665, and Pope Pius X named him a Doctor of the Church in 1877.

FOLLOWING CHRIST AS DEVOUT DISCIPLES

Francis confronts us with the dilemma every disciple faces: we can choose to will ourselves away from God and the wonder of creation or we can use, rather than misuse, our free will to move toward God by accepting his commands with resolve and fulfilling them with joy. Francis counsels us that our adherence to God's law of love, both in our everyday situations and in the tranquility of our heart, will bear fruit as we grow in service to God and others. Even in the dark nights of pain, suffering, and failure, we must find the courage to submit to God, whose mercy never fails us and whose love for us in the peaks and valleys of life remains steady and true:

> Even though everything turns and changes around us, we must always remain unchanging and ever looking, striving, and aspiring toward God. . . . Our soul may be overwhelmed with sorrow or joy, with sweetness or bitterness, with peace or trouble. . . . It may be scorched by the sun or refreshed by the dew—for all that, ever and always our heart's point, our spirit, our higher will . . . must unceasingly look and tend toward the love of God, its Creator, its Savior, its sole and sovereign good. (*IDL*, 256)

As love increases, fear decreases. Such is the secret of happiness Francis wants to share. Dying to our own egocentric willfulness enables us to exercise the loving and liberating will of God. Such "charity never enters a heart without lodging both itself and its train of all the other virtues which it exercises and disciplines as a captain does his soldiers" (*IDL*, 121).

Characteristic of Salesian spirituality is the adaptation of a particular virtue to a particular state of life. This specificity reveals the respect Francis had for every vocation, from family care in the world to monastic hiddenness from the world. Though God wants us to possess virtues in abundance, we are "not bound to exercise them in equal measure" (*IDL*, 122). What matters is that we remain faithful to the state of life to which God calls us.

This sensible, down-to-earth spirituality is what endears Francis to laity, clergy, and religious. He encourages us to aspire to a devout life of discipleship whatever our assignment in society may be. Wherever God places us, we are to act with prudence and discretion, with charity and courtesy. What we share in common is the remembrance that none of this good comes from us but from God's gifts to us. Such humility releases us from the danger of envious comparison; we celebrate the blessing that resides in every limit, provided we strive to follow Jesus and surrender our whole self into the Father's hands.

DEVOTION AS A DELIGHT

In his *Introduction to the Devout Life*, Francis composes a manual of meditation he believes anyone can follow.[4] He begins with a series of instructions intended to lead the soul from a desire for the devout life, through the resolve to embrace it, to a description of its purging of our interiority from inclinations to evil thoughts and acts. He then describes how to elevate the soul by means of prayer and reception of the sacraments, especially the Eucharist; how to practice virtue; how to resist temptations; how to cleanse our conscience; and how to confirm our commitment to live a devout life for the rest of our days.

Francis avoids any burdensome methodology that might interrupt the outflow of our love for God and neighbor in response to God's counsels and instructions. He reminds us to love our lowliness and to learn from our limits how to practice patience, meekness, and equanimity. Devotion for Francis is not a somber discipline associated with life-denying practices but "the delight of delights and queen of the virtues since it is the perfection of charity. If charity is milk, devotion is its cream; if it is a plant, devotion is its blossom; if it is a precious stone, devotion is its luster; if it is a rich ointment, devotion is its odor, yes, the odor of sweetness which comforts men and rejoices angels" (*IDL*, 43).

The course of action Francis prescribes enhances the devotion that is charity's finest fruit. He recommends good direction but admits it is not easy to find since the director must be full of charity, knowledge, and prudence. If any one of these three qualities is lacking, there is danger (see *IDL*, 47).

With or without a devout and skilled director, we must begin with purgation of sin as a precondition for engaging in the kinds of meditation—for example, on creation, death, judgment, hell, and paradise—that facilitate progress in holiness. For Francis, the test of devotion resides not in experiencing extraordinary phenomena such as rapture or ecstasy but in exercising the virtues our Savior modeled—obedience, poverty of spirit, and purity of heart—and acting according to God's good pleasure in whatever way it may be revealed to us. Avoiding procrastination or excessive deliberation and trusting in God's guidance quell needless anxiety. We honor the decisions we have made without worrying about the accuracy of the discernment process until such time when God shows us that they bring us neither personal tranquility nor a stronger commitment to charitable service.

He says in all cases that it is our duty before God to cultivate a servant-heart. By channeling the course of love from God to neighbor, we are better able to resist any diversion that tries to lure us away from our devotional life. Such love is the fruit of that interior movement by which we find ourselves by losing ourselves. Francis stresses the paradox that our will is only free when it is submissive to God's will. Citing the example of Catherine of Siena, he says that "she aroused herself to serve in spirit the whole court of heaven while joyously carrying out [her] humble tasks because she knew that such was God's will" (*IDL*, 214).

Master of devotion that he is, Francis commits himself to instruct those who live in town, within families, or at court to live an ordinary life in their outward appearances while inwardly remaining participants in the life of the

Trinity. Out of this reservoir of grace comes the commitment to practice constancy of heart and to embrace not our own plans but those destined for us by God. The affective/effective rhythm characteristic of the devout life leads to selfless acts of love for God and neighbor as well as to the production of good works: "After such affective acts you must consider the particular means necessary to maintain these cherished resolutions and determine to be faithful in making good use of them. . . . Affirm that you will never take them back again but leave them in the hand of his Divine Majesty in order to follow everywhere and always his holy ordinances" (*IDL*, 287–88).

At the conclusion of the *Introduction*, Francis gives us an unfailing counsel to follow: "Look upon Jesus Christ, and do not renounce him for all the world. And when the labors of a devout life seem hard to you, sing with St. Francis of Assisi: 'Such are the joys that lure my sight, / All pains grow sweet, all labors light'" (*IDL*, 291).

REFLECT NOW

1. How do you interpret the commandment to love your neighbor as you love yourself? What do you do to extend this love to all those entrusted to your care?
2. How would you assess the state of your heart, especially in regard to your obedience to God's commandments and your fidelity to your spiritual exercises?
3. What counsels come to mind when you desire to speak of God to others, to sing God's praises, and to witness to God's temporal and eternal glory?

READ MORE

John A. Abruzzese, *The Theology of Hearts in the Writings of St. Francis de Sales* (Rome: Pontifical University of St. Thomas Aquinas, 1985).

Maurice Henry-Coüannier, *St. Francis de Sales and His Friends*, trans. Veronica Morrow (Staten Island, NY: Abba House, 1964).

Wendy M. Wright, *Bond of Perfection: Jeanne de Chantal and François de Sales* (New York: Paulist Press, 1985).

22

CELEBRATE THE SACRAMENT
OF THE PRESENT MOMENT

BROTHER LAWRENCE OF THE RESURRECTION ON THE PRACTICE OF THE PRESENCE OF GOD

The holiest, most ordinary, and most necessary practice of the spiritual life is that of the presence of God. It is to take delight in and become accustomed to his divine company, speaking humbly and conversing lovingly with him all the time, at every moment, without rule or measure, especially in times of temptation, suffering, aridity, weariness, even infidelity and sin.

—Brother Lawrence of the Resurrection,
The Practice of the Presence of God, 36

In his first letter to the Thessalonians, the apostle Paul says that we must "pray without ceasing" (5:16). How is this possible? A fresh way of interpreting this command can be found in the down-to-earth directives Brother Lawrence of the Resurrection provides concerning the practice of the presence of God. For him, praying is comparable to the inhaling and exhaling of breath. It has to be nonstop or we die.

To pray ceaselessly does not require a set of techniques difficult for the average believer to master. Its practice is as mundane as it is profound. Brother Lawrence proves that to pray without ceasing is a sure, easy, and efficacious form of prayer. He says that the sense of God's nearness need never be lost since, from rising in the morning to retiring at night, we live in adoration of God and ask for his help.

MEET THE MASTER

Brother Lawrence of the Resurrection (1614–1691), named at birth Nicolas Herman, was the son of Dominic and Louise Herman, natives of a small village in Lorraine, France. Poor as they were, they passed on the human and religious qualities Lawrence never lost. Little is known of his upbringing, academic training, or employment. What we do know from his friend Abbé Joseph de Beaufort, a priest from Paris and his main biographer, is that he was only eighteen years old when he had a sweeping experience of God's presence, so sudden and profound that it stayed with him until his death in Paris in 1691. This was the call that would lead him to join the Discalced Carmelite community in Paris as a lay brother known for his devotion to the hidden life of Jesus of Nazareth.

The Carmelite tradition under the leadership of Teresa of Avila and John of the Cross was the window through which Brother Lawrence gazed upon the Savior of the world and begged to be his servant. He was particularly fond of St. Teresa's instructions in *The Way of Perfection*, where she reminded the religious who joined the discalced reform that they did not need to find special ways to go in search of the Lord. In the cloister where they lived, they could be present to him both in their inmost being and in the world around them.

Prior to Lawrence's entrance to Carmel, he enlisted in military service during the Thirty Years' War. While fulfilling his tour of duty, he was arrested by German troops, who accused him of being a spy and threatened to kill him. He was able to establish his innocence and rejoin the Lorraine army, but his wounds required him to return to his parents' home to recuperate.

In 1640, at the age of twenty-six, he heeded the call to become a Carmelite brother in their Parisian monastery; he took his solemn vows two years later, and for the next fifteen years served the community as cook and cobbler, weaving into the seamless garment of his religious life manual labor and contemplative prayer. Crippling gout made sitting and repairing sandals a source of joy for him. Many community members benefited from his sage homespun advice and his silent witness to the presence of God.

Brother Lawrence was captivated by the thought that prayer was in essence a way of being in the presence of God and open to God's transforming grace. Like all Carmelites, he identified with Christ's Cross and relished every chance to be as humiliated and forgotten as the Lord was. His secret was to turn with resolute conformity to the will of God and to serve others for God's sake. He saw charitable actions as the natural outflow of contemplative prayer. He sought and found the secret of spiritual maturity: that the sense of God's nearness never leaves the heart of a true lover of sanctity. Abbé Joseph de Beaufort reported how Brother Lawrence cultivated this sense of presence in a conversation they had on November 25, 1667:

> He told me that what matters is renouncing once and for all everything that we recognize does not lead to God, in order to become accustomed to a continual conversation with him, without mystery or finesse. We need only to recognize him present within us, to speak with him at every moment, and to ask for his help, so that we will know his will in perplexing events, and will be able to carry out those things we clearly see he asks of us, offering them to him before doing them, and thanking him afterward for completing them.[1]

Recognized as an exceptional spiritual director of monastics and laity alike, Brother Lawrence lived an exemplary life and died a holy death on February 12, 1691. Sixteen of his letters were preserved by Abbé Joseph, along with spiritual notes and maxims left in his cell, a collection that proved to be a legacy to both Catholic and Protestant readers around the world. Methodist founder John Wesley read Lawrence's writings aloud during his missionary journeys in America in the 1700s and recommended that they be studied by his colleagues and disciples.

Abbé Joseph added to Lawrence's own writings accounts of their conversations between 1666 and 1667. He published them along with the other
wisdom sayings of Brother Lawrence the year his friend died, little knowing
that they would eventually be translated from the original French into,
among other languages, English, German, Dutch, Spanish, Italian, Japanese,
Hebrew, and Korean. The reason so many readers love Brother Lawrence's
work might be that, as Abbé Joseph said in his eulogy, "In the midst of the
most demanding occupations, [Brother Lawrence] knew how to integrate
action with contemplation so well that for more than forty years he almost
never turned away from the presence of God" (*PPG*, 6).

Another trait that comes to the fore in his writings and helps account
for his universal appeal was his gentle manner—open and kind, never harsh
or judgmental; he elicited confidence in his listeners, who sensed that he
attended to them with the love Christ would show a friend. Simple as his
sayings were, they gave rise to reflection and a resolve to do better. Beyond
his rough exterior was an ordinary man with a good heart and an air of
affability. In him modesty and sanctity met. Nothing about him was con-
spicuous, yet everything he said was trustworthy. As he wrote to a nun in
1682: "We must never stop working, since in the spiritual life, not to advance
is to go backwards. Those who are empowered by the breath of the Holy
Spirit sail along even when asleep. If the ship of your soul is still beaten by
the winds or the storm . . . wake the Lord who is resting there, and he will
immediately calm the sea" (*PPG*, 50).[2]

SEVEN SPIRITUAL MAXIMS

Brother Lawrence's menial chores in the kitchen and the cobbler shop suit-
ed him. Going about his work with a spirit of peace and joy earned him a
reputation for holiness. Those with whom he shared his sage words and
good deeds became aware of their own Spirit-infused invitations to seek
God instead of paying attention to their fears and distractions. He outlined
the main ingredients that facilitated this practice in the seven chapters that
comprise his "Spiritual Maxims."

In chapter 1, "Principles," he tells us to "keep our eyes fixed on God in
everything we say, do or undertake" (*PPG*, 35). In chapter 2, he says that if

we want to remain in the presence of God, certain disciplines must be put in place, the central one being to stop as often as possible, amid work, reading, writing, and praying, "to adore God in the depths of our hearts, to savor him, even though in passing and stealthily" (*PPG*, 36).

Once we learn to practice these moments of stepping aside in order to start again, we may find ourselves, as he says in chapter 3, adoring God in spirit and truth "as if God were one with our souls and our souls were one with God" (*PPG*, 38). Chapter 4 confirms that the goal we long to attain is union with God, be it habitual, thanks to God's abundant grace; virtual, when we remain with him for the duration of one or the other deed; or actual, when a sense of union wells up from within with words such as, "My God, I love you with all my heart" (*PPG*, 39) said silently or aloud.

These preparatory principles and acts come to fulfillment when we are in the presence of God and when we practice this presence both intellectually and imaginatively. In chapter 5 he depicts this mode of being as a single act of love and a general awareness of God. We may converse with him in trust, asking for what we need and rejoicing "continuously with him in countless ways" (*PPG*, 40). Chapter 6 outlines the means to acquire this gift of presence, beginning with "great purity of life," followed by fidelity to this practice and detachment from whatever hinders "the holiest, the surest, the easiest, and the most efficacious form of prayer" (*PPG*, 41).

Brother Lawrence confirms the long-lasting benefits of this practice in chapter 7. There he says that our faith "becomes more intense and efficacious" thanks to the remembrance of God's presence. Without any strain or tension, our hope increases and our will is set aflame with "a sacred fire of love . . . that produces in [our] heart a holy ardor, a sacred zeal and a strong desire to see this God loved, known, served, and adored by all creatures" (*PPG*, 42).[3]

DISCIPLINES CONDUCIVE TO DISCIPLESHIP

Though Brother Lawrence admits with regret that few of us may take these disciplines to heart on a regular basis, he never doubts the generosity of God's grace. He encourages us to stay on track by doing our best to be in the presence of God. This intention is the first step toward our striving to reach the goal of Christian maturity.

In each of his sixteen letters, Brother Lawrence offers us at least one directive to commit to memory and to try with God's help to put into action. We learn in his first letter to a nun to say as often as possible little prayers such as "My God, I am all yours; Lord, fashion me according to your heart" (*PPG*, 49). In his second letter to a spiritual director, he advises him to try to express "a quiet and secret conversation of the soul with God that is lasting" (*PPG*, 53).

Letters 3 to 12, which he wrote to nuns, priests, and laypeople, offer steps to follow to attain conformity to Christ:

+ Do not practice God's presence for the sake of being consoled but out of love for God.
+ Stay recollected with God in the center of your soul and fear nothing.
+ Place your trust in God and let go of your cares.
+ When fears arise, cling to God with all your strength.
+ Remember, short as they may be, how pleasing to God these prayers of trust and inner adoration are.
+ However flighty your mind is, take hold of it and bring it back to God.
+ Renounce "for the sake of his love all that is not God" (*PPG*, 67).
+ You "do not always have to be in church to be with God. [You] can make of [your heart] an oratory where [you] can withdraw from time to time to converse with him" (*PPG*, 69).
+ Think of God often, night and day, when you are active and when you relax, and "do not leave him alone" (*PPG*, 71).
+ Be convinced that God is closer to you in sickness and suffering than when you are in perfect health, for God is the "sovereign doctor of body and soul" (*PPG*, 73).
+ Repeat these acts until they become second nature to you and never hesitate to ask God for the graces you need.

Brother Lawrence summarizes these counsels on how to advance to Christian maturity in Letter 13, written to a nun a year before his death:

> Be courageous. Continually offer [God] your sufferings
> while asking him for the strength to bear them. Most of

all, get used to conversing with him often, and try never to forget him. Adore him in your infirmities, offer him your sufferings from time to time, even in the midst of your greatest pain. Ask him humbly and lovingly, as a child does his kind father, to be conformed to his holy will, and for the help of his grace. I will help you with my poor, insignificant prayers. (*PPG,* 77)

Letters 14 to 16, written to the same nun, propose a fitting conclusion to the wisdom for holy living and holy dying coming from the pen of Brother Lawrence. As if he were speaking of himself, he expresses compassion for her pain. Abbé Joseph says in his eulogy for his friend that Brother Lawrence's fervor increased as the hour of his departure approached. Spiritually, it was well with his soul, though he felt mocked by the devil and so alone that he had to make continuous acts of love. He also offered his pain from severe gout and pleurisy for his own soul and the souls of those suffering in purgatory. His last words to a friar were, "I am doing what I will do for all eternity: I am blessing God, I am praising God, I am adoring him, and I am loving him with my whole heart" (*PPG,* 23).

He counseled the nun to whom he wrote during this time to ask God not for deliverance from her physical suffering but for the strength to endure it for as long as the Lord liked. Then in Letter 15, he joins her in thanking God for relieving her pain and for letting this gift make her more attentive to the privilege of being able to suffer with and for God. Through this suffering, he assured her, graces would be released to many needy members of his Body. He asks this same nun in Letter 16 to commit herself entirely to God and to banish everything else from her heart and mind. On the eve of his passing, he was able to say to her out of the fullness of his life of ceaseless prayer: "I cannot thank [God] enough for the relief he has given you. I hope for the merciful grace of seeing him in a few days" (*PPG,* 84).

REFLECT NOW

1. Do you sense God's presence in and around you? Have you begun to draw upon his grace wherever you are and in whatever you do?

2. Does your trust in God's presence increase or decrease in times of suffering physically or spiritually? How easy or how difficult is it for you to let go of your cares and place the past, the present, and the future in God's hands?

3. How does your practice of the presence of God enhance your prayer life and intensify your desire to follow Christ as an active contemplative and a contemplative-in-action?

READ MORE

Conrad De Meester, ed., *Writings and Conversations on the Practice of the Presence of God: Brother Lawrence of the Resurrection*, trans. Salvatore Sciurba (Washington, DC: ICS Publications, 1994).

Gerald C. May, *The Awakened Heart: Opening Yourself to the Love You Need* (San Francisco: Harper, 1991).

David Winter, *Closer Than a Brother: Brother Lawrence for Today* (Wheaton, IL: Harold Shaw Publishers, 1981).

23

FOLLOW IN FAITH THE WAY, THE TRUTH, AND THE LIFE

JOHN WESLEY ON
CHRISTIAN PERFECTION

Christian Perfection is (1) that love of God and our neighbor which implies deliverance from all sin; (2) that is received merely by faith; (3) that it is given instantaneously, in one moment; (4) that we are to expect it (not at death, but) every moment; that now is the accepted time, now is the day of this salvation.
—John and Charles Wesley, *Selected Writings and Hymns*, 326

The saintly founder of the Methodist faith tradition, John Wesley, devoted his life and ministry in England and America to the pursuit of Christian perfection. He shared with rich and poor, healthy and sick, the joy of knowing the Lord, who had strangely warmed his heart.

Were we among the flock he tended, we would in all likelihood hear him challenge us to face questions such as these: *Am I really a single-hearted lover and follower of Christ? In my decisions and deeds, do I desire to grow in likeness to the Lord, or have I become mainly a consumer of worldly goods? Do I know in my heart that the sum of being perfected as sons and daughters of God entails obedience to the Great Commandment?*

235

It is said that every sermon John preached brought his listeners to reflect on the truth that what saves us is not our human efforts but our faith in Jesus Christ, our Lord and Savior. Rather than entangle himself in endless argumentation, Wesley pledged to speak the plain truth of God's saving love to everyday people whose shared goal was the quest for holiness.

MEET THE MASTER

From the Anglican roots that shaped his devotional life, to the full flowering of his evangelical call, to the day of his death in London, John Wesley (1703–1791) felt at home with the great cloud of witnesses—the apostles, martyrs, and saints who taught him how best to formulate his methodical approach to Christian perfection.[1]

To aid him in this endeavor, Wesley turned to many Roman Catholic and Orthodox sources. He read the works of Gregory of Nyssa in the East and Augustine in the West. Pre-Reformation devotional texts such as *The Imitation of Christ* (1418) by Thomas à Kempis and post-Reformation masterpieces such as William Law's *Serious Call to a Devout and Holy Life* (1728) and Jeremy Taylor's *The Rules and Exercises of Holy Living* (1650) and *Holy Dying* (1651) taught him the importance of methodical prayer practices. It was Law's book that inspired the Holy Club at Oxford, in which the Wesley brothers, John and Charles, designed the blueprint for their evangelical revival in England. From Brother Lawrence of the Resurrection, John discerned that presence to the Divine Presence in daily life was the key to living with Jesus inwardly in worship and outwardly in work.

Born at Epworth in the northeast of England, John was one of ten children who survived into adulthood. His parents, Samuel and Susanna Wesley, drew upon the wellspring of their Puritan heritage to teach their sons and daughters a strict code of morality and to witness to the spiritual wealth found in frugal living.

Especially from his mother, John Wesley learned that the proper use of free will had to be tested by conformity to Christ, avoidance of sin, and the diligent pursuit of a life of sanctity and service. Important in this regard was the Society for Promoting Christian Knowledge, to which his parents belonged and whose members met in their home. This group was a proto-type for the Methodist societies he founded three decades later with the help of his brother Charles, whose hymns are sung to this day in churches throughout the world.[2]

As a young student in the charterhouse schools of London and later at Christ Church in Oxford, John Wesley led a disciplined life rooted in prayer and expressed in works of charity, penance, perseverance, and, above all, in exemplary adherence to God's Word in sacred scripture. He drew in private and public upon the abounding grace and mercy of God and attributed the first rise of Methodism from 1720 to 1735 to the actions of the Holy Spirit, to whom he became increasingly devoted.

Despite the Holy Clubs he and Charles started, this conviction did not spare them from the growing pains associated with spiritual renewal, ranging from self-doubt to dealing with misunderstandings of their motives, or from trying to combine their love of learning and their desire for God with a sacrificial way of life and social witness.

One of the main battles John Wesley fought and won was against the Calvinist doctrine of predestination, which "emphasized God's unlimited choice of those who would be saved or damned." By contrast, "the Wesleys promoted a dynamic understanding of salvation that embraced both divine initiative and human responsibility."[3] The Methodist societies' stance against slavery is but one example of the Wesleyan commitment to a lifetime of service to God and neighbor, a sentiment captured in John's dying words, "The best of all is, God is with us!"[4] He never forgot the dying words of his father, Samuel, to him, "The inward witness, son, the inward witness, that is the proof of Christianity."[5]

John's own life of discipleship grew under the inspiration of the "means of grace" he found in the *Book of Common Prayer*. Empowered as well was his commitment to social and communal involvement; it led him, following his ordination to the Anglican priesthood in 1728, to embark on visits to prisons, to offer assistance to the poor and rich, and to preach of the need to help those abandoned in body and soul to turn their trials over in total trust to God (see *SWH*, 13).

From England, the brothers extended their missionary efforts to America. In 1735, John received an unexpected opportunity to be missioned in

Savannah, Georgia, a move that constituted the second rise of Methodism. No matter where he was, the ground of John Wesley's belief remained the same: to love God with his whole heart, mind, soul, and strength and to feed with common-sense Gospel truth the lambs and the sheep entrusted to his care. He pictured them as bands of disciples coming together to ponder the imperfections that separated them from Christ and to renew their trust in God's saving grace. He felt convinced that only through fellowship and the celebration of faith could believers be perfected in Jesus Christ, put on his mind, and change their life.

LIVING IN FIDELITY TO CHRIST'S CALL

John Wesley stressed that the ideal of life in Christ does not exclude the errors into which we humans may fall. We need to face and overcome them with the help of God's grace. Only then can we fulfill the demands of discipleship and live in fidelity to Christ's call. He outlines these demands in his treatise, *A Plain Account of Christian Perfection* (see *SWH*, 299–377):

+ *Purity of intention*—by placing God first in all things and being single-hearted lovers and followers of Christ.
+ *Putting on the mind of Christ*—by basing our discernment of decisions and deeds on our desire for Christlikeness and thereby striving to follow his example always.
+ *Remembering that we were made in the image of God*—by letting this mark of human dignity annihilate in us whatever is not yet in conformity to Christ and by being obedient to him.
+ *Loving God and others in God*—by always listening to the greatest of Christ's commandments and thus pursuing the sum of Christian perfection.

Wesley's own conversion experience happened on Pentecost Sunday, 1738. That afternoon he went to St. Paul's Church in London. During the service, he heard with the ears of his heart an anthem from Psalm 30 that impressed him to the core of his being: "Out of the deep I have called unto thee, O Lord." Then, as he recounts:

In the evening, I went very unwillingly to a society in Aldersgate Street, where one was reading Luther's Preface to the Epistle to the Romans. About a quarter before nine, while he was describing the change which God works in the heart through faith in Christ, I felt my heart strangely warmed. I felt I did trust in Christ, Christ alone for salvation; and an assurance was given me that he had taken away *my* sins, even *mine* and saved *me* from the law of sin and death. . . . After my return home, I was much buffeted with temptations, but cried out and they fled away. They returned again and again. I as often lifted up my eyes and he *sent me help from his holy place*. And herein I found [in what] the difference between this and my former state chiefly consisted. I was striving, yea, fighting with all my might under the law, as well as under grace. But then I was sometimes, if not often, conquered; now, I was always conqueror. (*SWH*, 107)

Wesley understood that the quest for holiness cannot be confined to an occasional sojourn with the transcendent. It has to become a habitual state of being, enabling us to respond to the guidance of grace, to avoid sin, and to cultivate an abiding presence to the Spirit of the living God. In trying to describe the ideals to which he wanted believers to aspire, he wrote:

A Methodist is one who loves the Lord his God with all his heart, with all his soul, with all his mind, and with all his strength. God is the joy of his heart and the desire of his soul which is continually crying out, *Whom have I in Heaven but you; and there is none upon earth whom I desire besides you. My God and my all! You are the strength of my heart, and my portion forever.* He is therefore happy in God, yea always happy, as having in him a well of water springing up into everlasting life, and overflowing his soul with peace and joy. *Perfect love having now cast out fear, he rejoices evermore.* Yea, his joy is full, and all his bones cry out, *Blessed be the God and Father of our Lord Jesus Christ, who according to his abundant mercy has begotten me again unto a living hope of*

an inheritance incorruptible and undefiled, reserved in heaven
for me. (SWH, 303–4)

Faithful to his own unique blend of mystical theology, apostolic spirituality, and commonplace Christian wisdom and service, Wesley expected Methodists to "walk with the Lord" whether alone or in company, at work or in leisure. He wanted their hearts to be warmed by Christ so that they could fulfill the purpose for which they were created. This meant that every part of their life, not some of it only, had to be consecrated to Christ (*SWH*, 299). For him it was impossible to be *half a Christian*. In this verse, written in 1738, he summarizes his spirituality and prays that these sentiments will etch themselves on the heart of every believer:

> O grant that nothing in my soul may dwell but my *pure love alone!*
> O may thy love *possess* me whole,
> My joy, my treasure, and my crown;
> Strange fruits far from my heart remove:
> My *every act, word, thought,* be love! (*SWH*, 302)

To this end, Wesley provided counsels on how to pray in his doctrinal tracts, his sermons (including those on the Lord's Prayer), and his letters. Since God, so to speak, breathes into us his divine word, we ought to respond to it by breathing it out in every action of our daily life. He says that "our faithfulness in prayer is based on God's prior faithfulness to us displayed over and over again in our lives."[6] He interpreted Ephesians 6:18, "Pray in the Spirit at all times in every prayer and supplication," to mean that on every occasion our motivation must arise from the truth that neglect of prayer kills the soul. From the age of twenty-five onward for the rest of his life, Wesley began to collect prayers with as much passion as others might collect works of art. Excerpts from these collections sustained his own prayer life and helped him to guide those who came to him for help regarding how to commune with God.

In 1733, Wesley published *A Collection of Forms of Prayer for Every Day in the Week* (See *SWH*, 77–84). It provided a cycle of prayers for morning and evening, with additional questions for self-examination aimed at helping the supplicant to apply the principles voiced in the prayers themselves. According to Wesley's personal diary, he shared this collection with his students at Lincoln College, encouraging them to say the prayers for themselves and report the results to him. He was convinced that by praying in the context of some of the best examples of prayer in the Christian tradition, a person would discover the chief reasons for praying and develop a passion to pray in union with the saints.

This approach also prompted Wesley to recommend similar resources (devotional manuals, prayer books, and the *Book of Common Prayer*) as a complement to his collection. He did not intend this collection of classic prayers to produce a parroting or rote recitation of prayers; rather, he wanted to compose a concert in which the prayers of ages past blended with the prayers of individuals at present. He interspersed the printed prayers with advice pertaining to such forms of prayer as petition, thanksgiving, and intercession. He also reflected on the interior disposition conducive to becoming a man or woman of prayer by renouncing self-centeredness and living in Christ until he comes in glory. The advice he gave to one correspondent in 1732, after she confessed her inattention to prayer and some aridity, was not to put prayer aside but to pray more often. When Mary Pendarves said that she already addressed God twice a day, Wesley advised her to do so three times as simply and sincerely as she could.

UTTER DEPENDENCE ON DIVINE GRACE

Wesley's teaching on prayer stems from his unique perspective on the life of grace. New to many is his idea of prevenient grace, "the grace of God which operates before our experience of conversion"—that is to say, the grace that comes while we are yet sinners (Rom 5:8).[7] Such grace is undeserved and unmerited. God initiates this grace and bestows it upon us apart from our action. Prevenient grace goes before us, surrounds us, and leads us. It precedes our conscious impulses and prompts us to desire what most pleases God; it draws us from the death of sin to new life through repentance and faith in the Savior's promise of redemption.

"Justifying" or "converting" or "saving" grace, according to Wesley, gives us the blessed assurance that, though we are sinners, Christ forgave our sins and restored us to God's favor. Under the prompting and guidance of the Holy Spirit, our once-divided heart receives the undeserved gift of faith that reunites us to God.

The message of the Gospel, repent and believe, becomes for us a true conversion experience. Our new life in Christ then expresses itself in works of charity of benefit to every neighbor in need of help. As Wesley writes in his account of Christian perfection, "One of the principal rules of religion is to lose no occasion of serving God. And since he is invisible to our eyes, we are able to serve him in our neighbor" (*SWH*, 372). "Sanctifying" grace draws us to the higher reaches of what it means to be perfected in Christ. Wesley describes it as a heartfelt state of being habitually filled with the love of God and neighbor (see Mt 22:34–38). By it we learn to dwell in the presence of God, knowing that sin has no place in our life. When we do succumb to temptation, such occasions are due not to a failure of grace but to the misuse of our free will.

Wesley points to "perfecting" grace as that which leads us to pursue works of piety and mercy. It evokes in us a passion for justice and a commitment to bind our lives to Christ and fulfill his commission to renew the face of the earth. Such grace nurtures Christian fellowship and participation in the worshipping community. Giving glory to God is not a Sunday-only experience but a daily reality. In one of his hymns on the Nativity, Charles Wesley wrote a beautiful summary of John's teaching on this gracious gift of God:

> Made perfect first in love,
> And sanctified by grace,
> We shall from earth remove,
> And see his glorious face:
> Then shall his love be fully showed,
> And man shall then be lost in God. (*SWH*, 282)

What, then, must we do to ensure our progress toward holiness? In addition to cooperating with grace, John Wesley reminds us to examine the state of our soul; to pray always with both zeal and calmness of spirit; to lose no occasion to serve God; and to retain a sense of the presence of God. His pastoral sensitivity moves him to tell his bands of believers that even if they fall into sin, they must never despair, but forever repent. God himself shepherds our return to him by grace, which enables us to practice all of these spiritual disciplines in a methodical manner, in single-hearted love and fidelity to Christ's call. It is important to anticipate the eternal blessedness prepared for us by our crucified and risen Lord.

On New Year's Day, 1790, just a few days before he died, Wesley penned a fitting conclusion to his life. It testifies that he endured suffering, did the work of an evangelist, and carried out his ministry in the fullest way possible: "I am now an old man, decayed from head to foot. My eyes are dim; my right hand shakes much; my mouth is hot and dry every morning; I have a lingering fever almost every day; my motion is weak and slow. However, blessed be God, I do not slack my labour: I can preach and write still."[8]

REFLECT NOW

1. Is it easy or difficult for you, in your contemporary climate, to seek Christian perfection not as a remote ideal but as a way of life?
2. What evidence do you have of God's prevenient grace calling you to repentance and conversion?
3. Can you recall any instances of blessed assurance that helped you to chart the course of your life in obedience to Christ's call?

READ MORE

Paul W. Chilcote, *Praying in the Wesleyan Spirit: 52 Prayers for Today* (Nashville: Upper Room Books, 2001).

Kenneth J. Collins, *John Wesley: A Theological Journey* (Nashville: Abingdon Press, 2003).

Henry D. Rack, *Reasonable Enthusiast: John Wesley and the Rise of Methodism* (London: Epworth Press, 2002).

24

LET YOUR LIFE
BE ONE ACT OF LOVE

THÉRÈSE OF LISIEUX ON
THE LITTLE WAY OF
SPIRITUAL CHILDHOOD

I look upon myself as a *weak little bird*, with only a light
down as covering. I am not an *eagle*, but I have only an
eagle's EYES AND HEART. In spite of my extreme littleness
I still dare to gaze upon the Divine Sun, the Sun of Love,
and my heart feels within it all the aspirations of an *Eagle*.
— Thérèse of Lisieux, *Story of a Soul*, 198

Following any lecture I have ever given on the life and death of St. Thérèse
of Lisieux, it never fails to happen that someone comes to the podium to
share their story of how she helped them: "When my daughter was about to
breathe her last after a battle with brain cancer, I whispered to her the words
I learned from St. Thérèse, 'You are not dying, my darling, you are entering
into life.'" Another person said, "Please don't think I'm crazy, but I knew my
prayers for healing from severe scrupulosity had been heard through St.
Thérèse's intercession when I smelled the scent of roses in my room."
   Testimonies such as these should not surprise us. St. Thérèse is one
of the best known and most loved witnesses to the little way of spiritual

childhood that lets us feel the loving embrace of our Lord. Thérèse never hid her imperfections from God, nor must we. For her everything is grace. Life, she says, is one act of love. All the consolations we will ever need come from our abandonment to the mystery of God's mercy.

St. Thérèse found the essence of her vocation—to be love at the heart of the Church—from her reading of scripture and the masters. They drew her from inner adoration to self-donating action. They gave her the courage to move with her crucified Lord into the midnight moment of suffering, convinced that one day she would witness the dawning of an everlasting day. We love the Little Flower because she shows us what it means to uproot every trace of self-love, be a courageous defender of the faith, and become a new creation in Christ.

Meet the Master

Once an obscure Carmelite and now a Doctor of the Church, St. Thérèse of Lisieux (1873–1897) was born in Alençon, France, the youngest child of Louis and Zélie Martin, both of whom have been canonized.[1] After the death of her mother when she was only four years old, Thérèse moved with her father and her four sisters to Les Buissonnets, not far from Lisieux. The comfortable surroundings of her new home contrasted sharply with the inner turmoil Thérèse felt. She chose as her second mother her older sister Pauline, but for the next eight years she experienced dreadful mood swings from hyperactivity to lethargy, one moment being overly sensitive to the point of tears, the next exuding a joviality she did not feel. Added to her woes was a severe bout of scrupulosity.

After Pauline entered the Carmel of Lisieux in the winter of 1883, Thérèse began to experience continual headaches and insomnia. She became so sick that she went into convulsions, accompanied by nervous trembling and hallucinations. Then on May 13, 1884, the Feast of Pentecost, while she was praying before a statue of Our Lady of Victories, every prayer said for her seemed to be answered. Thérèse was sure that the Blessed Virgin smiled at her and cured her at once, although more spiritual trials followed her physical maladies.

Thérèse prepared for her first Holy Communion with deep devotion. When she partook of the Body and Blood of Christ for the first time, she felt the consoling warmth of his love, a feeling that repeated itself when in June she received the sacrament of Confirmation. Then, in 1885, a crisis of scrupulosity overtook her with full force, this time lasting for a year and a half. Little did she know that the decisive turning point of her life had been set in motion by Divine Providence.

At that time her sister Léonie left home to join the Poor Clares, though later she would become a Sister of the Visitation. Then Marie joined Pauline at Carmel, evoking in Thérèse a great sense of loss combined with an upsurge of hope that banished her scruples once and for all. She stood on the threshold of her conversion experience, which occurred following midnight Mass on Christmas Day of 1886. As she writes in her autobiography, she left her childhood and its childish demands for attention and committed herself, body and soul, to the Lord, who showed her that her mission from now on would change from one of being cared for to one of taking care of others.

Shortly thereafter, as she prayed before an image of the crucified Christ, she experienced a burning thirst for souls and the need to pour out upon them Christ's redeeming blood. She found proof of her mission in the fact that her first convert was the prisoner, Henri Pranzini, for whom she prayed with all her heart and who embraced the Cross before his execution.

Thanks to the bold request she made of Pope Leo XIII on a visit to Rome with her father, Thérèse was given permission to enter the Lisieux Carmel at the age of fifteen. There she would spend the remaining nine years of her life perfecting the apostolic mysticism she identified as her little way of spiritual childhood. Mainly by her ministry of presence, Thérèse taught her sisters, including Celine, who was also a Carmelite, how to live a life of joyful abandonment to Divine Providence. From the novices under her charge to the tens of thousands of people who would embrace her as their greatest advocate in heaven, she taught the uplifting message that even the smallest event of the day could be turned into an occasion of grace. Likewise, the darkest trial of suffering, such as the tuberculosis that took her in excruciating pain gasping for breath, could become a time of intense mystical transformation. On June 9, 1895, in her "Oblation to Merciful Love," she offered herself as a victim sacrifice for the salvation of others.

A prolific letter writer and an exquisite poet, Thérèse agreed, under obedience to her superiors, to write her autobiography. *Story of a Soul* was destined to become one of the most inspiring and best-loved books of all ages. Though she never left the enclosure, Thérèse was named, along with St. Francis Xavier, patron of the missions. She, who described herself as a grain of sand in the immensity of the ocean, became the greatest saint of modern times. Thérèse was beatified in 1923, canonized by Pope Pius XI in 1925, and proclaimed a Doctor of the Church in 1998 by Pope John Paul II, who called her a "living icon of God."[2]

LIVING THE ESSENTIALS OF CARMELITE SPIRITUALITY

In fidelity to her Discalced Carmelite charism, Thérèse chose to embody in the fullest way possible the teachings of the reformed order's founders, St. Teresa of Avila and St. John of the Cross. Like them, she sought guidance for her vocation in holy scripture, especially in the Gospel of John and the epistles of Paul. She specifies these traditional inspirations in her *Story of a Soul*:

> Ah! How many lights have I not drawn from the works of our Holy Father, St. John of the Cross! At the ages of seventeen and eighteen I had no other spiritual nourishment; later on, however, all books left me in aridity and I'm still in that state. . . . In this helplessness, Holy Scripture and the *Imitation* [*of Christ*] come to my aid; in them I discover a solid and very *pure* nourishment. But it is especially the *Gospels* which sustain me during my hours of prayer, for in them I find what is necessary for my poor little soul. I am constantly discovering in them new lights, hidden and mysterious meanings.[3]

This reading convinced her of the need to cultivate a one-on-one relationship of intimacy with "the Sun of Love" (*SS*, 198). She knew she could depend on him for everything and trust him unconditionally. Devotion to the Child Jesus, common in her era, would have been part of her own childhood as well as of her initiation in Carmel.[4]

This attraction to Jesus in his humanity and divinity counteracted the Jansenistic rigors plaguing the church of France. This heresy portrayed God not as a mild and tender child but as a harsh adult bent on punishing sinners and rarely showing merciful love. Thérèse had the opposite experience: "God was pleased all through my life to surround me with *love*, and the first memories I have are stamped with smiles and the most tender caresses. . . . [Jesus] also sent much love into my little heart, making it warm and affectionate" (*SS*, 17).

Thérèse celebrates with equal warmth her devotion to the Blessed Mother.[5] In her twenty-five-stanza poem titled, "Why I Love You, O Mary," she sees in "the ineffable treasure of *virginity*" the deepest meaning of her cloistered life.[6] Mary shows her that the best way to practice ardent charity is to forget about the vanity of worldly greatness and bind herself to Jesus with chains of humility. Of Mary's eloquent silence, modeled in her rule of life in Carmel, Thérèse says, "[It is] a sweet melodious concert / That speaks . . . of the greatness and power / Of a soul which looks only to Heaven for help."[7]

What attracted Thérèse was not the attainment of proficiency by mastering detailed rules and practices. She preferred to follow an accessible path to virtue, beginning with the acknowledgment of her nothingness. Thus she could approach God with total confidence, just as little children who leap into the arms of their beloved parents do.[8] Complementing this commitment to the pursuit of spiritual childhood was Thérèse's return to a life of evangelical simplicity. She recalls a conversation with one of the older nuns in the community, who said to her, "Your soul is extremely *simple*, but when you will be perfect, you will be even *more simple*; the closer one approaches to God, the simpler one becomes" (*SS*, 151).

Another Theresian virtue was that of detachment. As Teresa of Avila promises in *The Way of Perfection*, it gives her the freedom to attribute all that she possessed and all the good that she did to God, thus fostering both humility and charity. Since a little child is by definition weak and powerless, is it any wonder that she is incapable of self-assertion and lacks the strength to survive alone? The littleness Thérèse loved detached her from the myth of self-sufficiency and led her to live in the truth that she had nothing of which to boast. Everything is grace, and all that is comes from God (see *SS*, 266).

The chief characteristics of Thérèse's spirituality can be summarized in three words: *disinterested*, *inclusive*, and *discreet*. The thread that ties them together is the decision following her conversion that Jesus would possess her heart and enable her by the power of his grace to give her all to him. Her spirituality was *disinterested* in that she refused to put herself at the center of anyone's attention. Her love was *inclusive*, proving itself not by sweet words but by tireless deeds. Her life had to become "one act of love"[9] without undue reliance on sensible feelings and with the unwavering intention of doing her best to never lose her joy. Finally, *discretion* prompted Thérèse to hide her sufferings from others and even, so to speak, from God. Her faith assured her that no suffering was ever wasted in the Mystical Body of Christ. Love was the best means for correcting her faults as well as the best safeguard against future failings.

Far from grieving over the recognition of her own imperfections, Thérèse took delight in them. Detaching herself from the burden of possessiveness enabled her to live in readiness to receive the bounty of God's merciful love and to fulfill whatever duty God asked of her. There was no need to worry or be afraid as long as she walked in the truth of who she was. Her indigence posed no obstacle to God's actions through her. Thus she could say with full confidence that "happiness consists in hiding oneself, in remaining ignorant of created things. I understood that without *love* all works are nothing, even the most dazzling" (*SS*, 175). For her, sanctity was less about doing something and more about cultivating a disposition of the heart that makes us humble and that teaches us to accept our limits with confidence in the strength of God to sustain us. Since the Lord comes to us where we are, he will give us all that we still lack. He will take our nothingness and transform it into living fire.

DISCOVERING THE UNIQUENESS OF OUR VOCATION

Thérèse believed that the light of God within her was meant to radiate through her into the situations in which she found herself. Her story teaches us that God transforms us by grace so that we can bring the fruits of this transformation to others. At times our tendency to self-sufficiency may reassert itself, but this deceptive temptation weakens under the impetus of obedience. God seems to have instilled in us safeguards to protect his ultimate claim to the mystery of our call.

One sure safeguard to fidelity was in Thérèse's case frail health. She had no choice but to depend on God and to stay strong despite the suffering she endured. In her short life span, she came to understand that bearing our cross with joy surpasses all the pleasures the world has to offer since it leads us to simplicity of spirit and total trust in God's loving plan for our lives. The spirituality of a saint like Thérèse inspires us to move from a fragmented to an integrated life centered in the privilege of being adopted children of God (see Rom 8:15). Then with her we, too, can pray, "Jesus . . . draw me into the flames of [your] love . . . unite me so closely to [you] that [you] live and act in me" (SS, 257).

SECRETS OF SANCTITY

Thérèse's secret of sanctity consisted in the radical uprooting of all traces of self-love. Such renunciation did not mean that she took upon herself heroic mortifications. Her health prohibited any such feats. Eradicating selfishness was an interior disposition resulting in mortifying the self-love that makes us seek our own satisfaction in whatever we do. Thérèse knew that the love she had for others flowed through her from God and that it was to be returned to God.

The practice of self-forgetfulness is not an end in itself but a means to a more liberated way to love, a way freed from egoism and freed for service of God and neighbor. A process of pruning releases us from slavery to self and disengages us from everything that obstructs the ripening of selfless love. That is why Thérèse seized every opportunity for mortification that came her way. Her daily life was so full of crosses that she never had to look for special ones.

She loved beauty and neatness, but she learned to esteem the oldest and most oft-repaired habits. She suffered from the cold, but she never refused to do painful and disagreeable tasks whatever the season. A small mortification such as giving a book she wanted to read to another sister was for her such an aid to spiritual progress that the book passed instantly from her hands. As she relates:

> I applied myself to practicing little virtues, not having the capability of practicing the great. For instance, I loved to fold up the mantles forgotten by the Sisters, and to render them all sorts of little services. Love for mortification was given me, and this love was all the greater because I was allowed nothing by way of satisfying it. The only little mortification I was doing while still in the world, which consisted in not leaning my back against any support while seated, was forbidden me because of my inclination to stoop. Alas! My ardor for penances would not have lasted long had the Superiors allowed them. The penances they did allow me consisted in mortifying my self-love, which did me much more good than corporal penances. (*SS*, 159)

Charity compelled Thérèse to look only at the virtues of her sisters in the cloister, to see Christ in them. The more she matured, the less inclined she was to find fault in others or to feel resentful because of their failure to love. She loved them for Christ's sake, not because she expected to receive love in return. Not only did Thérèse render every service she could to a sister who seldom had a good word for her; she says, "I was content with giving her my most friendly smile, and with changing the subject of the conversation." Citing *The Imitation of Christ*, she adds, "For [it says], '*It is better to leave each one in his own opinion than to enter into arguments*'" (*SS*, 223). That is why, when trouble arose in the community, Thérèse did her best to restore tranquility. She kept a cheerful outlook and often found a humorous anecdote to raise everyone's spirit.

Another sign of maturation in Christ, lived and taught by Thérèse, is that of making ourselves available for God and letting him do with us as he wills despite our imperfections. Such humility explains why prayer for Thérèse "is an aspiration of the heart; it is a simple glance directed to heaven. It is a cry of gratitude and love in the midst of trial as well as joy; finally, it is something great, supernatural, which expands my soul and unites me to Jesus" (*SS*, 242). Her spirit of abnegation and self-sacrifice manifested itself to the full during her final, painful illness. She allowed her terrible suffering from consumption to lead her closer to Christ. In the darkest night of her existence, she discovered that true love bore lasting fruit in self-forgetfulness and in her choice to be other-oriented, with a smile on her face and a song in her heart. Thérèse never hides her limits. She remains candid and courageous, relying not on herself but on the Lord to lift her up, confessing to him:

> O Divine Word! You are the Adored Eagle whom I love and who alone *attracts* me! Coming into this land of exile, You willed to suffer and to die in order to *draw* souls to the bosom of the Eternal Fire of the Blessed Trinity. Ascending once again to the Inaccessible Light, henceforth Your abode, You remain still in this "valley of tears," hidden beneath the appearances of a white host. Eternal Eagle, You desire to nourish me with Your divine substance and yet I am but a poor little thing who would return to nothingness if Your divine glance did not give me life from one moment to the next. (*SS*, 199)

In pondering the meaning of her call, Thérèse came to a personal understanding of the doctrine that the Church is a Mystical Body composed of diverse cells, or members; the heart of the Mystical Body is the Holy Spirit, whose function is to give life and energy to all the members. This realization enabled her to clarify her vocation: since love is everything and contains all vocations, she had only to love and then to find the means of so loving God and causing him to be loved that it was equivalent to the task of all other apostolic labors. Thérèse's destiny was not to travel to distant lands but to pray for those who did.[10] It was to reclaim the one and only vocation that ultimately matters, and so she wrote:

> *Charity* gave me the key to my *vocation*. I understood that if the Church had a body composed of different members, the most necessary and most noble of all could not be lacking to it, and so I understood that the Church *had a Heart and that this Heart was* BURNING WITH LOVE. I *understood that it was Love alone* that made the Church's members act, that if *Love* ever became extinct, apostles would not preach the

Gospel and martyrs would not shed their blood. I understood that LOVE COMPRISED ALL VOCATIONS, THAT LOVE
WAS EVERYTHING, THAT IT EMBRACED ALL TIMES AND
PLACES . . . IN A WORD, THAT IT WAS ETERNAL! Then, in
the excess of my delirious joy, I cried out: O Jesus, my Love
. . . my *vocation*, at last I have found it . . . MY VOCATION IS
LOVE! (*SS*, 194)

REFLECT NOW

1. How would you describe the meaning of spiritual childhood and how
    would you distinguish it from childishness?
2. Have you come to see your imperfections not as blockages but as step-
    ping-stones to deeper holiness?
3. What do you do to mirror the mystery of God's love to others?

READ MORE

Guy Gaucher, *The Passion of Thérèse of Lisieux* (New York: Crossroad, 1990).
Thomas R. Nevin, *The Last Years of Saint Thérèse: Doubt and Darkness, 1895–1897*
    (New York: Oxford University Press, 2013).
Joseph F. Schmidt, *Everything Is Grace: The Life and Way of Thérèse of Lisieux*
    (Frederick, MD: Word Among Us Press, 2007).

25

ENJOY FULFILLING
WHATEVER DUTY
GOD GIVES YOU

JEAN-PIERRE DE CAUSSADE
ON ABANDONMENT TO
DIVINE PROVIDENCE

Yes, if only we had sense enough to leave everything to the guidance of God's hand, we should reach the highest peak of holiness. Everyone could do it, for the opportunity is offered to everyone. We have, as it were, only to open our mouths and let holiness flow in.

—Jean-Pierre de Caussade,
Abandonment to Divine Providence, 55

Attending faithfully to the duty of the day rather than ruminating about the past or worrying about the future is sound advice from a renowned spiritual master, Jean-Pierre de Caussade. His book *Abandonment to Divine Providence* encourages us to open our hearts to the peace of Jesus and move day by day in a graceful rhythm of worship and work. He advises us to remove obstacles to the flow of grace such as anxiety and discouragement that trail us like noxious vapors. Dangerous, too, is the false guilt we feel when we think we have failed God by not being prayerful enough. The truth is that God welcomes the smallest thing we do out of love since it signifies for him the highest degree of holiness. God is the artist; we are the canvas on which he paints a thousand brushstrokes of benevolence.

According to Caussade, to be abandoned to God is like being granted a new lease on life. Trials become catalysts to celebrate the victory of Christ over the worst limits life can inflict upon us. In God's guiding light, we see the fullest meaning of every task we perform. In the here-and-now situations in which we find ourselves, it is God's voice we hear and God's will we discern.

MEET THE MASTER

Jean-Pierre de Caussade (1675–1751) entered the Jesuit novitiate at Toulouse, France, in 1693. Ordained a priest in 1705, he professed his final vows in 1708. Throughout his religious life, he was a sought-after and respected teacher, preacher, and confessor. For many years, he gave conferences to the sisters of the Order of the Visitation at Nancy and undertook the spiritual direction of several of them. Notes of these conferences, together with examples of his extensive correspondence, were preserved by the order but remained unpublished for many years. They came to light in 1861 when they were published in the form of a treatise on the essence of holiness. In these texts, collected by Henri Ramière, S.J., Caussade expounded his teaching on appreciative abandonment and its applicability to everyone's spiritual life.[1]

In 1741, Caussade oversaw the publication of a book of spiritual instructions on various states of prayer in keeping with the doctrinal teachings of Jacques-Bénigne Bossuet (1627–1704), a renowned French preacher and bishop of Meaux and a stanch opponent, as was Caussade, of the quietest movement promoted by Archbishop François Fénelon (1651–1715) and Madame Guyon (1648–1717).[2] Caussade's book includes Bossuet's instructions pertaining to simple recollection and undistracted attention to God. Caussade says in no uncertain terms that "quietism is quite wrong" (*ADP*, I, 8:32) when it condemns spiritual disciplines like vocal prayer and the use of our senses. He adds, "It is a waste of time to try to picture any kind of self-abandonment which excludes all personal activity and seeks only quiescence, for if God wishes us to act for ourselves, the action makes us holy" (*ADP*, I, 8:32).

Caussade's teachings are traceable to the spirituality of Francis de Sales, especially to his *Treatise on the Love of God*, from which he learned the efficacy of "holy indifference," by which a soul makes itself pliable to God and ready to receive every impression of his will. He admired as well the works of John of the Cross, notably *The Spiritual Canticle*. From Carmelite spirituality, Caussade discovered the necessity of being open to the midnight moments of life, when faith alone unites us with God and intellectual reasoning recedes under the impetus of childlike trust.

The most trivial act done with love may please God more than great deeds devoid of abandonment to God. Fidelity to the Divine in the duty of the present moment is a surer path to spiritual maturity than great learning devoid of humility. In the smallest endeavor, it is wise to invite God to work through us. Trials then become catalysts for growing in faith, hope, and love. God gives us the power to overcome the seductions of the world, the flesh, and the devil.[3] In time, "[holiness] increases in proportion to the growth of our desire to obey [God's] will and his plans for us, no matter what they are" (*ADP*, I, 8:33).

That is why for Caussade contemplation includes the active performance of what God requires of us. We are to contemplate the invitations, challenges, and appeals the Lord sends our way since "the whole business of self-abandonment is only the business of loving, and love achieves everything" (*ADP*, VI, 9:113).

THE WAY OF PERFECTION FOR ABANDONED SOULS

From the nuns who transcribed his conferences on spiritual direction to the unnamed penitents he counseled, Caussade strove to open the way of perfection to the people of God. He showed only passing interest in exceptional states of prayer and bypassed complex techniques pertaining to the attainment of holiness of life. He insisted that this calling is open to all, thanks to the saving grace of Jesus Christ, whose love is the source of our capacity to combine communion with God and the commitment to serve our neighbor. Instead of assuming that the present moment passes by with little importance, he challenges us to interpret our situation in light of the deeper meaning obedience to God's will gives to every happening. When we look upon people, events, and things with the eyes of faith, we realize that God is not "out there" but here with us now. God comes to us under the guise of a task he needs us to do or a message he wants us to hear. Once we attend to each circumstance with a listening heart, we can detect the truth that "what God arranges for us to experience at each moment is the best and holiest thing that could happen to us" (*ADP*, I, 4:27).

No matter how humiliating or uplifting a situation may be for us, there is more meaning to it than meets the eye. Hidden beneath the ordinary details of daily life is a rich undercurrent of significance easily missed. We can hear with the inner ears of faith "the mysterious utterance of a still more mysterious God" (*ADP*, II, 4:42). His will at first appears to be incomprehensible, but the more we listen, the more we may decipher the meaning God wants to convey.

Caussade holds to the truth that each daily activity, faithfully attended to, may yield an unexpected revelation. Whether we realize it or not, the present situation in which we find ourselves is like an ever-flowing fountain from which we can quench our thirst for holiness. Its flow is inexhaustible because it emanates from the presence and power of God.

To pursue the way of perfection, we must accept the truth that we are only humble instruments in the hand of God, whose grace is enough for us. All that is required for the sanctification of our soul comes from God's unconditional love for us. We need to abandon ourselves to it like marble to a sculptor's chisel.

The benefits of abandonment to the mystery are beyond what Caussade can count. The posture of joyful surrender dispels self-centeredness, evokes heroic virtue, and radiates agapic love: "The soul finds the fullness of divine life, not offered drop by drop, but engulfing it instantly" (*ADP*, III, 4:64). Without reliance on God, our works risk becoming only outcomes of our own ego-projects. When our heart is abandoned to God, we do what pleases our Beloved, concerned neither about the failure of our performance nor about the praise we may receive for a success.

To subject ourselves to God's will under the present circumstances is for Caussade the best and easiest way to answer the call to unite holiness of life and service. Lifted from us is the always debilitating weight of worry. We do not fear the vicissitudes of existence or the certainty of death. We do not have to prove our goodwill to others because we are alert and active instruments of God wherever we are. We pursue Christian excellence as a rule, not as an exception, because we "do nothing but peacefully await the promptings of God" (*ADP*, IV, 4:79).

Because we see the hidden meaning behind whatever happens to us, we stand firm in the face of sharp reproaches, nagging criticisms, and unfair misunderstandings. As long as we keep our gaze fixed on the Lord, we can, in the blink of an eye, do whatever he asks of us without losing our peace. For us, wholehearted submission to Divine Providence "is the gospel and the whole Scripture and the law" (*ADP*, IV, 7:84).

FRUITS OF FIDELITY TO DIVINE GUIDANCE

Patient endurance is the virtue that enables us to persevere in the face of misfortune. Caussade advises souls who "weep and tremble . . . [to] make no attempt to escape from these divinely inspired terrors. Receive in the depths of your hearts the little streams which glow from the sea of sorrow which filled the most holy soul of Jesus. Keep advancing and let your tears flow under the influence of grace. . . . Then you will see, because of your abandonment, the full extent of what the divine action is accomplishing" (*ADP*, VI, 2:102).

Self-abandoned souls may appear to be defenseless, but this is not true. They know that God is their help and their protector. In our everyday experiences of loss and gain, sorrow and joy, we take nothing for granted. We realize how useless it is to behave according to our preconceived notions or natural impulses when the best course of action is never to "fight against the divine plans" (*ADP*, VI, 10:116). Once we accept the truth that God is alive and active in all that happens and that at no moment do we act outside of his grace and mercy, we approach the pinnacle of spiritual growth. We attain the "deepest knowledge we can have in this life of the things of God" (*ADP*, VI, 11:117).

It follows that we never mistake abandonment for mere passivity. This submissive trust in God's promise to provide what we need activates our creativity and heightens our attentiveness to divine dispensations revealed in the ordinary circumstances of daily life. It demands of us both a responsive readiness and a humble willingness to detect the presence of the mystery in our everyday surroundings as well as in the undeserved favors we receive from God. Only then can we say from the heart, "All will be well. God has the matter in hand. We need fear nothing" (*ADP*, VI, 1:101).

An abandoned life is a blessing because it leads us to union with God; it instills inner calm and grants us the gift of enlightened realism. In its benevolent light, we let things be. We accept their coming and their passing away. In midnight moments, as well as when the dawn breaks, we let God be God. We are at peace, knowing that we are not in control of our coming into existence or of our going forth from it. Our duty is to see what God wills in events as they unfold. They may be contrary to our expectations, but so be it. We harbor no illusion that life should be perfect. We accept our imperfections as teachable moments and try to do better in the future.

To take up the crosses that come our way is to embrace the Cross and to identify with the Paschal Mystery. We promote the good because we know our Redeemer lives in the just, peaceful, and merciful ways in which we think and act. We come to see that "the whole business of self-abandonment is only the business of loving, and love achieves everything" (*ADP*, VI, 9:113).

The six chapters of this masterpiece of classical Christian spirituality lead us to the following six conclusions:

1. *Let us do what we can* day by day to perform our duty and then, with equanimity and trust in Divine Providence, leave the rest to God.
2. *Let us behold the present moment as God's gift to us* and see it as an invitation to grow in holiness by matching our character to the Gospel truths Christ gave us.
3. *Let us recognize that surrendering to God is the start* of practicing every virtue. It is our best defense against pride and our surest path to humility.
4. *Let us go one step further* and concede with wonder that complete abandonment to the will of God is the essence of Christian spirituality.

5. *Let us ask God for the grace* to see that the first fruit of faith is to enable us to detect the deeper meaning of whatever happens to us and to accept it with joy.

6. *Let us validate day by day the revelation* that Christ's peace and joy can be ours the moment we abandon ourselves to the mystery of transforming love and to the light of God's unfailing guidance.

REFLECT NOW

1. How faithful are you to the designs of God revealed to you in the duty of the present moment?

2. What graces do you see flowing from abandonment to Divine Providence, and what is your personal experience of them?

3. Do you see the need to surrender to God's will in times of suffering as much as in times of joy?

READ MORE

Chiara Lubich, *Jesus: The Heart of His Message: Unity and Jesus Forsaken* (Hyde Park, NY: New City Press, 1985).

Bernardo Olivera, *The Sun at Midnight: Monastic Experience of the Christian Mystery* (Collegeville, MN: Liturgical Press, 2012).

Robert Cardinal Sarah, *God or Nothing: A Conversation on Faith with Nicolas Diat*, trans. Michael J. Miller (San Francisco: Ignatius Press, 2015).

26

PRAISE AND GLORIFY FATHER, SON, AND HOLY SPIRIT

ELIZABETH OF THE TRINITY ON INTIMACY WITH GOD

In the heaven of her soul, the praise of glory has already begun her work of eternity. Her song is uninterrupted, for she is under the actions of the Holy Spirit who effects everything in her; and although she is not always aware of it, for the weakness of nature does not allow her to be established in God without distractions, she always sings, she always adores, for she has, so to speak, wholly passed into praise and love in her passion for the glory of God.
—Elizabeth of the Trinity, *Complete Works*, I, 112–13

Answering the universal call to holiness seems to require length of years, but St. Elizabeth of the Trinity is a witness to the truth that the grace of God cannot be confined to chronology. She was a talented young pianist, a brilliant writer, and a Carmelite nun in love with the Trinity. She chose in her life of prayer to praise God's glory, believing that she had been destined during her twenty-six years on earth to forecast the joys of eternity.

We learn from Elizabeth that there is no abyss into which we can fall that is too deep for the Lord to offer us a helping hand out. Yielding to the embrace of the Cross gave her the strength to endure the inexorable suffering of her final days. She exemplified the commitment embedded in her vowed life to allow Christ to imprint himself on her like a seal on wax.

Elizabeth rejoiced that her name meant "house of God" and that by her prayers and actions she could fulfill her call to transform the world into God's dwelling place. The splendor of nature—every bird, bee, and flower, the starry sky and the deep blue sea—proved that he was the sovereign Lord of the loveliest house anyone could hope to behold. Elizabeth wanted the soul to become an incarnation of the Word that we might be another humanity in which God would renew his whole mystery.

MEET THE MASTER

Marie Elizabeth Catez (1880–1906), the daughter of a distinguished family known for their dedication to both civic and religious causes, was born in Bourges, France, on July 18, 1880. Her father, an officer in the French army, died when she was seven years old, leaving her mother to raise Elizabeth and her sister, Marguerite. The three of them moved to Dijon, where Elizabeth, a precocious child, grew more proficient in the exercise of her artistic gifts under the firm guidance of her widowed mother, Madame Catez.

When "Sabeth" (her nickname) made her First Communion on April 9, 1891, she received an inkling of her future vocation to the religious life. Unusually self-possessed for her age, she made a vow of virginity that foreshadowed her lifelong desire for intimacy with the Trinity. A gifted musician, a member of her parish choir, and a catechist, this future saint had many friends and admirers, but nothing this world had to offer displaced her attraction to interior prayer.

Following a visit to the Carmel in Dijon at the age of seventeen, Elizabeth knew she had found her vocation. Like her Carmelite sister Thérèse of Lisieux, whose autobiography she had read, Elizabeth mustered the courage to ask her mother for permission to enter the cloister, a request Madame Catez delayed until her daughter was twenty-one and had finished her education. Already in the postulancy, Elizabeth began to experience the dark nights of sense and spirit described by her spiritual father, John of the

Cross. The need to commit herself to humility, detachment, and fraternal charity, as described by her mother in Carmel, Teresa of Avila, in *The Way of Perfection*, had a profound influence on her.

In addition to Elizabeth's indebtedness to the Carmelite tradition, she was well schooled in the masterpieces of ascetical-mystical theology, ranging from the works of Pseudo-Dionysius to Jan van Ruysbroeck, both of whom confirmed her veneration for the mystery of the Trinity and her espousal to Christ. For her, the doctrine of Three Persons in One God was not an abstract theory but an expression of the Real Presence to be adored in the Eucharist. Her writings are replete with scriptural allusions, such as to Ephesians 2:19, where Paul tells us that we are no longer guests or strangers but citizens of the city of God. John 17:24 assured her that where the Lord was, there she would be. And, in Revelation 2:17, she found her new name to be a "praise of glory."

Elizabeth's love for holy scripture, especially the epistles of St. Paul, proved to her that before the foundation of the world, Christ had chosen her to be his bride. Under the pontificate of Leo XIII (1878–1903), the France of Elizabeth's time witnessed the influence of Christian social thought and the labor movement together with several conflicted Church-state relationships. In 1902, the prime minister strove to eradicate Catholicism from the country, going so far as to close all French parochial schools and placing restrictive measures on many religious orders, some of which had to leave the country, a fate that thankfully did not affect the Carmel of Dijon. The new pope, Pius X, initiated a renewed appreciation for the Word of God and encouraged Catholic laity to read the Bible.

Elizabeth compiled lists of biblical verses, committed them to memory, and practiced a vibrant lectio divina, inscribing hundreds of passages on her heart.[1] She also familiarized herself with the writings of Catherine of Siena, from whom she derived, even prior to her entrance to Carmel, her affinity for the cell of self-knowledge.[2] This Dominican influence continued during her retreat in 1902 with a priest of this order, who would have been steeped in the teachings of Thomas Aquinas on the indwelling Trinity. From a Jesuit retreat master in 1906 she may have learned more about the link between suffering and contemplation. By then she was an invalid in the last months of her life, hardly able to eat or drink but understanding more than ever how to share the Cross of her Beloved with confident faith in his compassionate care for her. She found solace and strength by reading the lives of the saints and identifying with their spirit of total trust in Divine Providence. In the sixteenth and final day of her last retreat, she concluded: "The soul will live, like the immutable Trinity, in an *eternal present,* 'adoring him always because of himself,' and becoming by an always more single, more unitive gaze, 'the splendor of his glory,' that is, the unceasing praise of glory of his adorable perfections" (*CW,* 162).

A year after her religious profession in 1903, Elizabeth composed her famous prayer, "O my God, Trinity Whom I adore." It synthesizes her spiritual doctrine and ends with the unforgettable words: "O my Three, my All, my Beatitude, infinite Solitude, Immensity in which I lose myself, I surrender myself to You as Your prey. Bury Yourself in me that I may bury myself in You until I depart to contemplate in Your light the abyss of Your greatness" (*CW,* 184).

By 1905, Elizabeth had begun to experience severe symptoms of the illness (Addison's disease) that would take her life. For the next several months, she could do nothing but abandon herself without reservation to the Divine Will. After a brief remission of her pain, she suffered yet another relapse. On May 24, 1906, a few months before her death, she reported having received the grace of feeling the presence of God. "I think," she wrote shortly before her death, "that in Heaven my mission will be to draw souls by helping them to go out of themselves to cling to God by a wholly simple and loving movement, and to keep them in that great silence within which that will allow God to communicate Himself to them and transform them into Himself."[3]

When Elizabeth was beatified on November 25, 1984, by Pope John Paul II, he confirmed her legacy to the Church by giving her as a guide to men and women who seek to simplify their lives in humility and charity and to make of them an experience of unceasing prayer. She was also hailed as a teacher of the doctrinal truth that the Trinity dwells within us. God is more intimate to us than we are to ourselves since "God's Spirit dwells in [us]" (1 Cor 3:16); we are hidden in Christ as Christ is hidden in God (see Col 3:3).

ENTERING THE LIBERATING LAND OF DIVINE INTIMACY

The interior castle described by Teresa of Avila constitutes the core of Elizabeth's spirituality. She believed it to be God's intention that we live in time in the presence of the Eternal so that "one day the veil will fall, [and] we will be introduced into the eternal court, and there we will sing in the bosom of infinite Love" (*CW*, 113).

Elizabeth knew that the price she had to pay to enter this liberating land of divine intimacy was to leave behind every remnant of natural egoism that prevented her from being united with the Beloved Spouse, who captivated her heart. The longing for intimacy that reveals the depth of Elizabeth's spirituality begins with her love of God's first revelation in creation.[4] Her artistic temperament drew her to see in forests, flowers, trees, and oceans manifestations of a mystery beyond words yet desirous of sweeping her into intimacy. This may have been the reason why she was able to bring out the good in everyone she encountered, especially her beloved sister, Marguerite, whose marriage and motherhood aroused her fondest affection: "Oh, my Guite, this Heaven, this house of our Father, is in 'the center of our soul'! . . . through everything, in the midst of your cares as a mother, while you give yourself to your little angels, you can withdraw into this solitude to surrender yourself to the Holy Spirit so he can transform you in God and imprint on your soul the Image of the divine Beauty, so the Father, bending over you lovingly, will see only his Christ and say, 'This is my beloved daughter, in whom I am well pleased.'"[5]

Undeniable is Elizabeth's discovery that nothing can distract us from God as long as we live in him and act for him. No matter where we are, we can listen to God's voice in the silence of our heart. Her ideal of sanctity was to live by love and to surrender herself, body and soul, to her Beloved. As a Carmelite nun, she knew that from this renunciation comes the liberation that frees us to conform to the Divine Will.

Especially in times of physical debilitation and spiritual desolation, Elizabeth chose to deepen her love for Christ crucified. For her, to live in praise of God's glory meant total identification with the Paschal Mystery, whether or not she would ever understand in her short life span what was happening to her. In a letter to her friend Madame de Sourdon, who was full of maternal concern, she wrote, "When everything was dark, when the present was so painful and the future seemed even more gloomy to me, I used to close my eyes and abandon myself like a child in the arms of this Father, who is in heaven."[6] Her advice to "dear Madame" was to surrender herself and all her preoccupations to the "Court of the King," trusting that the day would come when everything was clear and full of light.

THE DWELLING PLACE OF THE DIVINE

The spiritual nourishment we receive from St. Elizabeth can be found in her prayer to the Trinity she adores and to whom she says, "Help me to forget myself entirely that I may be established in you" (CW, 183). She reminds us that only to the degree that we forfeit our ego can we remember that we are children of God called to sink into the depths of the divine mystery as if our soul were already in eternity. She prays, "Give peace to my soul, make it . . . your beloved dwelling, your resting place" (CW, 183).

Elizabeth begs to be with Jesus from Calvary to Easter morn. She reminds us, nondescript as our lives may be, that Christ's light is in us and that we, too, may be a praise of his glory. This unity grows deeper when we vow to spend our life listening to him and becoming more docile to his leading. In sickness and in health, during the dark night of our soul and at the dawn of a new day, Elizabeth tells us to fix our gaze on Jesus.

Her boldest hope is that this consuming Fire, this spirit of Love, will come upon her and "create in [her] soul a kind of incarnation of the Word: that [she] may be another humanity for him in which he can renew his whole Mystery" (CW, 183). Do we dare to pray with her that the Word become flesh in us? Elizabeth believes with all her heart that this epiphany is possible. We, too, can be covered with the light of glory to such a degree that we delight the Father's eye as Jesus did.

To lose ourselves in the immensity of the Infinite in no way destroys our uniqueness. To bury ourselves with Jesus in the tomb is the only way that Jesus can bury himself in us and grant us the grace of intimacy with the Trinity that readies us, as it did Elizabeth, "to contemplate in [his] light the abyss of [his] greatness" (CW, 184).

When Elizabeth died at dawn on November 9, 1906, her last words were, "I am going to Light, to Love, to Life!" Though the disease that consumed her had drained her of energy, denied her sleep, and plunged her into the depths of silence, she reports having in the core of her being a conviction of being called to serve every member of the Body of Christ. Thanks to her concentration on the Trinity she adored, she was able to offer her suffering for the whole Church hungering for redemption. Thus she writes in her last retreat "the 'new song' which will most charm and captivate my God is that of a soul stripped and freed from self, one in whom he can reflect all that he is, and do all that he wills. This soul remains under his touch like a lyre, and all his gifts to it are like so many strings which vibrate to sing, day and night, the praise of his glory!" (*CW*, 157–58).

THE GRACE OF TRINITARIAN INTIMACY

Elizabeth's doctrine of intimacy with the Trinity reveals that though she was young in age, she had grown old in spiritual maturity. She points the way for us to stay in touch with the Infinite Mystery that dwells within us. Under her tutelage we learn the art and discipline of moving away from all that is less than God so that we can find our place in the embrace of Father, Son, and Holy Spirit. We ascend from what is seen to what is unseen, coming to such a depth of faith, hope, and love that we remain true to God in consolation and desolation, in joy and sorrow. The gift we receive from the Beloved gives us access to an abyss of blessedness without beginning or end. We stand at the threshold of that eternal present in awe and adoration, sensing that the eternity we seek is with us now and that the peace of God we feel surpasses all understanding (see Phil 4:7).

Elizabeth confided to her "Darling Mama" the conviction that she was loved exceedingly by God and that the secret to spiritual maturity resided in the knowledge that we cannot be separated from him.[7] She believed that mature Christians already live in the bosom of the Trinity and in communion with the heart of Christ. We abide at once in the *chronos* of each passing moment and in the *kairos* of Christ's promise of abundant life. To let ourselves be loved is a necessary step to living always in intimate union with the Father, the Son, and the Holy Spirit.

Elizabeth sees the practice of recollection as another sign of spiritual maturity. She gathers the little energy she has left into a gentle yet firm focus on God so that nothing distracts her attention from the tranquil presence of the Trinity. This abiding in awe-filled attention stays with her in whatever activity convent life requires of her. Even amid a multitude of visits, letter writing, and little chores, she does not lose her contemplative solitude. For her all facets of life are sacramental, offering us an opportunity to be in communion with God's indwelling presence. She makes this ingathering of her thoughts and actions a spiritual discipline and a source of her happiness. The finest fruit of this discipline is unceasing prayer, which Elizabeth describes as a "perpetual Sanctus," drawing our finite being into a relationship of deep love with the Infinite Being of God.

Elizabeth understood her vocation to be an abiding in love that both originates from and terminates in the Blessed Trinity. This conviction shaped her understanding of her mission and accounted for the fruitfulness of her spiritual life. Despite the waning of her physical stamina, she grew stronger in her understanding of the dignity granted to her due to her sharing in the "eternal Trinitarian formation and interformation event."[8]

Toward the end of her life, Elizabeth knew it was time to give herself a new name. She signed her letters *Laudem Gloriae* (Praise of God's Glory). Conformity to Christ, complemented by her devotion to Our Lady of Mount Carmel, inspired her to offer her sufferings and approaching death to be another humanity in which Christ renewed his whole mystery.[9] Echoing the apostle Paul, she concluded that Jesus lived in her and she no longer wanted to live her own life but to be transformed into his so that her life would be more divine than human. Two months before her death, she wrote from the infirmary, "I feel already as if I were almost in heaven in my little cell, alone with Him alone, bearing my cross with my Master" (*CW*, 123).

Reflect Now

1. Do you read scripture with a listening heart, open to receiving God's Word as God's word for you?

2. Do you feel that you are growing in intimacy with the Trinity and in praise of God's glory?
3. In what way does living the Paschal Mystery aid your prayer life and help you to personalize the dying and rising of Jesus?

READ MORE

Hans Urs von Balthasar, *Two Sisters in the Spirit: Thérèse of Lisieux & Elizabeth of the Trinity* (San Francisco, CA: Ignatius Press, 1992).

Conrad De Meester, O.C.D., *Elizabeth of the Trinity: Light Love Life: A Look at a Face and a Heart* (Washington, DC: ICS Publications, 1987).

Marian T. Murphy, ed., *Elizabeth of the Trinity: Always Believe in Love* (Hyde Park, NY: New City Press, 2009).

27

CLEANSE YOUR PERCEPTION
AND SEE WHAT IS
REALLY REAL

EVELYN UNDERHILL ON
PRACTICAL MYSTICISM

Is there not here, then, abundance of practical work for you
to do; work which is the direct outcome of your mystical
experience? Are there not here, as the French proverb has
it, plenty of cats to comb? And isn't it just here, in the new
foothold it gives you, the new clear vision and certitude—in
its noble, serious, and invulnerable faith—that mysticism
is "useful"; even for the most scientific of social reformers,
the most belligerent of politicians, the least sentimental of
philanthropists?
—Evelyn Underhill, *Practical Mysticism*, 184

Spirituality is reality. Such is the conclusion reached by Evelyn Underhill, an
English master of the mystical life, who stands shoulder to shoulder with the
saints and scholars we have encountered so far. All insist that contemplative
presence must be the ground of active participation in everyday life.

Underhill subordinated her love of learning to her desire for God; she probed the historical treasures of Christianity for the purpose of coming to know Jesus Christ. As a result, her body of work bridges pre- and post-Reformation spirituality. She is as much at home with the Carmelite master John of the Cross as she is with the founder of Methodism, John Wesley.

We owe Underhill a debt of gratitude for her authorship of the Christian classic *Practical Mysticism*. In it she addresses such questions as *How do I go beyond the mediocrity of a Sunday-morning-only Christianity? Can contemplative prayer enhance practical effectiveness? What must I do to find in the routines of the day a refreshing sense of the Sacred?*

Underhill offers sensible answers to these questions based on her own experience of longing for God and her passionate commitment to selfless service. Her writings are a wake-up call inviting us to encounter the Divine Reality amid the nuts and bolts of everydayness. Her practical approach generates a breath of fresh air in the stuffy rooms of abstract speculation. She assures us that, if we cleanse the channels of our perception, we will see from alps to insects pointers to God's presence.

MEET THE MASTER

Evelyn Underhill (1875–1941) chose as her mission in life to heal the disharmony between practicality and spirituality. She grew up in a middle-class family in Britain and remembers them as having had no particular interest in religion. Yet she believed that this indifference served to awaken her quest for the depth dimension of the spiritual life, displayed in the imagery and intellectual splendor of the Christian mystical tradition. Visiting a Franciscan convent in 1907 so impressed her that she decided to convert to the faith. Though she felt at first that this decision pointed to joining the Roman Catholic Church, she adhered to her husband's objections and remained with the Church of England. More years would pass before she acknowledged the fullness of her commitment to Christ, but for her, every facet of the journey revealed the poverty of her own will compared to the guidance of the Holy Spirit.

Once she graduated from King's College in London, Underhill became the first woman to attain a lectureship in religion at Oxford University. There she combined her scholarly interests with her skills as a bookbinder and her knack for sailing. Her goal was to link ordinary religious practices to the extraordinary richness of the mystical tradition. For Underhill, the wisdom of the past had to inspire believers in the present. What people professed in their faith tradition had to bear fruit in their everyday formation. There was for her no separation between contemplative living and charitable giving.[1]

Under the guidance of Baron Friedrich von Hügel (1852–1925), her spiritual director, Underhill became one of the main architects of the mystical revival in Western Europe and America following World War I. Among its proponents, in addition to Underhill herself, were C. S. Lewis, Cardinal John Henry Newman, and the Quaker spiritual writer Rufus Jones. Though the ravages of the war had shaken her to the core, she drew strength from her faith and her encounter with the mystics. Until this hellish period of history ended, she relied on the direction of von Hügel to help her unearth the treasures of the faith. She found that the academic world she had entered limited her aspiration to embrace Jesus with childlike candor and to craft a spirituality of adoration and action.

Intriguing to Underhill was the thought, held by the mystics, that reality was both near and far: "far from our thoughts, but saturating and supporting our lives. Nothing would be nearer, nothing dearer, nothing sweeter, were the doors of our perception truly cleansed."[2] For her, at the age of thirty-six, this cleansing process resulted in the publication of what would become her most famous book, *Mysticism* (1911).[3] Soon thereafter she wrote *The Mystic Way* (1913)[4] and published *Practical Mysticism* in 1915. Two decades later, she revealed in her books *Worship* (1936) and *The Spiritual Life* (1937) her lucidity as a gifted spiritual guide and her serenity as a woman who had found the way to combine contemplative composure with selfless compassion.[5]

Though religious studies did not interest Underhill in her college years, that outlook changed dramatically during the sixteen trips she and her mother made to Italy and France. She became intrigued by the Christian art and architecture of the Middle Ages and wondered what prompted such people to produce beauty on this scale. Could she come to understand their faith and its outflow in good works?

In her landmark book, *Mysticism*, she manifested her grasp of Thomistic philosophy and its insistence that grace enlightens and uplifts human nature. Her quest to discover the depth dimension of the soul's longing for intimacy with the Trinity led her to the works of the Flemish mystic Bl. Jan van Ruysbroeck as well to the life and writings of Catherine of Genoa (1447–1510) and Catherine of Siena, both of whom taught her how to embody in works of charity the efficacy of contemplative prayer. She said of this kind of reading and meditative reflection that it was the way to experience how the insights and findings of the communion of saints can be felt by people of all ages seeking union with God.[6]

Toward the end of her life, when she was bed-bound due to chronic asthma and other illnesses, Underhill drew strength from her decision to live in abandonment to the mystery. Without knowing it, she might have written her own eulogy when she said in *Practical Mysticism*, "As to the object of contemplation, it matters little. From Alp to insect, anything will do, provided that your attitude be right: for all things in this world towards which you are stretching out are linked together, and one truly apprehended will be the gateway to the rest" (*PM*, 119).

SPIRITUALITY AS THE KEY TO RENEWED VITALITY

Underhill believed that the presence of the Holy Spirit in our human spirit readies us for ordinary contemplation, characterized not by ecstatic uplifts or blissful departures from the demands of the real world but by acts of charity and self-giving service. She says that it is always false to reduce mysticism to the "status of a spiritual plaything" (*PM*, 12). In her words, contemplation ought not to "wrap its initiates in a selfish and other-worldly calm, [or] isolate them from the pain and effort of the common life. Rather it gives them renewed vitality" (*PM*, 13). A mystical or contemplative outlook on life involves each of us in a spiritual adventure to which the nearest human analogy is the experience of falling in love.

To fall in love with God is to be drawn by grace beyond the mediocrity of a Sunday-only spirituality to the maturity of a life of intimacy with the Divine. According to Underhill, women as diverse as Joan of Arc and Florence Nightingale acted under the same "mystical compulsion" (*PM*,

14). She believes that "their intensely practical energies were the flowers of a contemplative life" (*PM*, 14). In other words, contemplative prayer stills the heart, guards the soul, and liberates us from evil thoughts, words, and actions; it helps us to focus on divine grace, which empowers us to emphasize the virtues and overcome the vices that disrupt our interior life.

Steady growth in presence to the Divine Presence ought not to be equated with an impoverishment of the sense life in favor of a supersensual denial of reality. Underhill warns us to be wary of private mystical experiences, so otherworldly that they lead to the neglect of daily duty. Our active life flourishes when we complement it with contemplative wonder and praise of God, thereby bestowing upon our otherwise routine days a refreshing sense of the Sacred beneficial to everyone we encounter.

According to Underhill, the path to such mature spirituality proceeds through five distinct phases. The first is *awakening*. It signifies a wake-up call to the self to become conscious of the Divine Reality, if only for a brief duration. Awakened in us is a feeling of intense joy that may cause a crisis of separation from the unawakened life we used to live.

What follows this awakening experience and the conversion it evokes is a time of *inner purification*. A spirit of detachment from anyone or anything idolized more than God liberates the soul to pursue union with the Sacred. Essential to this inward movement is the virtue of mortification, or daily dying to our self-will. This discipline has both negative and positive implications. The negative entails stripping away or negating all that is superfluous, illusionary, or distracting. The evangelical counsel pertaining to poverty of spirit entails a deliberate withdrawal of attention from the bewildering multiplicity of things. The positive side of mortification involves a reorientation of our heart in which anything less than God no longer captivates our attention. We begin to form new habits such as surrendering ourselves to God in humility and joy and discovering behind our formerly conflicted life of inordinate attachments a call to freedom from selfish sensuality.

In the third stage of *illumination*, God allows us glimpses of what deeper union with the Really Real might mean. The quality of these revelations varies from person to person. In this game of love (*ludus amoris*) God treats each soul uniquely. Some experience a sense of oneness with nature. Others hear voices or see visions. Still others note only a further solidifying of belief.

What matters to Underhill is that all true lovers of God seek God alone; they do not pursue spiritual phenomena that only point to the Uncreated Light. Illumination assures souls that they are on a quest for the Eternal that will never be satisfied with lesser expressions of transcendence. The illumined soul attunes itself to the calming power of remaining in recollection and inner stillness in presence to the Divine Presence. At this point in the process, our personality is not lost; instead, its hard edges of willfulness and arrogance undergo a notable softening.

Now the soul enters the fourth stage, in which the felt sense of God's nearness vanishes and we must struggle across the desert of inner aridity guided by *pure faith*. As the soul travels toward union, it enters what in classical Christian literature are the dark nights of sense and spirit. We may be assailed by doubts and temptations that arise from within. Consolations cease. Replacing them may be a sense of our nothingness without God. Awareness of our imperfections may be accompanied by a feeling of mental and emotional exhaustion. Those who persevere through this time of testing may enter into the unitive life seen in faith as a gift of God's grace and not the result of any human effort.

The mystical tradition identifies the fifth and final stage of union with God as *spiritual marriage*. The soul, having been plunged into the living flame of love, enters a transformed state characterized by energetic action. Catherine of Siena became a peacemaker between warring papal states, Teresa of Avila reformed her order, and Francis of Assisi rebuilt God's troubled Church. All of the mystics especially meaningful to Underhill from earliest times to the present age led productive lives of love and service. They were living proof of her conviction that *"mysticism is the art of union with Reality. The mystic is a person who has attained that union in a greater or less degree; or who aims at and believes in such attainment"* (PM, 23).

EXPERIENCING UNION WITH THE REAL

In response to the oft-repeated question "What is mysticism?" Underhill answers that it is neither a philosophy nor an illusion nor a kind of religion, and it is certainly not a disease! It does not mean having visions; performing conjuring tricks; leading an idle, dreamy, self-absorbed life; neglecting ordinary business; wallowing in vague spiritual emotions; or posturing a special attunement to the Eternal. It is the art of union with Reality or with the Really Real. It prevents us from reducing life to a series of static routines controlled by our willful efforts to arrange and rearrange the threads that up to now have formed the tapestry of our life. A crisis of transcendence, painful as it may be, lifts us out of this stagnant plane of complacency and places us in a richer world of meaning.

Underhill views us as poised between two orders of reality: being and becoming, eternity and time, unity and multiplicity, and the spiritual and the natural worlds. Contemplatives live in these two orders at one and the same time and try to respond to both of them. They see the seeming disharmony between the parts and the whole as an illusion. Freedom from viewing vital drives and functional ambitions as ends in themselves results in freedom for a transcendent vision of all things in God and of God in all things. One moves from looking at the world through windows coated with the grime of dusty, idle, disintegrated thoughts and narrow self-interests to seeing a new heaven and a new earth (see Rv 21:1).

Underhill reminds us that *recollection* begins with the deliberate and regular practice of *meditation*, or mental prayer. Once we commit ourselves to taking a closer look at the meaning of the beliefs and devotions inherent in our faith tradition, it ought not to surprise us that our undisciplined attention will waver. This back-and-forth swing should not worry us. We must trust that progress is being made and that we are entering a place of fresh perception. We are less inclined to take things for granted. We become as appreciative as children of the wonders of daily life. We feel shame and sorrow for our sins. We are more resourceful in disciplining our attention when it wavers and in renewing our commitment to live in simplicity of heart.

These graced encounters with the Really Real result in a kind of seeing that renders the sense world a theophany of the Most High. We perceive in the many the presence of the One just as Julian of Norwich, gazing upon a hazelnut, found in it the epitome of creation and a pointer to the divine embrace that sustains life.

A shift now occurs from the so-called active effort of our will by means of self-discipline, control of thoughts, and longing love to infused or effortless contemplation. We seek to obey God's will while becoming conscious of the constricting force of our own selfishness. While it may feel as if everything is being taken away, in truth a transformation occurs in which God's action takes the place of our activity. This realization marks the mysterious and life-changing contact between the lover and the Beloved. We are asked to eradicate the last traces of self-interest, even of a spiritual nature, and wait upon what has been given to us in the Eternal Now that bestows upon the world of time its validity and meaning.

As Underhill observes, this graceful rhythm of being and doing adds to, rather than subtracts from, our practical efficiency. Heightened by contemplation is our sensitivity to the abundance of work we have yet to do, such as avoiding the spectacular in favor of the give-and-take of duty and dedication. Underhill summarizes the marks of Christian maturity:

+ *Reading and studying* the classical literature of spirituality, which, in her words, is the way to stretch our spiritual muscles.
+ *Going on retreat* at least once a year.
+ *Being committed to some mode of service* in our familial and faith community and remembering that the test of contemplation is the charity that flows from it.
+ *Not letting the ups and downs of daily life discourage us* and trusting that all shall be well.
+ *Scheduling the spiritual disciplines* of reading, meditation, prayer, and contemplation into our day.
+ *Training ourselves to accept* the unfolding of God's providential plan in the circumstances of our life.
+ *Remaining convinced that there is a reason for everything* and that embedded in every obstacle is a formation opportunity.
+ *Maintaining a balance of body, mind, and spirit*, and trying our best to live a healthy human and Christian life.
+ *Practicing mental prayer and recollection* as if we were "standing back from the whirl of the earth, and observing the process of things" (*PM*, 72–73).
+ *Living in humility*, so that rather than boasting of any success we may have, we remember to thank God for any good we might do.[7]

Underhill witnesses in an exemplary way to what it means to be open to the presence and action of God in our ordinary life and in the whole spectrum of creation. She cautions us not to be entrapped in secularity or to lose our sense of the Sacred. Progress in the spiritual life happens when we recognize the larger horizon against which everything we see points to a deeper meaning. Only then can both our spiritual consciousness and our practical energy be "the flowers of a contemplative life" (*PM*, 14). Only then, "like the blessed one of Dante's vision," can the clearness of the mystic's flame respond "to the unspeakable radiance of the Enkindling Light" (*PM*, 191).

REFLECT NOW

1. How do you resolve the tension between having to live at once in two orders of reality, the temporal and the eternal?
2. How do you respond to the disharmony in your interior life due to sin and selfishness?
3. When the great unknowns of life rush in upon you, are you able to create a ring of silence around yourself in which to ponder their meaning and discern the providential direction God invites you to follow?

READ MORE

Christopher J. R. Armstrong, *Evelyn Underhill (1875–1941): An Introduction to Her Life* (Grand Rapids, MI: Eerdmans, 1975).
Margaret Cropper, *The Life of Evelyn Underhill: An Intimate Portrait of the Groundbreaking Author of "Mysticism"* (Woodstock, VT: First Skylight Paths, 2003).
John Stoffart, *The Wisdom of Evelyn Underhill* (London: A. R. Mowbray, 1951).

28

Let God Lead You to the Dawn of a New Day

THOMAS R. KELLY ON THE LIGHT WITHIN

Eternity is at our hearts, pressing upon our time-torn lives, warming us with intimations of an astounding destiny, calling us home unto Itself. Yielding to these persuasions, gladly committing ourselves in body and soul, utterly and completely, to the Light Within, is the beginning of true life. ... Here is the Slumbering Christ, stirring to be awakened, to become the soul we clothe in earthly form and action. And He is within us all.

    —Thomas R. Kelly, *A Testament of Devotion*, 3

In the silence of a Quaker meetinghouse, Thomas R. Kelly discovered the Light Within. He found that the source of truth he sought resided in the words proclaimed by the psalmist: "Be still, and know that I am God!" (Ps 46:10). He resolved in his personal and professional life to overcome the tension between outer business affairs and the inner longing he felt to follow the Quaker custom of allowing presence to the Divine Presence to permeate every activity.

Into the devotional tapestry he weaves, Kelly threads such essentials of discipleship as following Jesus in holy obedience, simplifying our worship experiences by placing them under the guidance of the Holy Spirit, and treating one another as members of the Mystical Body of Christ. Through the writings of the pre-Reformation master Brother Lawrence of the Resurrection and the post-Reformation mystic Evelyn Underhill, Kelly was able to return to the silent depths of what it means to be formed, reformed, and transformed by Christ.

MEET THE MASTER

Thomas R. Kelly (1893–1941) was born and raised in Ohio, but after his father's death, when he was only four years old, he and his widowed mother moved to the college town of Wilmington, Delaware. There, by dint of her tireless labor and Kelly's own vigilance, he attended Haverford College as an undergraduate and went on to earn his PhD in philosophy at Hartford Theological Seminary. Though he taught initially at Earlham College, he returned to Haverford, teaching there from the age of thirty-six until his death of a heart attack in January of 1941.

Late in the autumn of 1937, he underwent what he named an event of "crushing disappointment." It brought him not to despair, as he thought it would, but into an experience of the Presence that was so powerful he felt melted down by the love of God. Here was a true awakening that prompted him over the next three years to try to describe what had happened to him in a number of Quaker publications that proved to be as prophetic as they were confessional.

A few months after Kelly's death, his editor, Douglas V. Steere, published a selection of his essays in a book he titled *A Testament of Devotion*.[1] Twenty-five years later, his son Richard Kelly published several more of his late father's inspired works under the title *The Eternal Promise*.[2] In both these classics, Kelly confirms the necessity of finding a center of stillness amid the myriad distractions of modern life. The soul converted to Christ can enjoy the lasting peace granted by this inner spiritual journey. In typical Quaker fashion, Kelly challenges us to find the silence that is the source of sound, saying:

> Many of the things we are doing seem so important to us. We haven't been able to say "no" to them, because they seemed so important. But if we center down, as the old phrase goes, and live in that holy Silence which is dearer than life, and take our life program into the silent places of the heart, with complete openness, ready to do, ready to renounce according to his leading, then many of the things we are doing lose their vitality for us. I should like to testify to this, as a personal experience, graciously given. There is a reevaluation of much that we do or try to do, which is done for us, and we know what to do and what to let alone. (*TD*, 95)

The founder of Quakerism, George Fox (1624–1691), lives anew in his modern-day counterpart. Fox, too, excelled in prayer, discovered the Light Within, and taught the Quakers why it is necessary to stand for justice, peace, and mercy in family life, church, and society. Fox's legacy lived on in William Penn's *Charter of Privileges* for Pennsylvania (1681); in John Woolman's condemnation of slaveholding by the Society of Friends (1758); in the first Peace Society in England (1816); and in the establishment of Haverford College (1833) and Swarthmore College (1864). In 1947 the American Friends Service Committee received the Nobel Peace Prize, a culmination of the vision George Fox made a reality.

Kelly acknowledges his indebtedness to Fox for his disclosure of the Light Within, which was their way of identifying the Living Christ. He also drew inspiration from Woolman, the Quaker tailor and author of a famous journal, who taught him how to be about the business of the day while paying attention to his inner life of prayer.[3] Other representatives of his faith tradition who inspired Kelly were Isaac Penington (1616–1679), along with his wife, Mary, both of whom committed themselves to "centering down" and allowing friendship with the Lord to permeate every activity.[4] Kelly cites in his testament the writings of Rufus Jones (1863–1998), author

of the six-volume history of the Religious Society of Friends and a teacher
of philosophy at Haverford College. Jones left such a stamp on Kelly's soul
that he attributes to Jones his notion of the "Double Search," by which the
Father draws his prodigal son home to himself even while his wayward son
wanders in the wilderness, restless and lonely and searching for a "wiser
Shepherd" (*TD*, 25).[5]

What Kelly resisted most was a secular mindset that neglected the
deepest part of us—our religious nature. He drew upon scripture, especially
the psalms, and teachings of the spiritual masters to ensure that he and his
students would keep "close to the foundations of divine creativity ... [to the]
peace and assurances, that are utterly incomprehensible to the secular mind
... bestirred to an outward life of unremitting labor" (*TD*, 9–10).

To uphold the master–disciple relationship, as his teachers of old did,
Kelly surrounded himself with groups of students whom he designated
message bearers. Their lives had to be grounded in ceaseless prayer and in
love and respect for one another. He taught them by example that economic
poverty was a much lesser problem than poverty of spirit, or "deprivation of
God's recreating, loving peace. ... The primary step is a holy life, transformed
and radiant in the glory of God" (*TD*, 99).

Resting in God, Kelly says, is the only way to give meaning to our work.
Without adhering to the Light Within, we labor in vain. For him, as well as
for Dietrich Bonhoeffer, the key to following Jesus is holy obedience. Costly
as it is, only when we take up the crosses he asks us to bear can we enkindle
"embers of faith in the midst of a secular world" (*TD*, 44).

FIVE FACETS OF THE DIAMOND OF DIVINITY

As plainspoken as it is inspirational, Kelly's *Testament* presents in five com-
pelling essays why we need to practice the presence of God and devote
ourselves to the task of doing whatever God asks of us. In the spirit of his
Christian mentors, Kelly experiences prayer as a way of being in conversation with God. Even when we flounder, he assures us: "There is an infinite
fountain of lifting power, pressing within us, luring us by dazzling visions,
and we can only say, the creative God comes into our souls. An increment
of infinity is about us. Holy is imagination, the gateway of Reality into our

hearts. The Hound of Heaven is on our track, the God of Love is wooing us to His Holy Life" (*TD*, 33).

What we find in this short but powerful text are the main tenets of the Quaker tradition—among them, simplicity in forms of worship; opposition to violence; and, above all, faith in the personal and corporate guidance of the Holy Spirit, witnessed in the assembly of believers.

From their beginning in seventeenth-century England through the religious persecutions that led them to the New World, Quakers have treasured the presence of God's Spirit in their hearts and have tried to practice the five themes Kelly summarizes in his *Testament*. It provides an ideal companion to that highest of all human acts—lifelong communion with God.

The Light Within. Deep within us there is an amazing inner sanctuary of the soul, a holy place, a divine center to which we may return. According to Kelly, committing ourselves to the Light Within is the beginning of a mature spiritual life. Our responses to the light vary from internal adoration to pure joy, from thanksgiving to worship, and from self-surrender to obedient action.

To practice this perpetual return to our inner sanctuary is what it means to pray without ceasing. We listen to God with the ears of our heart. We hear God's whispered directives in the depths of our soul. Kelly's advice to us, however distracted we may be, is to "admit no discouragement, but ever return quietly to Him and wait in His Presence" (*TD*, 13).

Holy Obedience. To obey the Inner Voice requires that we proceed in two directions at the same time: we must be detached from the world and yet never lose our concern for the world. As Kelly explains, "The life that intends to be wholly obedient, wholly submissive, wholly listening, is astonishing in its completeness. Its joys are ravishing, its peace profound, its humility the deepest, its power world-shaking, its love enveloping, its simplicity that of a trusting child. It is the life and power in which the prophets and apostles lived. It is the life and power of Jesus of Nazareth. . . . And it is a life and power that can break forth in this tottering Western culture and return the Church to its rightful life as a fellowship of creative, heaven-led souls" (*TD*, 28–29).

Holy listening remains the core of a God-intoxicated life. Some of its imperatives are as follows:

- *Begin where you are:* obey now!
- *Pray silently and steadily* in wordless submission to God. Don't say "I will"; rather, let life be willed through you.
- *Have a passion for personal holiness,* a sense of humility, a God-directed mind.

The simplicity that marks us as children of God is the beginning of Christian adulthood. The lasting fruit of this obedience is the peace that comes to us after the awkward stage of religious activism. The internal simplification of our personality happens when we center down, and live with a singleness of eye from this holy center, at home with God and free from every sliver of anxiety.

The Blessed Community. The fellowship of love we share as Christians guarantees that we will never be alone. Our lives, enveloped as they are by God, have a common meeting point. We are at home with ourselves and with one another. The center of authority that makes a faith community alive resides not in human inventiveness but in God. We believe, says Kelly, that "until the life of men in time is, in every relation, shot through with Eternity, the Blessed Community is not complete" (*TD*, 61). Our entrance to this community of faith is not granted by a certificate we earn; it is a gift given to us by God. When one of us suffers, we all feel the pain; when one of us rejoices, our joy abounds.

The Eternal Now and Social Concern. An experience of the Eternal breaking into time is the ground of every social endeavor. From this point of view, the inward and the outward life are one whole: "Thus in faith we go forward, with breath-taking boldness, and in faith we stand still, unshaken, with amazing confidence. For the time-nows are rooted in the Eternal Now, which is a steadfast Presence, an infinite ocean of light and love which is flowing over the ocean of darkness and death" (*TD*, 80).

The tendency today is to suppose that the religious life must prove its worth insofar as it changes the social order, but time is no judge of the Eternal; rather the Eternal is the judge and tester of time. Given this intersection of heaven and earth, the Christian, as Evelyn Underhill said, must live on two planes of reality at once: in time (*chronos*) and in time as pierced by the Eternal (*kairos*). We must learn to say *no* to what is not of God while saying *yes* to God's will at work in the world. In this way we can be sure that our concerns remain God-oriented and not merely self-initiated. The origin of our actions is not our own efforts but the prevenient grace of God.

Simplification of Life. We tend to think that our lives are complex due to the complexity of the world in which we live. This explanation, ruled as it is by the outward order, leads us to turn to thoughts of life on, let us say, a quiet South Sea Island! We harbor the illusion that escape from reality will guarantee our peace.

Simplification of life does not follow upon simplification of our environment. The real root of our problem lies in the inner condition of our heart. In other words, our outer distraction reflects a lack of inner integration. We try to be several selves doing several tasks at once without any of them being ordered by a single, mastering purpose within us. Chaos results if our life does not flow from and return to its center in God. At every moment, outward affairs must be attentive to a sense of inward order. We must maintain tender love for the Beyond amid the ups and downs of everydayness. Only when we yield to this divine center does our life become simple, serene, and radiant. Even in the fiercest storm, we do not feel frantic. God is at the helm of our ship. The day comes and goes. At nightfall we lie down in peace, asleep at our Lord's feet.

FINDING OUR DEEPEST GROUND IN GOD

Having come through the crucible of suffering in his own life, including bouts with anxiety and depression, Kelly assures us that joys beyond telling await us when we return to that holy center and from there approach every activity. Our greatest joy is to make certain that the life of God is at work in the world. Nothing ought to distract us from this lofty aim. A contemporary Quaker influenced by Kelly tells us that in the united stillness of a truly "gathered" meeting, there is a power, known only by experience, that enables the mysterious to become more familiar. Nearness to the Divine Presence flows from "vessel to vessel" in the quiet presence of fellow worshippers.[6]

Kelly's experience of group worship manifests his love for the "holy hush" that descends over the gathering: "A blanket of divine covering comes over the room, a stillness that can be felt is over all, and the worshipers are gathered into a unity and synthesis of life which is amazing indeed."[7] He speaks of this Presence as a quickening, as a breaking down of the walls of isolated individuality, as a blending of our human spirits with a life-giving Spirit that is beyond us. It enfolds all of us; it nourishes and comforts our souls, arousing once slumbering longings we can no longer deny. As Kelly says, "The Burning Bush has been kindled in our midst, and we stand together on holy ground."[8]

Kelly urges us to develop the habit of orienting ourselves to the Light Within, which he sees as the point of integration of worship and work. No matter how busy we are, we can turn to this inward center in awe and adoration. Simple phrases such as "How great thou art," repeated with love, help us to overcome our lapses in attention. Kelly does not want us to waste time in self-recrimination or useless worry. Even when we are asleep, we can remain alive in God.

The following tenets of Quaker spirituality found in Kelly's works embellish the two-thousand-year treasury of our faith and formation tradition:

+ *Trust the promptings of the Spirit* in your heart and let them seal your maturity in the spiritual life.
+ *Place your being and your doing under the authority* of Jesus Christ.
+ *Take time each day to center down* and sink into the embrace of the Eternal Now.
+ *Stand up against injustice* by witnessing to the peace of Jesus.
+ *Try your best to alleviate unjust conditions* of tyranny, fear, and suppression of freedom.
+ *Live simply* and show loving concern for all creatures.
+ *Foster reverence for life.*
+ *Rejoice* in the splendor of God's gift of creation in and around us.

Kelly successfully articulated the anxiety and strain of modern life because he saw himself as part of it. In "The Simplification of Life," the final essay in *A Testament of Devotion*, he describes how his feverish existence was transformed into a life of joy and serenity. The solution to the habit of trying to do it all is not found in isolating ourselves from what God calls us to do; the remedy Kelly offers to our unintegrated lives is to attend to the Spirit of God within us and submit to the guidance we receive. When we take the many activities that seem important to us down into the center of who we are, we learn to say no for the sake of a greater yes. The solution to activism is not to retreat from life but to contemplate the leadings of God.

Only then can we cultivate a life so hidden with Christ that amid the business of the day we "inwardly [lift] brief prayers, short ejaculations of praise, subdued whispers of adoration and of tender love to the Beyond that is within. . . . One can live in a well-nigh continuous state of unworded prayer, directed toward God, directed toward people and enterprises we have on our heart . . . an inner world of splendor within which we, unworthy, may live. Some of you know it and live in it; others of you may wistfully long for it; it can be yours" (*TD*, 98).

REFLECT NOW

1. Despite the busy life you lead, can you retire to that place within and remain receptive to the "divine breathing" (*TD*, 9)?
2. What happens when you let go of anxiety and unrest and walk hand in hand with the Lord?
3. Do you believe that an infinite ocean of light and love flows over the rough waves of darkness and death? Are you free enough to share this belief with others?

READ MORE

J. Brent Bill, *Holy Silence: The Gift of Quaker Spirituality* (Grand Rapids: Eerdmans, 2016).

Gleanings: Selected Writings of Douglas V. Steere (Nashville, TN: The Upper Room, 1986).

D. Elton Trueblood, *The People Called Quakers* (New York: Harper's, 1966).

29

TAKE UP YOUR CROSS
AND FOLLOW JESUS

DIETRICH BONHOEFFER ON
THE COST OF DISCIPLESHIP

Christianity without the living Christ is inevitably Christianity without discipleship, and Christianity without discipleship is always Christianity without Christ.
—Dietrich Bonhoeffer, *The Cost of Discipleship*, 63–64

In *The Cost of Discipleship*, Dietrich Bonhoeffer restates the truth of St. Paul's teaching: "If we live, we live to the Lord, and if we die, we die to the Lord; so then, whether we live or whether we die, we are the Lord's" (Rom 14:8). He resisted the Nazi culture of death, even at the cost of his own life.

To read his writings is to be confronted by such unavoidable questions as *What in my life do I still refuse to surrender to the Lord? What must I do to let the yes of Jesus to the Father be the guiding light of my life? Do I have the courage to forfeit my life on earth for the sake of my eternal salvation?*

MEET THE MASTER

Dietrich Bonhoeffer (1906–1945), a native of Breslau, Germany, a Lutheran pastor, and a zealous opponent of Nazi tyranny, stands with other missionary martyrs such as St. Maximilian Kolbe (1894–1941) and St. Edith Stein (1891–1942), who gave their lives in defense of the faith. All understood what it meant to respond without reservation to the life-changing power of Christ's call, cast away fear, and accept the duty asked of them as his disciples.

Paying the cost of discipleship was at the forefront of Bonhoeffer's life's work and legacy. He began by distinguishing three groups of would-be disciples. The first group rush to follow Jesus without being called and end up not knowing what they are doing or why what they do does not bear lasting fruit. The second group makes lists of what they must attend to before they obey the Master's call. They place their business before his invitation to the banquet. The third group listens to the Lord and then takes the initiative, assuming that their plans are surely better than his and that they can stipulate the terms of discipleship. The cost of the Cross is not their first consideration; reducing discipleship to the level of human management is.[1]

True disciples follow a different path. As soon as they say yes to Jesus, they know they will have to leave their previous existence behind them. The old situation has departed; the new knocks at their door. The first cost of the Cross is this drastic relinquishment of how we used to be and of what we used to do. We enter not the first stage of a new career but an entirely new life. Obedience to the call defies human understanding, but it evokes no resistance, only a peace and joy the world cannot give. The call, once assented to, may lead us to places we never anticipated; having the Master at our side is enough for us. Our only thought is to be faithful to his call, all the way to the foot of the Cross (see *Cost*, 66–69).

While Bonhoeffer could have excelled as a professor in any academic arena, he chose the road less traveled in obedience to his divine destiny. He earned a doctor of theology degree at the University of Berlin at the age of twenty-one, graduating summa cum laude. Shortly thereafter, in 1930–1931, he traveled by invitation to the Union Theological Seminary in New York City, where, in addition to his teaching, he ministered at the Abyssinian Baptist Church in Harlem.

Early in his ministry, he became involved in ecumenical activity in both England and America, but the situation in his home country reinforced his decision to resist the destructive forces of fascism engulfing Europe. National Socialism propagated a heinous ideology of pseudoscientific racism, anti-Semitism, and totalitarianism. Doctors, lawyers, military officers, and certain ministers strove to propagate and implement its version of racial purity that would lead during World War II to the "Final Solution"—the extermination of six million Jews.

Bonhoeffer returned to Europe, serving German-speaking congregations in London from 1933 to 1935, where he came under the influence of Bishop George Bell of Chichester and his Anglican religious community. He returned to Germany to lead a preachers' seminary in Finkenwalde and to form a faith group (House of the Brethren) around it. Had he stayed abroad, he might have assured his own safety, but that was an option he never entertained. God led him in due time to become a leader in the Confessing Church and to take a stand against the fanatical anti-Semitism that kept the Nazi Party in power. By the mid-1930s Adolf Hitler and his followers were well on the way to subduing Poland and other neighboring lands and to promoting an ever-vaster network of propaganda and raw power.

Forbidden by the Nazis in 1936 to teach, Bonhoeffer decided to accept several lecture tours in America. He stayed among friends and colleagues until the war broke out in 1939. That was the decisive year he refused a teaching post in America in the belief that it was his duty to return to Germany and suffer with his people. Only then, when the war was over, did he feel he would have earned the right to take part in rebuilding Germany. Little did he realize that he would do so with his own blood. Despite the duress of being spied on constantly, after his return to Germany he continued to teach in the underground seminary in Finkenwalde. There he offered spiritual direction to the students and wrote his book *Life Together* (1938), in which he describes the essentials of Christian community.[2]

Influenced by the Lutheran theologian Karl Barth (1886–1968), who declared that only Jesus is Lord of the Church, not Hitler, Bonhoeffer decided at great personal peril to work with associates in the intelligence services to try to overthrow the dictator and his widespread reign of terror. He helped as many Jews and Christians as he could find safe havens and escape deportation to concentration camps while encouraging friends, family members, and colleagues not to lose hope. He wrote numerous letters on a wide range of spiritual, theological, and ethical issues. His refusal to compromise his beliefs brought him to the attention of the secret police, who arrested him in 1943. Bonhoeffer spent the remaining two years of his life in various Gestapo prisons. For him there would be no escape. He was executed at Flossenbürg on April 9, 1945, at the age of thirty-nine. A doctor who witnessed his death told a friend of Bonhoeffer's that he saw him kneeling on the floor of his cell praying fervently. When led to the place of execution, he uttered a brief prayer and climbed the steps to the gallows, standing tall, brave, and composed. He died within seconds, submissive, as this witness reported, not to his executioners but to the merciful love of God.

PAYING THE PRICE OF FOLLOWING CHRIST

Bonhoeffer tried in person and through his correspondence to fight against the evils of fascism and to enkindle the spiritual ideals represented by the Confessing Church. He encouraged his students never to allow the enemy to strip them of their Christian convictions. Unbeknownst to him, his letters and other works, once collected and published, would influence the postwar development of theology in Europe and the Americas. His teachings on prayer, on discipleship, on "costly grace," and on the necessarily prophetic role of the Christian community brought to light the treachery of accommodating the eternal truths of the Gospel to temporal points of view.

In *The Cost of Discipleship*, Bonhoeffer confirms that Christ must be not only the center of our personal life but also the epicenter of human history. Only in the light of the Incarnation can past, present, and future ages be interpreted. Christ's Word must be accepted in faith, pondered in hope, and embodied in love. Only then can we fulfill the divine commission to keep his presence alive in the community and in the Church.

The mark of honor Bonhoeffer left on postwar Christianity proves that radical obedience to the Word made flesh must never be compromised. Though the evils of Nazism cost him his life, Bonhoeffer witnessed to the lordship of Christ that in the end crushed the false gods of Blood, Soil, and Volk, promulgated by the Nazi Party. Adherence to Christ, not an abstract

Christology, was for him the cornerstone of discipleship. However efficacious doctrinal systems on subjects of grace or the forgiveness of sins may be, they render the following of Christ superfluous unless we accept the call to be a witness to the truth of the Gospel, even to the point of martyrdom. No amount of religious knowledge can replace personal obedience. As he says:

> The actual call of Jesus and the response of single-minded obedience have an irrevocable significance. By means of them Jesus calls people into an actual situation where faith is possible. For that reason his call is an actual call and he wishes it so to be understood, because he knows that it is only through actual obedience that a man can become liberated to believe. (*Cost*, 91–92)

LIVING IN RADICAL FAITH

Bonhoeffer's belief in the Word of God suffused all that he did, wrote, and suffered. From this depth of radical adherence to Gospel truth came the wisdom and vision that enabled him to ponder and practice a life of prayer, virtue, and discipleship, characterized by constancy of mind and persistency of purpose, by compassion for suffering humanity, and by a commitment to pursue the good whatever the cost. Worldly fame held no attraction for him. The disciple of Jesus had to be willing, as he was, to follow Christ under the humiliating sign of the Cross.

He expresses this ideal in his *Letters and Papers from Prison*.[3] Remarkable among them is the letter he wrote to his dear friend, Eberhard Bethge, from Tegel prison, shortly before his death. In it, he describes *metanoia*, or ongoing conversion of heart, as the living proof of how radical our faith must be. In this letter, dated July 21, 1944, he tells his friend:

> I remember a conversation that I had in America thirteen years ago with a young French pastor. We were asking ourselves quite simply what we wanted to do with our lives. He said he would like to become a saint (and I think it's quite likely that he did become one). At the time I was very

impressed, but I disagreed with him, and said, in effect, that I should like to learn to have faith. For a long time I didn't realize the depth of the contrast. I thought I could acquire faith by trying to live a holy life, or something like it. . . .

I discovered later, and I'm still discovering right up to this moment, that it is only by living completely in this world that one learns to have faith. One must completely abandon any attempt to make something of oneself, whether it be a saint, or a converted sinner, or a churchman (a so-called priestly type!), a righteous man or an unrighteous one, a sick man or a healthy one. . . . In so doing we throw ourselves completely into the arms of God, taking seriously, not our own sufferings, but those of God in the world— watching with Christ in Gethsemane. That, I think, is faith; that is *metanoia*; and that is how one becomes a man and a Christian. (*LPP*, 369–70)

Following this letter, Bonhoeffer penned a poem in four stanzas that has come to be seen as his final legacy:

STATIONS ON THE ROAD TO FREEDOM

Discipline

If you set out to seek freedom, then learn above all things
to govern your soul and your senses, for fear that your passions
and longing may lead you away from the path you should follow.
Chaste be your mind and your body, and both in subjection,
obediently, steadfastly seeking the aim set before them;
only through discipline may a man learn to be free.

Action

Daring to do what is right, not what fancy may tell you,
valiantly grasping occasions, not cravenly doubting—
freedom comes only through deeds, not through thought taking
    wing.
Faint not nor fear, but go out to the storm and the action,
trusting in God whose commandment you faithfully follow;
freedom, exultant, will welcome your spirit with joy.

Suffering

A change has come indeed. Your hands, so strong and active,
are bound; in helplessness now you see your action
is ended; you sigh in relief, your cause committing
to stronger hands; so now you may rest contented.
Only for one blissful moment could you draw near to touch
    freedom;
then, that it might be perfected in glory, you gave it to God.

Death

Come now, thou greatest of feasts on the journey to freedom
    eternal;
death, cast aside all the burdensome chains, and demolish
the walls of our temporal body, the walls of our souls that are
    blinded,
so that at last we may see that which here remains hidden.
Freedom, how long we have sought thee in discipline, action,
    and suffering;
dying, we now may behold thee revealed in the Lord. (*LPP*,
    370–71)

Bonhoeffer names discipline, action, suffering, and death as the four steps to freedom. The discipline inherent in discipleship sets us free from the illusion of self-sufficiency. We accept in humility that we can only meet the demands of daily duty when we forget about success or failure and cast ourselves into the outstretched arms of the Crucified. Jesus took upon himself the sufferings of the world, and what are our sufferings compared to his?

RELYING ON COSTLY GRACE

Self-stripping is a gift of grace given to us by God to disclose the poverty of our existence and to prove once and for all that without God we can do nothing. To understand this depth of humility, Bonhoeffer articulated the difference between "cheap grace" and "costly grace":

Cheap grace is the preaching of forgiveness without
requiring repentance, baptism without church discipline,

Communion without confession, absolution without personal confession. Cheap grace is grace without discipleship,
grace without the cross, grace without Jesus Christ, living
and incarnate.

Costly grace is the treasure hidden in the field; for the
sake of it a man will gladly go and sell all that he has. . . . It
is the kingly rule of Christ, for whose sake a man will pluck
out the eye which causes him to stumble. It is the call of
Jesus Christ at which the disciple leaves his nets and follows
him. (*Cost*, 47)

Even if this act of love meant forfeiting his life, Bonhoeffer pledged to
follow Christ to the end of his days. He would do so with joy, availing himself of the grace that condemns sin and justifies the sinner. After all, "God
did not reckon his Son too dear a price to pay for our life, but delivered him
up for us. Costly grace is the incarnation of God" (*Cost*, 48).

The outcome of the good we do is not under our control because costly
grace leads us where we would not go. It calls us out of death to self to a new
life of obedience so that we "can become liberated to believe" (*Cost*, 92). To
follow this call is to be moved beyond everything our life used to be. It may
only be comprehensible to us in its incomprehensibility.

SUFFERING AT THE FOOT OF THE CROSS

To follow Jesus is to forsake our old life and the security it purported to
guarantee and to surrender to the inevitable insecurity of fellowship with
the Lord and the community of believers, who cherish and embody his
model of sacrificial love.

In his book *Life Together*, Bonhoeffer tells us what Christian community is and is not. He notes with certainty that "by sheer grace God will not
permit us to live in a dream world even for a few weeks and to abandon
ourselves to those blissful experiences and exalted moods that sweep over
us like a wave of rapture. For God is not a God of emotionalism, but the
God of truth."[4]

Ever the disciple, Bonhoeffer decries "religionless Christianity" as a replacement for the living God, who demands of us sacrificial lives of love and service. He says, "If we refuse to take up our cross and [refuse to] submit to suffering and rejection at the hands of men, we forfeit our fellowship with Christ and have ceased to follow him. But if we lose our lives in his service and carry our cross, we shall find our lives again in the fellowship of the cross with Christ. The opposite of discipleship is to be ashamed of Christ and his cross and all the offence which the cross brings in its train" (*Cost*, 101).

Union with the suffering of Jesus changes our life on every level. That is why, for Bonhoeffer, Christianity without the living Christ is the reverse of discipleship. It remains an abstract idea, not a living relationship so intense and wondrous that it becomes transforming to the highest degree: "To go one's way under the sign of the cross is not misery and desperation, but peace and refreshment for the soul, it is the highest joy. Then we do not walk under our self-made laws and burdens, but under the yoke of him who knows us and who walks under the yoke with us. Under his yoke we are certain of his nearness and communion. It is he whom the disciple finds as he lifts up his cross" (*Cost*, 103).

To lift up our crosses, we must be willing to ask if there is some part of our life that we still refuse to surrender to Christ—some sinful passion, animosity, expectation, ambition, or any other reason. According to Bonhoeffer, the main mark of Christian maturity is to learn the meaning of obedience by letting go of the inordinate attachments that prevent our flight to freedom. Progress means to stop academic discussions about the meaning of the call of the Lord and to become "partakers in the perfect joy and bliss of fellowship with him" (*Cost*, 101). Then we are ready to be sent forth as ambassadors for Christ, as messengers of the mystery of suffering love in small matters as well as in life-changing ones. Then no prison can hold our spirit in bondage; then no loss of earthly fame and fortune can erode our commitment to live and die as true disciples of the Lord because we believe with undying certitude that "beside Jesus nothing has any significance. He alone matters" (*Cost*, 63).

Throughout *The Cost of Discipleship*, Bonhoeffer names several steps to follow if we want to become mature disciples of the Master. They include the following:

- *Leaving the security of our comfort zone* to seek fellowship with Christ, to rise up and follow him in an act of radical obedience.

- *Letting the call of discipleship lend meaning* to all that we are and do, knowing that this costly existence has a quality of its own, which may lead us where we would not have chosen to go.

- *Being willing to ask life-changing questions* such as, "Is there some part of my life which I refuse to surrender at Christ's behest, some sinful passion, some animosity, some expectation, perhaps my ambition or my reason?"

- *Refusing to keep control* of some part of our life or to absolve ourselves from what we know in our heart to be wrong.

Discipleship discloses the poverty of our existence; it prepares us for radical detachment from all that separates us from God and draws us to an intimate relationship with the Divine Master, who alone can satisfy our spiritual hunger. Human hungers pale in comparison to our hunger for God. That is why a disciple as true as Bonhoeffer was has to forsake his old life with its relative security and surrender to the inevitable insecurity of following Jesus.

REFLECT NOW

1. Are you willing to pay the cost of discipleship?
2. How would you explain the difference between cheap grace and costly grace?
3. Why is it that Christianity can never be understood without adherence to the Cross?

READ MORE

Stephen R. Haynes, *The Bonhoeffer Phenomenon: Portraits of a Protestant Saint* (Minneapolis: Fortress Press, 2004).

Eric Metaxas, *Bonhoeffer: Pastor, Martyr, Prophet, Spy* (Nashville, TN: Thomas Nelson, 2010).

Elizabeth Raum, *Dietrich Bonhoeffer: Called by God* (London: Burns and Oates, 2002).

30

FOSTER THE CONNECTION BETWEEN SANCTITY AND SERVICE

THOMAS MERTON ON INTEGRATING CONTEMPLATION AND ACTION

I have got in the habit of walking up and down under the trees or along the wall of the cemetery in the presence of God. And yet I am such a fool that I can consent to imagine that in some other situation I would quickly advance to a high degree of prayer. If I went anywhere else I would almost certainly be much worse off than here. And anyway, I did not come here for myself but for God. God is my order and my cell. He is my religious life and my rule. He has disposed everything in my life in order to draw me inward, where I can see Him and rest in Him. He has put me in this place because He wants me in this place, and if He ever wants to put me anywhere else, He will do so in a way that will leave no doubt as to who is doing it.

—Thomas Merton, *The Sign of Jonas*, 22

As a man of prodigious learning, Thomas Merton drew upon the wisdom of the two-thousand-year treasury of Christian classics, and as a monk and a spiritual master he chose for his main work contemplative prayer. He struggled, as we do, to find the balance between too much work and not enough prayer, on the one hand, and too much prayer and not enough work on the other. He concluded that if we allow God to draw us inward, we will be made ready to serve him anywhere.

Our false self causes a split between being and doing; our true self heals it. Merton had to learn the rhythm of going off to a quiet place to pray and returning to ministry without losing the peace of contemplation. One moment he engages in spiritual reading, the next he plows a field. Each activity is edifying in the eyes of God, since God is the center of everything.

Merton wants us to open our eyes to see that in tedious chores there is mystical depth and that we must never confine contemplative life to a cloister. Why do we persist in living in airtight compartments when we are immersed in a mercy beyond telling? Why is it so hard for us to discover Christ in new and unexpected places? Are we willing to submit ourselves unconditionally to the Master? Do we want him to free us from the prison of ego-centricity? Can we accept the paradox that self-emptying is the surest pathway to self-fulfillment?

In seeking the answers to these questions, Merton assures us that transformation begins in the hermitage of our heart and that true power can only be found in the powerlessness of the Cross.

MEET THE MASTER

The Sign of Jonas is the journal in which Thomas Merton details the first five years of his life in the monastery of Gethsemani; he reveals in it his quest to integrate contemplation ("draw me inward") and action ("put me anywhere").[1]

To appreciate the depth of his conversion, we need to return to his biography before the thought of becoming a monk even crossed his mind. Thomas Merton (1915–1968) was born in Prades in southern France at the outbreak of World War I. His father was from New Zealand, his mother from the United States. Throughout his upbringing, he enjoyed a cosmo-politan background, being educated first in French schools, later in English ones, including Cambridge University. In his best-selling autobiography, *The Seven Storey Mountain,* he depicts the loneliness he felt as a young man when he left Europe and went to New York to find himself.[2] There he took the decisive step to stop testing life's borders and to enter the Roman Catholic Church. Despairing of a world at war and seeking the meaning of life, he concluded that the most fitting outcome of his conversion would be the bold step to leave behind the society that had nearly swallowed him like Jonas, the prophet, in the belly of the whale and enter the Trappist monastery at Gethsemani, Kentucky. He did so in 1941 with the full intention of follow-ing the Benedictine ideal (see chapter 6 herein) of *ora et labora,* worship and work, for the rest of his life.

As much as he wanted to lose himself in God, he admitted suffering from a desire to be noticed, to be a somebody rather than a nobody. Of the various conflicts in his life, none was more burdensome to him than that between silence and speaking. Yet he believed the Trappist abbey to be a place that probably kept the universe from falling apart. There he found him-self in the court of the Queen of Heaven, albeit with a growing awareness of his own shortcomings and those of his fellow monks. He details these experiences in journals and books, ranging from the theological depth of *The Ascent to Truth* to the depiction of his spiritual struggles in, for example, *Contemplation in a World of Action, No Man Is an Island,* and *The Seeds of Contemplation.*[3]

His interest in the dialogue between Buddhism and Christianity led him to Bangkok and the meeting with God for which he longed. He died there accidentally on December 10, 1968, electrocuted due to a faulty lamp in his room. The date of his passing was the anniversary of his monastic profession in 1941. In a passage from *The Sign of Jonas,* he speaks of God as "mercy within mercy within mercy," picturing a Russian matryoshka doll: to open one is to find the surprise of another nestled within it (*Sign,* 362).

Merton loved to meet with his fellow monks, with friends near and far, and with strangers. He welcomed into his circle mentors, artists, poets, and photographers, all of whom shed light on the mystery of the presence and absence of God, of the dying and rising of Christ. He enjoyed the way they broke open the shell of God's words for eternal seekers of truth like him; their work revealed to him the face of our Merciful Maker, always present and ready to embrace souls as wayward as his own, whether in the solitude of his cell or with the community reciting the Divine Office. It was his library of mystics and spiritual masters that guided him from falsehood to truth.[4] In these writings from ancient times onward, he found proof of the twofold movement that marked the deepest rhythm of his life: from the ebb of contemplation to the flow of action in service to the sons and daughters of God.

In the celebration of the Eucharist, in praying the psalter, and in his disciplined delving into the great traditions of Christianity, Merton found not only himself but also "the Priest who is the Center of the soul of every priest, shaking the foundations of the universe and lifting up—me, Host, altar, sanctuary, people, church, abbey, forest, cities, continents, seas, and worlds to God and plunging everything into Him" (*Sign*, 189).

THE RIGHT RHYTHM OF SPIRITUAL LIVING

Integrating contemplation and action is a pervasive theme in the life and writings of Thomas Merton. For instance, on the feast of St. Benedict, March 21, 1950, on a day like any other in the monastery, he writes, "I am sitting on a pile of lumber by the ruins of the old horse barn. There is a beautiful blue haze in the sky beyond the enclosure wall, eastward and over the brow of the hill. There is going to be a new garden there, and I see the furrows Frater Nehemias has been plowing with the John Deere tractor. I guess I will stop and read Origen" (*Sign*, 293).

The emphasis, even in a short passage such as this, is on how we humans in the ordinary course of daily life can remain open to the mystery disclosed in tedious chores and in a text of great mystical depth. How can we be united to one another as members of the Body of Christ, in service of Church and society? Merton refused to confine contemplative life to the cloister; it was for him an awakening to the presence of God in and around us. We are not total strangers confined to separate compartments of life but sons and daughters of God, who blankets all of us with mercy beyond telling. He writes on March 3, 1950:

The Christian life—and especially the contemplative life—
is a continual discovery of Christ in new and unexpected
places. And these discoveries are sometimes most profitable
when you find Him in something you had tended to overlook and even despise. Then the awakening is purer and its
effect more keen, because He was so close at hand and you
neglected Him. I am ashamed that it has taken me so long
to discover Him. (*Sign*, 282)

The central message of Merton's spirituality is that our life is a continuous seeking and finding of God that we might share God's love with others.
We submit ourselves to the Master for the sake of letting him work in us
despite our limits. When he entered the monastic life, Merton did not realize
that being a monk and a mystic was not being more than what he was before
but realizing that there was to be nothing left of him but God. The prayer of
abandonment freed him from the prison of ego-centeredness and widened
his understanding of the truth that ascetical self-emptying was the surest
pathway to mystical self-fulfillment: "By giving up what I wanted I ended
up by having more than I had thought of wanting" (*Sign*, 343).

Realization of our true self begins when our false self faces its inherent
vulnerability and dissolves as if it were a bad dream.[5] For Merton this meant
that instead of being overly concerned with experiences and techniques of
prayer, he had to grow in the grace of seeing things in God as they really
are, from the crucifix in the chapel to the furrows in a newly plowed field.

Contemplative seeing reveals all of life as coming from God, held in
being, and bound to return to God. There is a flow from supplication to
service, from solitude to solidarity. Merton saw the monastery as the place
in which he could disappear from the world as the ultimate source of fulfillment so that he could in his hiddenness and by the power of his prayer
be everywhere help was needed: "The important thing is not to live for
contemplation but to live for God" (*Sign*, 30). Solitude taught him to love
others for who they were, not for any satisfaction he might receive from his
encounters with them.

As Merton grew in the understanding of his vocation, he saw that "the
speech of God is silence. His word is solitude . . . we are travelers from the
half-world of language into solitude and infinity . . . yet there is a return from

solitude, to make manifest His name to them who have not known it. Then to re-enter solitude and dwell in silence" (*Sign*, 267–68). These essentials of his cloistered life taught Merton to love his brothers and sisters by participating "in the solitariness of God." Solitude marks a withdrawal "from an artificial and fictional level of being which men, divided by original sin, have fabricated in order to keep peace with concupiscence and death" (*Sign*, 269). Thus the solitary, the monk in all of us, must find our way to union with God in the hermitage of our heart and then transform the world, brick by brick, into the house of God.

Merton's spirituality drew him to the conclusion that he had "no time to be anything but a contemplative or a teacher of the contemplative life. . . . There is nothing left for me but to live fully and completely in the present, praying when I pray, and writing and praying when I write, and worrying about nothing but the will and glory of God, finding these as best I can in the sacrament of the present moment" (*Sign*, 270).

OVERCOMING OBSTACLES TO CONTEMPLATION

Merton teaches us the freeing truth that contemplation is the work of the Holy Spirit acting in our souls through the gifts of wisdom and understanding that increase our love for God and neighbor and that draw us to the joy only union with God can grant. In the epilogue to *The Sign of Jonas*, he hears the voice of God say to him, "*What was fragile has become powerful. I loved what was most frail. I looked upon what was nothing. I touched what was without substance, and within what was not, I am*" (*Sign*, 362).

For Merton, infused contemplation is not a matter of receiving extraordinary gifts that pass as swiftly as they are bestowed by grace but the means God uses to increase our love for him that we may nourish the human and Christian needs of others. This deep and intimate knowledge of God by means of the union of love is received on earth, but it will never be understood fully until we gaze on the face of God in the life to come.

What feeds our soul here is the desire to know God as we are known. It is to give up our yearning for things that can never satisfy us so that we are free to pursue the one and only good that can bring rest to our restless hearts. Merton wants us to see that the greatest obstacle to contemplation and its beneficial fruits is the foolish and willful decision to keep our distance from God, forgetting that he is mercy, not cruelty, and that he has "forgiven the universe without end" (*Sign*, 362).

What starves our interior life are routine exercises of piety, external acts of worship, begrudging moments of service, and the avoidance of sin not out of love of God but from the fear of violating a moral duty. We bow to God as an impersonal commander, but our heart does not belong to him as would that of a disciple to a beloved master. We focus on reward and punishment, but our real concern is for the fulfillment of our own ambitions, the cessation of troubles, and the increase of worldly pleasure. We let God into this circle of concern to resolve difficulties and dispense rewards but not to crush our false self so that we can find our true self in the mind and heart of God.

The proof of love, the decisive factor, that distinguishes the mystic from the mediocre Christian is, according to Merton, total and uncompromising docility to the will of God. Merton finds this passageway to spiritual maturity in the five vows he made at the time of his profession: "poverty, chastity, obedience, stability, and conversion of manners" (*Sign*, 9). To make and keep these vows strengthens the monk to consecrate his life to God; they deliver him from the cares and illusions that beset him in the world. What they demand is the bedrock of the spirituality of Thomas Merton: complete self-renunciation. His life had to be hidden in Christ if he were to be chosen to embrace the whole of life and give witness to the freedom only trust in the providential action of God can grant. That is why he shares his conviction that the "life of every monk, of every priest, of every Christian is signed with the sign of Jonas, because we all live by the power of Christ's resurrection. But I feel that my own life is especially sealed with this great sign, which baptism and monastic profession and priestly ordination have burned into the roots of my being" (*Sign*, 11).

FOSTERING CONDITIONS THAT FACILITATE UNION WITH GOD

Merton reminds us that we must allow God to take possession of our intellect, memory, and will and to guide them according to his plan. This kind of practical mysticism echoes the teaching of Evelyn Underhill, who holds that

God graces us where we are while giving us a taste of the supernatural order characterized by those in-breaking moments designated by the mystics as infused contemplation. This life of virtue finds its root system in humility, detachment, and obedience, the windows on reality that make us attentive to what pleases God and what happens when we abandon ourselves to him. Merton discovers that "what monks most need is not conferences on mysticism but more light about the ordinary virtues, whether they be faith or prudence, charity or temperance, hope or justice or fortitude. And above all what they need and what they desire is to penetrate the Mystery of Christ and to know Him in His Gospels and in the whole Bible" (*Sign*, 337).

In *The Sign of Jonas*, Merton makes note of seven marks of his own journey to a Christ-centered life. He says (1) that he ought to be grateful for his attraction to prayer and remain quiet before the tabernacle; (2) that he ought to try to understand mystical writers such as the Flemish master Jan van Ruysbroeck and continue to read him; (3) that he ought to teach contemplation to other people and try to convince them how accessible it is, provided they exercise generosity and strive for sanctity; (4) that he must remember that his love for silence does not mean he has to leave the monastery and pursue his vocation as a Carthusian; (5) that he has to learn to profit from the crosses Jesus sends him in connection, for example, with adverse criticism; (6) that he needs to focus more on the joy it gives Jesus to see him acting out of love and doing good for others; and (7) that he must continue his devotion to spiritual reading as a means to discern what is and what is not God's will for him (see *Sign*, 20).

Such marks of growing in Christ offer lessons for every disciple. Blinded though we may be by the effects of original sin, the light of God's love shines on our soul, clarifying the fault lines in our character and preparing us for a life courageous enough to embrace the Cross and to be born anew in the depths of our being: "You are found in communion: Those in me and I in Thee and Thou in them and they in me . . . the Father and I are One" (*Sign*, 362).

Though we may feel afflicted and defeated, as Merton often did, we need not be afraid. God is as near to us in aridity as he is in awe. Mysteriously, we find light inaccessible in this night of pure faith, united with the living God no earthly explanation can exhaust. The darkness remains dark, yet it seems brighter than the day. We may not know where the road leads, but we have no urgency to abandon it.

Directed by Holy Providence, we undertake the works God entrusts to us; we allow God, through the graces of active contemplation and contemplation in action, to use us to offer others the help they need and to give them a taste of the eternity they seek. As Merton concludes:

> When your tongue is silent, you can rest in the silence of the forest. When your imagination is silent, the forest speaks to you, tells you of its unreality and of the Reality of God. But when your mind is silent, then the forest suddenly becomes magnificently real and blazes transparently with the Reality of God; for now I know that the Creation which first seems to reveal Him, in concepts, then seems to hide Him, by the same concepts, finally *is revealed in Him*, in the Holy Spirit; and we who are in God find ourselves united, in Him, with all that springs from Him. This is prayer, and this is glory! (*Sign*, 343)

REFLECT NOW

1. When obstacles stand in the way of your trying to pray with a recollected mind and heart, what conditions help you not to be overcome by them?
2. What must you do to be more faithful to the practice of contemplative prayer?
3. If devotional reading of the Bible and the Christian classics has become an important part of your life, what can you do to encourage the same practices in the lives of others?

READ MORE

Richard Cashen, *Solitude in the Thought of Thomas Merton* (Kalamazoo, MI: Cistercian Publications, 1981).

Patricia Hart and Jonathan Montaldo, eds., *The Intimate Merton: His Life from His Journals* (New York: Harper, 1999).

Victor A. Kramer, *Thomas Merton: Monk and Artist* (Kalamazoo, MI: Cistercian Publications, 1984).

EPILOGUE

Through the writings of the holy men and women featured in this book, we have discovered many treasures that, taken together, comprise a veritable feast of faith deepening. The thirty masters I have chosen to reflect upon offer choice morsels on the table of formation wisdom spread before us from ancient to modern times. From whatever place setting we view this table, it inspires us to deepen our spiritual life and to let go of whatever hinders the forming, reforming, and transforming power of grace in our lives. No matter where we sit, we acknowledge that this feast verifies the necessity of openness to the inspiration of the Holy Spirit, profound surrender to the grace and providence of God, and the willingness to incarnate the guidance we receive in the mundane trials and tasks of daily life.

Not represented here, but of great importance in any collection of wisdom literature, are the works of mystics and spiritual masters from the Dominican school, such as St. Thomas Aquinas, and from the English school, such as Richard Rolle and Walter Hilton. The Rhineland school, with Hadewijch; and the French school, with John Eudes and Jean-Baptiste de La Salle, merit our attention, as do the earlier classics emanating from the Ignatian school of spirituality, starting with the founder of the Jesuits, St. Ignatius of Loyola.

What, then, have we learned that we want to take away with us from the table and treasure forever? Here is a brief summary of these timeless and timely themes that feed our hungry souls:

1. **The Desert Tradition.** We may not be able to flee to an actual desert, but we can retire in stillness to the hermitage of our heart, to that quiet place that frees us to encounter the Divine Presence and grow in compassion.

2. **Evagrius Ponticus.** On the battlefield in our heart where virtue contends with vice, we should strive for *apatheia*, or liberation from the passions that have dominated our lives.

3. **Gregory of Nyssa.** Thanks to our orientation to the transcendent, we are constantly being drawn upward to God. The spiritual life is a

never-ending journey of ascent toward God. Because of our limited human condition, we never arrive but are always arriving.

4. **Augustine of Hippo.** Experience confirms that our heart is restless until it rests in God. The treasure we seek awaits within us. To experience there the dwelling place of the Lord, we must counter pride with humility and allow our hearts to be broken open by the reality of God.

5. **John Cassian.** To pray unceasingly, we must keep the thought of God always in our mind while humbly asking the Lord under all circumstances to hasten to our rescue. In this way, we move from merely saying prayers to *becoming* living prayer.

6. **Benedict of Nursia.** None of us want to live a split existence: worship on Sunday, and then for the rest of the week work, work, work. We long to live the holy and holistic life crafted in the Rule of St. Benedict by integrating contemplation and action, *ora et labora.* Humility is key to the life of Christian maturity that is essential for discipleship.

7. **Pseudo-Dionysius.** Despite all we know, we really know so little. It is good for us to be drawn into the way of unknowing and to remain silent before the mystery—caught up in awe of the ultimately indescribable essence of God.

8. **John Climacus.** Step by step, we ascend toward the summit of Christian life: contemplative union with God. Every vice we reject reveals the depths of self-deception and the subtle ways in which we try to escape the consequences of sin. Every virtue we cultivate leads us upward and onward in conformity to Christ.

9. **Maximus the Confessor.** We were created to love God and to love one another. Mastering our passions and following God's will in simplicity and love deliver us from wickedness and lead us to prefer good over evil.

10. **Gregory the Great.** The healing work that spiritual directors do represents a special vocation within the general call to follow Christ. Spiritual caregivers must work to recognize that a virtue displayed by those under their care may actually conceal a corresponding vice—greed may disguise itself as frugality, wastefulness as generosity, and so on. The goals of pastoral care are to help us follow the divine directives of God and to show us by example how to grow in virtuous living.

11. **Bernard of Clairvaux.** There is no limit to how much we ought to love God because God loves us without limit. When we find our center in God, we discover the truth St. Bernard proclaimed: that the measure of love is to love without measure.

12. **Aelred of Rievaulx.** Friendship must begin in Christ, continue with Christ, and be perfected by Christ. True friendship is motivated by charity and expels character faults, enabling us to grow in virtue.

13. **Francis and Clare.** Imitating Christ in every possible way, as these two saints did, allows us to know our own sinfulness and beseech God for mercy while delighting in the goodness of creation. In every circumstance of life, God's love for us is reason enough to radiate joyful optimism and sacrificial generosity while depending totally on God for all our needs.

14. **Bonaventure.** Our journey through life is an ascent into ever greater knowledge of God and conformity to Christ crucified and glorified. As we advance through the stages of our journey into God, we learn the practices of detachment from excessive materialism, reverential respect for creation, and zeal for a life of prayer and participation through preaching, healing, and teaching.

15. **Jan van Ruysbroeck.** Our Bridegroom comes to greet us. If we unclutter our interior life, we can go forth amid the mundane demands of the day and meet Christ, who longs to encounter us and reveal to us a glimpse of the sublime nature of God.

16. **Catherine of Siena.** Obedience is the hallmark of our Christian lives. We must do our best to say "Yes, Father" with Jesus. Entering the cell of self-knowledge teaches us who we are, and who God is. We discover that our obligation is not only to hear the Word of God in our heart, but also to proclaim it to the world.

17. *The Cloud of Unknowing.* Awe places us in the presence of a mystery no mind can fathom. To accept in humility the darkness of unknowing raises us up to God in silent wonder and fervent love. The insight attained through this form of contemplation bestows upon us a sense of knowing God rather than merely knowing about God.

18. **Julian of Norwich.** Pain is passing. When we think God is absent from us, that is when God is most near. We can and must trust in Divine

Providence. Each period of pain or purgation in our lives is a movement toward transfiguration. God is always with us, and all shall be well.

19. **Teresa of Avila.** Three paving stones line the path to union with God and communion with others: humility, detachment, and fraternal charity. Freedom of spirit depends on our willingness to be detached from anything or anyone to whom we cling instead of giving priority to God. Humility means to walk in the truth of who we are and to learn the most valuable lesson of all: that of selfless love.

20. **John of the Cross.** The dark nights of sense and spirit grant us the divine favor of bearing the cross of self-denial as an opening to oneness with the Lord. The sad night becomes a glad night when we flee from all that displeases God and begin to experience the grace that heals our aching heart with tender and sublime touches of love.

21. **Francis de Sales.** To live a devout life is not an extraordinary feat but the ordinary outcome of our being faithful to God's call wherever we are. People in all walks of life can pursue holiness. What matters is that we remain faithful to the state of life to which God calls us.

22. **Brother Lawrence of the Resurrection.** The only way to pray unceasingly is to practice the presence of God in everyday circumstances. We become adept at conversing lovingly with our Beloved about the details of our daily life. With each breath we take, we discover that the Lord is near and that sharing in this companionship of love is the source of true healing and lasting joy.

23. **John Wesley.** Whatever our faith tradition, we all share the desire to grow in holiness and in our relationship with the Lord. To be found worthy of answering the call to follow Jesus, we must love the Lord with all our heart, with all our soul, with all our mind, and with all our strength. Under the guidance of grace, we avoid sin and cultivate an abiding presence to the Spirit of the living God.

24. **Thérèse of Lisieux.** The little way of spiritual childhood begins with an acknowledgment of our nothingness and ends with the feeling of our being held in the loving embrace of God. Thérèse never hid her imperfections from God, nor must we. If, as she believed, everything is grace, then our life can be one act of love, and we can abandon ourselves to the mystery of God's mercy.

25. **Jean-Pierre de Caussade.** Let us move day by day in a graceful rhythm of worship and work. Hidden beneath the ordinary details of daily life is a rich undercurrent of significance, which we can see with God's guiding light. Fidelity to the Divine in the duty of the present moment is a sure path to spiritual maturity.

26. **Elizabeth of the Trinity.** To see ourselves as the dwelling place of the Trinity causes us to pause and pray that we may be found worthy of this awesome favor. Nothing can distract us from God as long as we live in him and act for him. No matter where we are, we can listen to God's voice in the silence of our heart. Nondescript as our lives may be, Christ's light is in us, and we, too, may be a praise of his glory.

27. **Evelyn Underhill.** The practical work we do is the outcome of our being present to a transcendent order of reality, beheld perhaps in moments of reflection but with us always. We need to cleanse our perception to see life as it really is—not apart from, but a part of, God. There must be no separation between contemplative living and charitable giving.

28. **Thomas R. Kelly.** Deep within us there is an amazing inner sanctuary of the soul, a holy place, a divine center to which we may return. This is the Light Within, which gives us insight into the deepest truth of who we are and radiates outward to the Blessed Community to which we belong. Unless we adhere to the Light Within, we labor in vain.

29. **Dietrich Bonhoeffer.** No cost is too much to pay for the privilege of being a true disciple. To deny ourselves, take up our cross, and follow Jesus are the cornerstones of both our Christian life and our human history. To choose the path of costly grace, the choice Bonhoeffer made, compels us to ponder what we would do were we asked to defend our faith to the death.

30. **Thomas Merton.** To find the balance between not enough prayer and too much work and vice versa may elude us until we experience that contemplation and action are two sides of the same coin of our being centered in God. Each activity is edifying in the eyes of God. To be drawn inward is to be made ready to serve God anywhere. Our life is a continuous seeking and finding of God that we might share God's love with others.

The great cloud of witnesses whose main themes I have traced throughout these thirty chapters concur with the truth that a life that is all head and no heart is as unbalanced and shallow as one that is all heart and no head.

We need to be both thoughtfully astute and spiritually inspired in pursuit of our active and contemplative lives.

The masters we have met want us to become so interiorly liberated that no cross we have to carry, no material constraint or spiritual challenge we must endure, no incident of worldly failure or success can deter us from living in the light and love that lead to intimacy with the Trinity. There the radical restlessness of our human heart culminates in a mystical experience of resting in God, momentarily here on Earth and forever in eternity.

ACKNOWLEDGMENTS

The book you are holding in your hands represents for me the culmination of a lifetime of study and instruction in the life and writings of great holy men and women from throughout Church history, from the most ancient to the contemporary Christian authors and teachers. Because it is impossible to fully convey the significance and eloquence of their writings without drawing directly from them, on behalf of Ave Maria Press and the Epiphany Association I would like to thank the following publishers, who have agreed to allow me to quote extensively from the previously published works of these great masters and mystics.

Excerpts from *The Sayings of the Desert Fathers: The Apophthegmata Patrum: The Alphabetical Collection* by Benedicta Ward, SLG, trans, CS 59 (Collegeville, MN: Cistercian Publications, 1975). Used by permission of Liturgical Press. All rights reserved. *Spiritual Friendship*, by Aelred of Rievaulx, ed. Marsha L. Dutton, trans. Lawrence C. Braceland (2010). Copyright 2010 by Cistercian Publications, Inc. © 2008 by Order of Saint Benedict, Collegeville, Minnesota. Used with permission.

Excerpts from the following works were published by Image Books, and have been reprinted with permission from Doubleday Dell Publishing Group: St. Francis de Sales, *Introduction to the Devout Life*, as translated by Reverend Monsignor John K. Ryan (1966), copyright permission was granted by "The Society for the Propagation of the Faith/www.missio.org"; and Jean-Pierre de Caussade, *Abandonment to Divine Providence*, trans. John Beevers (1975).

Selected texts from Thomas Merton's *The Sign of Jonas* (A Harvest Book, 1981) have been reprinted with permission of Harcourt, Inc. Passages from Thomas R. Kelly's *A Testament of Devotion* (1992) have been reprinted with permission of Harper Collins Publishers.

I am especially grateful to ICS Publications for granting permission to reprint selected passages from the following works: *The Collected Works of St. Teresa of Avila, Volume Two*, translated by Kieran Kavanaugh and

Otilio Rodriguez. Copyright © 1980 by Washington Province of Discalced Carmelites ICS Publications, 2131 Lincoln Road, N.E. Washington, DC 20002-1199 U.S.A. www.icspublications.org; from *The Collected Works of St. John of the Cross*, translated by Kieran Kavanaugh and Otilio Rodriguez Copyright © 1964, 1979, 1991 by Washington Province of Discalced Carmelites ICS Publications 2131 Lincoln Road, N.E. Washington, DC 20002-1199 U.S.A. www.icspublications.org; from *On The Practice of the Presence of God* translated by Salvatore Scuirba, O.C.D. Copyright © 1994 Washington Province of Discalced Carmelites ICS Publications 2131 Lincoln Road, N.E. Washington, DC 20002-1199 U.S.A. www.icspublications.org; from *Story of a Soul*, translated by John Clarke, O.C.D. Copyright © 1975, 1976, 1996 by Washington Province of Discalced Carmelites ICS Publications 2131 Lincoln Road, N.E. Washington, DC 20002-1199 U.S.A. www.icspublications.org; from *The Complete Works of Elizabeth of the Trinity Volume One* translated by Sr. Aletheia Kane, O.C.D. Copyright © 1984 by Washington Province of Discalced Carmelites ICS Publications 2131 Lincoln Road, N.E. Washington, DC 20002-1199 U.S.A. www.icspublications.org.

Our gratitude is also extended to Paulist Press for permission to excerpt a number of works, including Gregory of Nyssa, *The Life of Moses*, trans. Abraham J. Malherbe and Everett Ferguson (1978); John Cassian, *Conferences*, trans. Colm Luibheid (1985); *Pseudo-Dionysius: The Complete Works*, trans. Colm Luibheid (1987); John Climacus, *The Ladder of Divine Ascent*, trans. Colm Luibheid and Norman Russell (1982); *Maximus Confessor: Selected Writings*, trans. George C. Berthold (1985); Bernard of Clairvaux, *Selected Works*, trans. G. R. Evans (1987); *Francis and Clare: The Complete Works*, trans. Regis J. Armstrong and Ignatius C. Brady (1982); John Ruusbroec, *The Spiritual Espousals and Other Works*, trans. James A. Wiseman (1985); Catherine of Siena, *The Dialogue*, trans. Suzanne Noffke (1980); *The Cloud of Unknowing*, ed. James A. Walsh (1981); Julian of Norwich, *Showings*, trans. Edmund Colledge and James Walsh (1978); *John and Charles Wesley: Selected Writings and Hymns*, ed. Frank Whaling (1981).

Excerpts from *Dietrich Bonhoeffer: Letters and Papers from Prison*, ed. Eberhard Bethge (1971), have been reprinted with permission from Macmillan Publishing Co.

BIBLIOGRAPHY OF
MAJOR SOURCES

PART ONE: ANCIENT MASTERS

Athanasius. *The Life of Anthony and the Letters to Marcellinus*. Translated by Robert C. Gregg. New York: Paulist Press, 1980.

Augustine of Hippo: Selected Writings. Translated by Mary T. Clark. New York: Paulist Press, 1984.

Cassian, John. *Conferences*. Translated by Colm Luibheid. New York: Paulist Press, 1985.

———. *The Institutes*. Translated by Boniface Ramsey. New York: Newman Press, 2000.

Chittister, Joan D. *The Rule of Benedict: Insights for the Ages*. New York: Crossroad, 1996.

Confessions of Saint Augustine, The. Translated by John K. Ryan. Garden City, NY: Image Books, 1960.

Daly, Lowrie J., S.J. *Benedictine Monasticism: Its Formation and Development through the 12th Century*. New York: Sheed and Ward, 1965.

Dreuille, Mayeul de, O.S.B. *The Rule of Saint Benedict: A Commentary in the Light of World Ascetic Traditions*. Translated by Mark Hargreaves, O.S.B. Mahwah, NJ: Newman Press, 2000.

Ellsberg, Robert. *All Saints: Daily Reflections on Saints, Prophets, and Witnesses for Our Time*. New York: Crossroad, 1997.

Evagrius Ponticus. *The Mind's Long Journey to the Holy Trinity*. Translated by Jeremy Driscoll, O.S.B. Collegeville, MN: Liturgical Press, 1993.

———. *The Praktikos, and Chapters on Prayer*. Translated by John Eudes Bamberger. Spencer, MA: Cistercian Publications, 1970.

———. *On Prayer: One Hundred and Fifty-Three Texts* in *The Philokalia: The Complete Text*, compiled by St. Nikodimos of the Holy Mountain and St.

Makarios of Corinth, vol. 1. Translated by G. E. H. Palmer, Philip Sherrard, and Kallistos Ware. London: Faber and Faber, 1979.

From Glory to Glory: Texts from Gregory of Nyssa's Mystical Writings. Translated by Herbert Musurillo. Crestwood, NY: St. Vladimir's Seminary Press, 1979.

Funk, Mary Margaret. *Thoughts Matter.* New York: Continuum, 1998.

Gregory the Great. *Dialogues.* Translated by Odo John Zimmerman. Washington, DC: Catholic University of America Press, 1959.

———. *Pastoral Care (Regula Pastoralis),* vol. 11. Translated by Henry Davis. New York: Newman Press, 1950.

Gregory of Nyssa. *Ascetical Works.* Translated by Virginia Woods Callahan. Washington, DC: Catholic University of America Press, 1966.

———. *The Life of Moses.* Translated by Abraham J. Malherbe and Everett Ferguson. New York: Paulist Press, 1978.

———. *The Lord's Prayer, The Beatitudes.* Translated by Hilda C. Graef. New York: Newman Press, 1954.

Hausherr, Irénée, S.J. *Penthos: The Doctrine of Compunction in the Christian East.* Kalamazoo, MI: Cistercian Publications, 1982.

John Climacus. *The Ladder of Divine Ascent.* Translated by Colm Luibheid and Norman Russell. New York: Paulist Press, 1982.

Leclercq, Jean, O.S.B. *The Love of Learning and the Desire for God: A Study of Monastic Culture.* Translated by Catherine Misrahi. New York: Fordham University Press, 1960.

Maximus Confessor: Selected Writings. Translated by George C. Berthold. New York: Paulist Press, 1985.

McBrien, Richard P. *Lives of the Saints: From Mary and St. Francis of Assisi to John XXIII and Mother Teresa.* San Francisco: Harper, 2001.

Muto, Susan. *Words of Wisdom for Our World: The Precautions and Counsels of St. John of the Cross.* Eugene, OR: Wipf and Stock, 2009.

Mystical Theology, in *The Pseudo-Dionysius: The Complete Works.* Translated by Colm Luibheid. New York: Paulist Press, 1987.

Nault, Jean-Charles, O.S.B. *The Noonday Devil: Acedia, the Unnamed Evil of Our Times.* Translated by Michael J. Miller. San Francisco: Ignatius Press, 2015.

Nichols, Aidan. *Byzantine Gospel: Maximus the Confessor in Modern Scholarship.* Edinburgh: T&T Clark, 1993.

Rule of the Master. Translated by Luke Eberle. Kalamazoo, MI: Cistercian Publications, 1977.

Sayings of the Desert Fathers: The Alphabetical Collection. Translated by Benedicta Ward, S.L.G. Kalamazoo, MI: Cistercian Publications, 1975.

Spiritual Canticle in *The Collected Works of St. John of the Cross*. Translated by Kieran Kavanaugh and Otilio Rodriguez. Washington, DC: ICS Publications, 1991.

Van der Meer, F. *Augustine the Bishop: The Life and Work of a Father of the Church*. Translated by Brian Batteshaw and G. R. Lamb. London: Sheed and Ward, 1961.

PART TWO: MEDIEVAL MASTERS

Aelred of Rievaulx. *The Mirror of Charity*. Translated by Elizabeth Connor. Kalamazoo, MI: Cistercian Publications, 1980.

————. *Spiritual Friendship*. Edited by Marsha L. Dutton. Translated by Lawrence C. Braceland. Collegeville, MN: Liturgical Press, 2010.

Alvarez, Thomas, and Fernando Domingo. *The Divine Adventure: St. Teresa of Avila's Journeys and Foundations*. Edited by Patricia Morrison. Washington, DC: ICS Publications, 2015.

Augustine of Hippo: Selected Writings. Translated by Mary T. Clark. New York: Paulist Press, 1984.

Bernard of Clairvaux. *On the Song of Songs*. Translated by Kilian Walsh. Kalamazoo, MI: Cistercian Publications, 1971.

————. *Selected Works*. Translated by G. R. Evans. New York: Paulist Press, 1987.

Bodo, Murray, O.F.M. *Tales of St. Francis*. Cincinnati, OH: St. Anthony Messenger Press, 1988.

Bonaventure. *The Soul's Journey into God, The Tree of Life, The Life of St. Francis*. Translated by Ewert Cousins. New York: Paulist Press, 1978.

Bouyer, Louis. *The Cistercian Heritage*. Translated by E. Livingston. Westminster, MD: Newman Press, 1958.

Butler, Cuthbert. *Western Mysticism*. New York: Harper & Row, 1966.

Catherine of Siena. *The Dialogue*. Translated by Suzanne Noffke. New York: Paulist Press, 1980.

Chesterton, G. K. *Saint Francis of Assisi*. New York: Image Books, 1924.

Cloud of Unknowing, The. Edited by James A. Walsh. New York: Paulist Press, 1981.

Collected Works of St. John of the Cross, The. Translated by Kieran Kavanaugh and Otilio Rodriguez. Washington, DC: ICS Publications, 1991.

Collected Works of St. Teresa of Avila, The. Vol. 1, *The Book of Her Life*. Translated by Kieran Kavanaugh and Otilio Rodriguez. 1976; rev. ed. Washington, DC: ICS Publications, 1987.

————. Vol. 2, *The Way of Perfection*. Translated by Kieran Kavanaugh and Otilio Rodriguez. Washington, DC: ICS Publications, 1980.

Curtayne, Alice. *Saint Catherine of Siena*. Rockford, IL: Tan Books, 1980.

Dreyer, Elizabeth A. *Accidental Theologians: Four Women Who Shaped Christianity*. Cincinnati, OH: Franciscan Media, 2014.

Francis and Clare: The Complete Works. Translated by Regis J. Armstrong and Ignatius C. Brady. New York: Paulist Press, 1982.

Gilson, Etienne. *The Mystical Theology of St. Bernard*. Translated by A. H. C. Downes. New York: Sheed and Ward, 1939.

Giordani, Igino. *Saint Catherine of Siena: Doctor of the Church*. Translated by Thomas J. Tobin. Boston: Daughters of Saint Paul, 1975.

Hardy, Richard. *Search for Nothing: The Life of John of the Cross*. New York: Crossroad, 1982.

John Ruusbroec: The Spiritual Espousals and Other Works. Translated by James A. Wiseman. New York: Paulist Press, 1985.

Julian of Norwich. *Showings*. Translated by Edmund Colledge and James Walsh. New York: Paulist Press, 1978.

McCreary, Robert, O.F.M. Cap. *Medieval Mysticism: Francis and Clare*. Wickliffe, OH: St. Mary Seminary, 2008.

Muto, Susan. *Dear Master: Letters on Spiritual Direction Inspired by Saint John of the Cross*. Liguori, MO: Liguori/Triumph, 1999.

————. *Deep into the Thicket: Soul-Searching Meditations Inspired by Saint John of the Cross*. Pittsburgh, PA: Epiphany Association, 2001.

————. *Where Lovers Meet: Inside the Interior Castle*. Washington, DC: ICS Publications, 2008.

O'Mara, Philip. *The Character of a Christian Leader*. Ann Arbor, MI: Servant Books, 1978.

Pursuit of Wisdom, and Other Works by the Author of the Cloud of Unknowing, The. Translated and edited by James A. Walsh. New York: Paulist Press, 1988.

Raymond of Capua. *The Life of Catherine of Siena*. Translated by Conleth Kearns. Wilmington, DE: Michael Glazier, 1980.

Rolf, Veronica May. *Julian's Gospel: Illuminating the Life of Revelations of Julian of Norwich*. Maryknoll, NY: Orbis Books, 2013.

St. Francis of Assisi: Writings and Early Biographies: English Omnibus of the Sources for the Life of St. Francis. Edited by Marion A. Habig. Chicago: Franciscan Herald Press, 1973.

Steps of Humility, The. Translated by G. Bosworth Burch. Notre Dame, IN: Notre Dame University Press, 1963.

Sweeney, Jon. *The Saint and the Scholar: The Fight between Faith and Reason.* Cincinnati, OH: Franciscan Media, 2017.

Triple Way, or Love Enkindled, The, in St. Bonaventure, *Mystical Opuscula.* Translated by José de Vinck. Paterson, NJ: St. Anthony Guild Press, 1960.

Tuchman, Barbara. *A Distant Mirror: The Calamitous 14th Century.* New York: Random House, 1978.

Works of Bernard of Clairvaux, The. Vols. 1–5. Translated by M. A. Conway. Washington, DC: Cistercian Publications, 1974.

Works of St. Bonaventure, The. Vol. 2: *Itinerarium Mentis in Deum.* Translated by Philotheus Boehner. St. Bonaventure, NY: Franciscan Institute, 1956.

PART THREE: MODERN MASTERS

Ahern, Patrick. *Maurice and Thérèse: The Story of a Love.* New York: Image/Doubleday, 1998.

Bérulle and the French School: Selected Writings. Translated by Lowell M. Glendon. New York: Paulist Press, 1989.

Birkel, Michael L. *Silence and Witness: The Quaker Tradition.* Maryknoll, NY: Orbis Books, 2004.

Bonhoeffer, Dietrich. *The Cost of Discipleship.* New York: Macmillan Publishing, 1963.

———. *Life Together.* San Francisco: Harper and Row, 1954.

Caussade, Jean-Pierre de. *Abandonment to Divine Providence.* Translated by John Beevers. Garden City, NY: Image Books, 1975.

———. *Treatise on the Love of God.* Vol. 1, books 1–6, and vol. 2, books 7–12. Translated by John K. Ryan. Rockford, IL: Tan Books, 1974.

Dietrich Bonhoeffer: Letters and Papers from Prison. Edited by Eberhard Bethge. New York: Macmillan, 1971.

Elizabeth of the Trinity: The Complete Works. Vol. 1, *General Introduction and Major Spiritual Writings.* Translated by Aletheia Kane. Washington, DC: ICS Publications, 1984.

Elizabeth of the Trinity: The Complete Works. Vol. 2, *Letters from Carmel.* Translated by Anne Englund Nash. Washington, DC: ICS Publications, 1995.

Fénelon: Selected Writings. Translated by Chad Helms. New York: Paulist Press, 2006.

Finley, James. *Merton's Palace of Nowhere: A Search for God through Awareness of the True Self.* Notre Dame, IN: Ave Maria Press, 1978.

Francis de Sales. *Introduction to the Devout Life.* Translated by John K. Ryan. New York: Image Books, 1966.

Francis de Sales, Jane de Chantal: Letters of Spiritual Direction. Translated by Péronne Marie Thibert. New York: Paulist Press, 1988.

John and Charles Wesley: Selections from Their Writings and Hymns. Annotated by Paul Wesley Chilcote. Woodstock, VT: Skylight Paths, 2011.

Jones, Rufus. *Spiritual Reformers of the 16th and 17th Centuries.* Boston: Beacon Press, 1959.

Kelly, Thomas R. *The Eternal Promise.* New York: Harper, 1966.

———. *A Testament of Devotion.* San Francisco: Harper, 1992.

Laveille, August Pierre. *The Life of St. Thérèse of Lisieux: The Original Biography Commissioned by Her Sister.* Translated by Rev. Michael Fitzsimmons. Notre Dame, IN: Ave Maria Press, 2017.

Lawrence of the Resurrection, Brother. *The Practice of the Presence of God.* Translated by Salvatore Sciurba. Washington, DC: ICS Publications, 1994.

Merton, Thomas. *The Ascent to Truth.* New York: Harcourt, Brace, and Co., 1951.

———. *Contemplation in a World of Action.* New York: Doubleday, 1973.

———. *No Man Is an Island.* Garden City, NY: Image Books, 1967.

———. *The Seeds of Contemplation.* Norfolk, CT: New Directions, 1949.

———. *The Seven Storey Mountain.* New York: Signet Books, 1948.

———. *The Sign of Jonas.* New York: Harcourt, 1981.

Miguel de Molinos: The Spiritual Guide. Translated by Robert P. Baird. New York: Paulist Press, 2010.

Mosley, Joanne. *Elizabeth of the Trinity: The Unfolding of Her Message.* Vol. 1, *In the World & in Community,* and vol. 2, *In the Infirmary & After Her Death.* Oxford, Eng.: Teresian Press, 2012.

Muto, Susan. *Gratefulness: The Habit of a Grace-Filled Life.* Notre Dame, IN: Ave Maria Press, 2018.

———. *Then God Said: Contemplating the First Revelation in Creation.* Eugene, OR: Wipf and Stock, 2014.

Plays of St. Thérèse of Lisieux, The. Translated by Susan Conroy and David J. Dwyer. Washington, DC: ICS Publications, 2008.

Poetry of Saint Thérèse of Lisieux, The. Translated by Donald Kinney. Washington, DC: ICS Publications, 1996.

Pourrat, Pierre. *Christian Spirituality: From Jansenism to Modern Times,* vol. 4. Westminster, MD: Newman Press, 1955.

Schmidt, Joseph F. *Walking the Little Way of Thérèse of Lisieux: Discovering the Path to Love.* Frederick, MD: Word of God Among Us Press, 2012.

Steere, Douglas V., ed. *Quaker Spirituality: Selected Writings*. New York: Paulist Press, 1984.

Story of a Soul: The Autobiography of St. Thérèse of Lisieux. Translated by John Clarke. Washington, DC: ICS Publications, 1975.

Tomkins, Stephen. *John Wesley: A Biography*. Grand Rapids, MI: Eerdmans, 2003.

Underhill, Evelyn. *Abba: Meditations Based on the Lord's Prayer*. London: Longmans Green, 1940.

———. *Modern Guide to the Ancient Quest for the Holy*. Edited by Dana Greene. Albany, NY: State University of New York, 1988.

———. *The Mystic Way: A Psychological Study in Christian Origins*. London: J. M. Dent, 1913.

———. *Mysticism: A Study of the Nature and Development of Spiritual Consciousness*. London: Methuen, 1941.

———. *Practical Mysticism*. Columbus, OH: Ariel Press, 1942.

———. *The Spiritual Life*. Homebush, Australia: Society of St. Paul, 1976.

———. *Worship*. Edited by W. R. Matthews and H. W. Robinson. New York: Harper, 1959.

van Kaam, Adrian, and Susan Muto. *Living Our Christian Faith and Formation Traditions*, vol. 4 of the Formation Theology Series. Pittsburgh, PA: Epiphany Association, 2007.

Wesley, John and Charles. *Selected Writings and Hymns*. New York: Paulist Press, 1981.

NOTES

PART ONE: ANCIENT MASTERS

1. TEACHINGS FROM THE DESERT TRADITION:
QUIET YOUR HEAD AND HEAR WITH YOUR HEART

1. See Athanasius, *The Life of Anthony and the Letters to Marcellinus*, trans. Robert C. Gregg (New York: Paulist Press, 1980).

2. Two excellent treatments of the desert tradition are David G. R. Keller, *Oasis of Wisdom: The Worlds of the Desert Fathers and Mothers* (Collegeville, MN: Liturgical Press, 2005), and Stelios Ramphos, *Like a Pelican in the Wilderness* (Brookline, MA: Holy Cross Orthodox Press, 2000). See also William Harmless, *Desert Christians: An Introduction to the Literature of Early Monasticism* (Oxford: Oxford University Press, 2004), and John Chryssavgis, *In the Heart of the Desert: The Spirituality of the Desert Fathers and Mothers* (Bloomington, IN: World Wisdom Press, 2003).

3. These and other excerpts on desert wisdom can be found in *The Sayings of the Desert Fathers: The Alphabetical Collection*, trans. Benedicta Ward, S.L.G. (Kalamazoo, MI: Cistercian Publications, 1975), 30:21–22. Hereafter cited as *Sayings*, followed by paragraph and page number.

4. See Irénée Hausherr, S.J., *Penthos: The Doctrine of Compunction in the Christian East* (Kalamazoo, MI: Cistercian Publications, 1982).

5. See Susan Muto, *Words of Wisdom for Our World: The Precautions and Counsels of St. John of the Cross* (Eugene, OR: Wipf and Stock, 2009), and "Desert Messages," in *Pathways of Spiritual Living* (Pittsburgh, PA: Epiphany Books, 2004), 39–50.

2. *EVAGRIUS PONTICUS: RUN AWAY FROM EVIL AND RUN TOWARD THE GOOD*

1. See Evagrius Ponticus, *The Praktikos, and Chapters on Prayer*, trans. John Eudes Bamberger (Spencer, MA: Cistercian Publications, 1970). According to Bamberger, the influence of Evagrius remains and continues to grow today because of his belief that a person who truly prays is a person who has seen the face of God and is thus innately a spiritual theologian, that is to say, a mystic. Hereafter cited as *Praktikos* or *On Prayer*, followed by chapter and page number.

2. Origen was an early Christian scholar and theologian (ca. 185–254). He wrote commentaries on many books of scripture and developed an understanding of the soul's ascent to and union with God as a "mysticism of light." Unfortunately, certain doctrines of Origen were deemed heretical by the Fifth Ecumenical Council of 553. Among his problematic discourses were those that involved the hierarchy of the Trinity, the redemption of demons, and the "preexistence of souls." He is still credited, however, with pioneering a framework for the whole of the Christian mystical tradition.

3. The treatise by Evagrius Ponticus titled *On Prayer: One Hundred and Fifty-Three Texts* can also be found in *The Philokalia: The Complete Text*, compiled by St. Nikodimos of the Holy Mountain and St. Makarios of Corinth, vol. 1, trans. G. E. H. Palmer, Philip Sherrard, and Kallistos Ware (London: Faber and Faber, 1979), 55–71. Evagrius's works commonly appear in the "Chapter" or "Century" form, meaning a collection of often enigmatic sayings organized in groups of hundreds. Evagrius was the first Christian author to employ this genre.

4. See Evagrius Ponticus, *The Mind's Long Journey to the Holy Trinity*, trans. Jeremy Driscoll, O.S.B. (Collegeville, MN: Liturgical Press, 1993). This work is a collection of 137 proverbs by Evagrius, whose biblical style and precise language evoke meditation on the mystery of faith and its everyday application.

5. In the sixth century, St. Gregory the Great recodified the eight vices of Evagrius into the more familiar seven capital sins of pride, anger, avarice, envy, sloth, lust, and gluttony.

6. Ponticus, *Mind's Long Journey*, 23. Driscoll remarks, "The remedy against this system of demonic attacks is a constant vigilance over thoughts, never allowing them to linger. *Prakitiké* is learning this art." See also Mary Margaret Funk, *Thoughts Matter* (New York: Continuum, 1998), and Jean-Charles Nault, O.S.B., *The Noonday Devil: Acedia, the Unnamed Evil of Our Times*, trans. Michael J. Miller (San Francisco: Ignatius Press, 2015).

7. See Louis Bouyer, *Introduction to Spirituality*, trans. Mary Perkins Ryan (Collegeville, MN: Liturgical Press, 1961), 204.

3. GREGORY OF NYSSA: SEEK THE LORD AND LET YOURSELF BE FOUND

1. Citing the proclamations of these historic councils, we read in the *Catechism of the Catholic Church* (Washington, DC: United States Conference of Catholic Bishops, 1997), "The Church thus confesses that Jesus is inseparably true God and true man. He is truly the Son of God who, without ceasing to be God and Lord, became a man and our brother" (469).

2. Gregory of Nyssa, *The Life of Moses*, trans. Abraham J. Malherbe and Everett Ferguson (New York: Paulist Press, 1978). Although its dating is uncertain, *The Life* was probably written around 390. It is divided into two books, Book I concerning perfection in virtue and Book II on contemplation of the life of Moses. Gregory's shorter, historical overview of the exodus event complements his longer interpretation of the spiritual sense of the story. Hereafter cited as *Life*, followed by book, paragraph, and page number.

3. See also *From Glory to Glory: Texts from Gregory of Nyssa's Mystical Writings*, trans. Herbert Musurillo (Crestwood, NY: St. Vladimir's Seminary Press, 1979), 56–71.

4. In his introduction to *From Glory to Glory*, Jean Daniélou says that for Gregory, "perfection consists in this perpetual penetration into the interior, a perpetual discovery of God," 61. He remarks that to seek God without end, to never cease in our ascent, is the heart of Gregory's spiritual doctrine and that "the awareness of [the] inaccessibility [of the divine essence] constitutes the highest form of contemplation," 27.

5. Gregory's treatment of what he calls "traveler's equipment" (tunic, shoes, staff, and food) can be found in *Life*, Book II, 107–108:79.

6. This false doctrine was like a razor-sharp sword that cut a deep wound in the heart of Christianity and necessitated the need for healing provided by the Church Fathers. It takes its name from Arius (256–326), a priest of Alexandria, who taught that Christ was not the equal of the Father, nor was he true God. Christ was a creature more perfect than others but still a part of the creation of God. Arianism was condemned at the Council of Nicaea in 325.

7. See Gregory of Nyssa, *Ascetical Works*, trans. Virginia Woods Callahan (Washington, DC: Catholic University of America Press, 1966), for, among other

texts, *On Virginity* (3–75); *On Perfection* (93–122); and *The Life of Macrina* (161–91). See also Gregory of Nyssa, *Homilies on the Song of Songs*, trans. Richard A. Norris Jr. (Atlanta, GA: Society of Biblical Literature, 2013).

8. Gregory's contribution to our understanding of the *via negativa*, or the apophatic stream, in Christian spirituality complements the teachings of Pseudo-Dionysius, the anonymous author of *The Cloud of Unknowing*, and St. John of the Cross. These masters, inspired by St. Gregory, crafted their classical versions of the threefold path of purgation, illumination, and union.

9. *On Virginity*, in *Ascetical Works*, 23:68.

10. *On Virginity*, introduction, 4.

11. *On Virginity*, 2:11.

12. See Callahan's introduction to *On What It Means to Call Oneself a Christian* in *Ascetical Works*, 80. There we read that the mark of being true Christians is to assimilate ourselves to God and to live insofar as possible lives of prayer and perfect virtue. See also Gregory of Nyssa, *The Lord's Prayer, The Beatitudes*, trans. Hilda C. Graef (New York: Newman Press, 1954). Gregory notes at the beginning of his treatise on the Our Father that "if work is preceded by prayer, sin will find no entrance into the soul," 23.

13. See Gregory's treatise on the Sermon on the Mount in *The Lord's Prayer, The Beatitudes*, 159.

4. AUGUSTINE OF HIPPO: SAY YES TO GRACE AND CHANGE YOUR LIFE

1. *The Confessions of St. Augustine*, trans. John K. Ryan (Garden City, NY: Image Books, 1960). Hereafter cited as *Confessions*, followed by book, chapter, paragraph, and page number.

2. See F. van der Meer, *Augustine the Bishop: The Life and Work of a Father of the Church*, trans. Brian Batteshaw and G. R. Lamb (London: Sheed and Ward, 1961), which offers an excellent analysis of Augustine's anti-Manichean, anti-Donatist, and anti-Pelagian writings; and Henry Chadwick, *Augustine* (Oxford: Oxford University Press, 1986), which serves as an introduction to Augustine's life and thought. Of particular interest are the chapters titled "Vocation" and "Confession." See also Mary T. Clark, *Augustine* (New York: Continuum, 1994), which, instead of addressing *The Confessions* directly, focuses on such topics as "Happiness and Human Existence," "Christ and Trinity," "Church and Sacraments," "Monasticism," "City of God," and "Augustine and Neoplatonism."

3. Noteworthy in this regard is the fact that Augustine, along with St. Thomas Aquinas, is one of the two masters most cited in the *Catechism of the Catholic Church*.

4. See Jean-Marc Laporte, *Patience and Power: Grace for the First World* (New York: Paulist Press, 1988).

5. See *Augustine of Hippo: Selected Writings*, trans. Mary T. Clark (New York: Paulist Press, 1984). Augustine wrote his fifteen-volume work *On the Trinity* between 400 and 416. From 413 to 425 he wrote his other masterpiece, *The City of God*, trans. Gerald G. Walsh et al. (Garden City, NY: Image Books, 1958). Both works reveal his passion for holy scripture and his belief in the providential plan of God for humankind moving onward to the kingdom of heaven.

6. "When, therefore, a person who knows how to love himself is bidden to love his neighbor as himself, is he not, in effect, commanded to persuade others, as far as he can, to love God?" (*The City of God*, Book X, 3:191). This love, according to Augustine, is the only force powerful enough to subdue the "lust for dominion" that so despoils our relationship with God and others.

7. *Augustine of Hippo: Selected Writings*, 302. See also the first encyclical of Pope Benedict XVI, *Deus Caritas Est*, to appreciate the contribution of Augustine to the Church of our own and all previous ages. In his general weekly audience in February 2008, the pope meditated on Augustine's "triple conversion." The first turn, of course, marks his singular acceptance of Jesus in 386, followed by his baptism by Bishop Ambrose in Milan in 387. His second conversion, stirred to life by his friendship with Christ and his formation of a school of love in Africa, has as its hallmark the shift from learned lectures to simple preaching in Hippo, his hometown. In simplicity and humility, he took upon himself the duty to bring the people of God closer to their Creator. His third conversion, shortly before his death, brought him to a living attunement to the Sermon on the Mount, to the need he felt to be washed clean by Christ and constantly renewed in him.

5. JOHN CASSIAN: REJOICE ALWAYS AND GIVE THANKS

1. John Cassian, *Conferences*, trans. Colm Luibheid (New York: Paulist Press, 1985). Hereafter cited *Conference*, followed by its number, paragraph, and page number. See also John Cassian, *The Institutes*, trans. Boniface Ramsey (New York: Newman Press, 2000), where Cassian described monastic life as he had seen it lived in the deserts of Egypt and Syria. Designed for beginners in this way of life,

The Institutes deals with the eight obstacles to perfection in the style of the eight vices described by Evagrius Ponticus. In *Conferences*, Cassian offers expositions on a variety of spiritual topics, including the objective of the monastic life (Conference One); discernment (Conference Two); and prayer (Conferences Nine and Ten). In all, he wrote twenty-four conferences, nine of which are in the Paulist Press edition. Both of these works were written in Latin between the years 425 and 428.

2. For a review of these and other writers influenced by Cassian, see the introduction to *Conferences* by Owen Chadwick in the Paulist Press edition, 1–16.

3. Cassian's treatise on gluttony, unchastity, avarice, anger, dejection, listlessness, self-esteem, and pride can be found in *The Philokalia: The Complete Text*, compiled by St. Nikodimos of the Holy Mountain and St. Makarios of Corinth, vol. 1, trans. G. E. H. Palmer, Philip Sherard, and Kallistos Ware (London: Faber and Faber, 1979), 72–93.

4. Both Pelagianism and semi-Pelagianism emphasized that works, not grace, can save us. These false doctrines were condemned by the Council of Orange in 529.

5. In his description of this demon found in *The Philokalia*, 87, Cassian says that the treachery afflicted upon us is severe because it obscures the soul's capacity for spiritual contemplation and keeps it from good works.

6. See Book 9 of *The Institutes* on sadness, 211–14, and Book 10 on the spirit of acedia (the noonday devil), 217–34.

6. BENEDICT OF NURSIA: REMAIN AT THE SAME TIME CONTEMPLATIVE AND ACTIVE

1. See Joan D. Chittister, *The Rule of Benedict: Insights for the Ages* (New York: Crossroad, 1993). Hereafter cited as *Rule*, followed by chapter and page number. See also *The Rule of Saint Benedict in Latin and English*, trans. Abbot Justin McCann (London: Sheed and Ward, 1962).

2. See Lowrie J. Daly, S.J., *Benedictine Monasticism: Its Formation and Development through the 12th Century* (New York: Sheed and Ward, 1965). In addition to the scriptures, the Rule of St. Benedict, either directly or indirectly, draws upon *The Institutes* and *Conferences* of John Cassian and the rules composed by Pachomius, St. Basil the Great, and St. Augustine. The most immediate source of Benedict's Rule is the anonymous *Rule of the Master*, which is a synthesis of all the material and spiritual aspects of monastic life in the region of Rome. Secondary sources include the sayings of the Desert Fathers, the *Rule of Pseudo-Macarius*, and the letters of St. Jerome. The Rule composed by St. Benedict is a creative and original

blending of the essential theory and practice of the Eastern and Western monastic traditions that preceded it. Because of its intrinsic worth and obvious originality, the Benedictine Rule gradually supplanted these predecessors and became the living norm for monks of the West to the present. See *The Rule of the Master*, trans. Luke Eberle (Kalamazoo, MI: Cistercian Publications, 1977).

3. See Claude J. Heifer, O.S.B., "Forming Men Today for Life according to the Rule," in *Rule and Life: An Interdisciplinary Symposium*, ed. M. Basil Pennington, O.C.S.O. (Spencer, MA: Cistercian Publications, 1972), 206. See also Mayeul de Dreuille, O.S.B., *The Rule of Saint Benedict: A Commentary in the Light of World Ascetic Traditions*, trans. Mark Hargreaves, O.S.B. (Mahwah, NJ: Newman Press, 2000).

4. Gregory the Great, *Dialogues*, trans. Odo John Zimmerman (Washington, DC: Catholic University of America Press, 1959).

5. *Dialogues*, Book 2, 103.

6. *Dialogues*, Book 2, 103–4.

7. PSEUDO-DIONYSIUS: LIVE IN AWE OF THE MYSTERY

1. See *The Mystical Theology*, in *Pseudo-Dionysius: The Complete Works*, trans. Colm Luibheid (New York: Paulist Press, 1987), 135–41. Hereafter cited as *The Complete Works*, followed by the page number.

2. See *The Cloud of Unknowing*, ed. James Walsh (New York: Paulist Press, 1981), 138–39.

3. *The Spiritual Canticle*, in *The Collected Works of St. John of the Cross*, trans. Kieran Kavanaugh and Otilio Rodriguez (Washington, DC: ICS Publications, 1991), Stanza 1, 3:479.

4. See *The Divine Names*, in *The Complete Works*, 49–131.

5. St. Gregory of Nyssa anticipates this sense of God's unknown splendor in *The Life of Moses*, trans. Abraham J. Malherbe and Everett Ferguson (New York: Paulist Press, 1978). Moses enters the cloud on Mount Sinai, freed from what is seen, and is swept up in the intangible and invisible glory of God.

6. See John Paul II, *Fides et Ratio* (*On Faith and Reason*), October 15, 1998, rpr. in *Inside the Vatican* (Rome, 1998), 1–41. In the words of the Holy Father, "Faith and reason are like two wings on which the human spirit rises to the contemplation of truth" (Opening Salutation, 3).

8. JOHN CLIMACUS: COMMIT YOURSELF TO CLIMB UP TO GOD

1. John Climacus, *The Ladder of Divine Ascent*, trans. Colm Luibheid and Norman Russell (New York: Paulist Press, 1982). Hereafter cited as *Ladder*, followed by the page number.

2. *The Ladder* resembles another enduring spiritual classic of the Western Church, Walter Hilton's fourteenth-century masterpiece *The Scale of Perfection*, trans. John P. H. Clark and Rosemary Dorward (New York: Paulist Press, 1991). It, too, aims to help souls practice a life of Christian virtue that they may attain an enduring likeness to the Son of God.

3. John's teaching on how to discern thoughts, passions, and virtues leads beginners to true self-knowledge. Those midway on the road to perfection develop a spiritual capacity to distinguish between what is truly good and what in nature is opposed to the good. Knowledge among the perfect results from divine illumination, which with its lamp dispels the shadows of sin associated with our fallen condition.

4. By way of review, a sincerely seeking soul has to break with the worldliness of the world through renunciation (1), detachment (2), and exile (3). Then the seeker must begin in the active life to practice the basic virtues of obedience (4), penitence (5), remembrance of death (6), and sorrow (7). Now the struggle with the nonphysical passions of anger (8), malice (9), slander (10), talkativeness (11), falsehood (12), and despondency (13) begins in earnest. Fast on its heels are the physical and material passions of gluttony (14), lust (15), and avarice (16–17). Not to be underestimated on this battlefield of the heart are other attacks from such nonphysical passions as insensitivity (18–20), fear (21), vainglory (22), and pride and blasphemy (23). Enter into the fray the higher virtues of the active life—simplicity (24), humility (25), and discernment (26)—and the soul is on the way to union with God, transitioning on wings of grace to the contemplative life in stillness (27), prayer (28), dispassion (29), and love (30).

9. MAXIMUS THE CONFESSOR: LEARN HOW TO BE WITH AND FOR OTHERS

1. *The Four Hundred Chapters on Love*, in *Maximus Confessor: Selected Writings*, trans. George C. Berthold (New York: Paulist Press, 1985), 1,27:38. Hereafter cited as *Love*, followed by chapter, paragraph, and page number. *The Four Hundred Chapters on Love* is a collection of short paragraphs (*apothegms*), arranged in four

groups of one hundred (centuries) and patterned after the four gospels. While Maximus acknowledges his dependence on such distinguished predecessors as Evagrius Ponticus, he strove in his own original way to write in an evangelical spirit appealing to monks and laity alike, covering a range of topics from Trinitarian theology to the demands of discipleship.

2. In his description of deification, Maximus echoes the classic expression of St. Athanasius: "[Christ] became man that we might become God." For Maximus, the Incarnation of Jesus Christ was the fulfillment of God's providential plan leading to our deification.

3. See Rebecca Letterman, "Dispositions of the Heart in *The Four Hundred Chapters on Love,*" in *Epiphany International*, August 2007, 78–98. See also Aidan Nichols, *Byzantine Gospel: Maximus the Confessor in Modern Scholarship* (Edinburgh: T&T Clark, 1993), and Lars Thunberg, *Man and the Cosmos: The Vision of St. Maximus the Confessor* (Crestwood, NY: St. Vladimir's Seminary Press, 1985).

4. In another poetic turn of phrase, Maximus says, "The one who has joined the body to the soul through virtue and knowledge has become a lyre and a flute and a temple. A lyre, firstly, because he beautifully maintains the harmony of the virtues; next, a flute because through the divine experiences he receives the Spirit's inspiration; finally, a temple because through the purity of his mind he has become the Word's dwelling place" (*Chapters on Knowledge*, in *Selected Writings*, 100:170).

5. Maximus frequently confirms his preference for the apophatic way (the *via negativa*) that aligns him, among other masters, with Pseudo-Dionysius.

10. GREGORY THE GREAT: ACKNOWLEDGE YOUR NEED FOR DIRECTION AND BECOME MORE COMPASSIONATE

1. Gregory the Great, *Dialogues*, trans. Odo John Zimmerman (Washington, DC: Catholic University of America Press, 1959). See Book 2, 56–110, on St. Benedict, who inspired St. Gregory's own monastic life.

2. See Gregory the Great, *Pastoral Care (Regula Pastoralis)*, vol. 11, trans. Henry Davis (New York: Newman Press, 1950). Hereafter cited as *Care*, followed by part, chapter, and page number.

3. In the East as well, St. Gregory the Great is one of the most read of the Latin Fathers. John Climacus, author of *The Ladder of Divine Ascent*, cites his indebtedness to Gregory's doctrine of compunction. In the West, after Aristotle and Augustine, Gregory is the most quoted author in Aquinas's *Summa Theologica*.

4. See Jean Leclercq, O.S.B., *The Love of Learning and the Desire for God: A Study of Monastic Culture*, trans. Catherine Misrahi (New York: Fordham University Press, 1960), 33. As Leclercq reminds us, St. Anselm of Canterbury and St. Bernard of Clairvaux owe a great debt to St. Gregory. He adds that if ideas of the past are to remain fresh and vital, each generation must think them through and rediscover them in their pristine newness.

5. See *Dialogues*, Book 2, 70–71.

6. See Robert Ellsberg, *All Saints: Daily Reflections on Saints, Prophets, and Witnesses for Our Time* (New York: Crossroad, 1997), 379–81.

7. See Richard P. McBrien, *Lives of the Saints: From Mary and St. Francis of Assisi to John XXIII and Mother Teresa* (San Francisco: Harper, 2001), 359–62.

8. See Leclercq, 35.

9. Leclercq, 42.

PART TWO: MEDIEVAL MASTERS

11. BERNARD OF CLAIRVAUX: WALK IN THE TRUTH OF WHO YOU ARE

1. These sermons can be found in the three-volume series by Bernard of Clairvaux, *On the Song of Songs*, trans. Kilian Walsh (Kalamazoo, MI: Cistercian Publications, 1971). Exemplary is Sermon 18, in which Bernard distinguishes two gifts of the Holy Spirit: infusion and effusion. He says that we must first be filled (like a reservoir) and then control the outpouring. He warns that in the Church today there are far too many canals and not enough reservoirs.

2. See Jon Sweeney, *The Saint and the Scholar: The Fight between Faith and Reason* (Cincinnati, OH: Franciscan Media, 2017).

3. See Etienne Gilson, *The Mystical Theology of St. Bernard*, trans. A. H. C. Downes (New York: Sheed and Ward, 1939).

4. See *The Steps of Humility*, trans. G. Bosworth Burch (Notre Dame, IN: Notre Dame University Press, 1963).

5. Cuthbert Butler, in his book *Western Mysticism* (New York: Harper & Row, 1966), reminds us that Bernard was identified as the "Last of the Fathers" because he combated the beginnings of the scholastic movement and preferred to focus on the doctrine and practice of mystical theology. Though the mind is reduced to silence, "the soul itself is full of light and operating with an intense activity," 106.

6. See Terence L. Connolly, *On the Love of God* (Techny, IL: Mission Press, 1943), and Edmund Garrot, *The Book of St. Bernard on the Love of God* (New York: Dutton, 1916).

7. These themes are vividly portrayed and repeated throughout *The Works of Bernard of Clairvaux*, vols. 1–5, trans. M. A. Conway (Washington, DC: Cistercian Publications, 1974). See also Louis Bouyer, *The Cistercian Heritage*, trans. E. Livingston (Westminster, MD: Newman Press, 1958).

8. Bernard of Clairvaux, *Selected Works*, trans. G. R. Evans (New York: Paulist Press, 1987), 166. Hereafter abbreviated *SW*, followed by the page number.

9. "On Loving God," in *Treatises II*, in *Works of Bernard of Clairvaux*, vol. 5, no. 13 (Washington, DC: Cistercian Publications, 1974), 115–16.

10. "On Loving God," 118.

11. "On Loving God," 119–20.

12. "The Steps of Humility and Pride," in *Treatises II*, 55.

12. AELRED OF RIEVAULX: BE FRIENDS OF GOD AND THEN BEFRIEND ONE ANOTHER

1. Aelred of Rievaulx, *Spiritual Friendship*, ed. Marsha L. Dutton, trans. Lawrence C. Braceland (Collegeville, MN: Liturgical Press, 2010). Hereafter abbreviated *SF*, followed by part, paragraph, and page number.

2. Aelred of Rievaulx, *The Mirror of Charity*, trans. Elizabeth Connor (Kalamazoo, MI: Cistercian Publications, 1980), 298.

3. See "On the Trinity," in *Augustine of Hippo: Selected Writings*, trans. Mary T. Clark (New York: Paulist Press, 1984), 311–59.

13. FRANCIS AND CLARE OF ASSISI: DEPEND ON GOD FOR EVERYTHING

1. See G. K. Chesterton, *Saint Francis of Assisi* (New York: Image Books, 1924); Omer Engelbert, *St. Francis of Assisi: A Biography* (Cincinnati, OH: St. Anthony Messenger Press, 1979); and St. Bonaventure, *The Life of St. Francis*, ed. Henry Cardinal Manning (Rockford, IL: Tan Books, 1988).

2. See Murray Bodo, O.F.M., *Tales of St. Francis* (Cincinnati, OH: St. Anthony Messenger Press, 1988), for a presentation of the edifying ways in which God answered the prayers of his servant Francis.

3. "Canticle of Brother Sun," cited in *Francis and Clare: The Complete Works*, trans. Regis J. Armstrong and Ignatius C. Brady (New York: Paulist Press, 1982), 38–39. Hereafter abbreviated *FC*, followed by the page number. See also *St. Francis of Assisi: Writings and Early Biographies: English Omnibus of the Sources for the Life of St. Francis*, ed. Marion A. Habig, O.F.M. (Chicago: Franciscan Herald Press, 1973).

4. See Robert McCreary, O.F.M. Cap., *Medieval Mysticism: Francis and Clare* (Wickliffe, OH: St. Mary Seminary, 2008).

5. *English Omnibus of Sources*, 242–43.

6. Alexander IV, *Clara Claris praeclara*, *Bullarium Franciscanum* 2 (Rome, 1761), 81. See also *FC*, 169.

14. BONAVENTURE: SEE IN EVERY ENDING A NEW BEGINNING

1. *The Life of St. Francis*, in Bonaventure, *The Soul's Journey into God, The Tree of Life, The Life of St. Francis*, trans. Ewert Cousins (New York: Paulist Press, 1978), 179–327. Hereafter cited by title, followed by the page number.

2. See *Major and Minor Life of St. Francis*, trans. Benen Fahy, O.F.M., in *St. Francis of Assisi: Writings and Early Biographies: English Omnibus of the Sources for the Life of St. Francis*, ed. Marion A. Habig, O.F.M. (Chicago: Franciscan Herald Press, 1973), 627–851. See also Ilia Delio, *Crucified Love: Bonaventure's Mysticism of the Crucified Christ* (Cincinnati, OH: Franciscan Media, 1998).

3. See *The Works of St. Bonaventure*, vol. 2, *Itinerarium Mentis in Deum*, trans. Philotheus Boehner (St. Bonaventure, NY: Franciscan Institute, 1956), for another excellent translation of this masterpiece.

4. Bonaventure follows the medieval technique of the four modes of scriptural interpretation: *literal*, the letter of the text; *allegorical*, the faith it connotes; *topological*, the moral lesson it contains; and *anagogical*, its depiction in human words of heavenly truths. He also practiced the dialectics of scholastic argumentation, whereby the seeker searches texts for reasons that lead to a fuller understanding of the faith.

5. See *The Triple Way, or Love Enkindled*, in St. Bonaventure, *Mystical Opuscula*, trans. José de Vinck (Paterson, NJ: St. Anthony Guild Press, 1960), 61–94.

6. *The Triple Way*, 88.

7. "The Six Wings of the Seraph," in *The Works of St. Bonaventure*, vol. 3, trans. José de Vinck (Paterson, NJ: St. Anthony Guild Press, 1966), 133–96. See

also Philip O'Mara, *The Character of a Christian Leader* (Ann Arbor, MI: Servant Books, 1978).

8. "The Six Wings of the Seraph," 196.

15. JAN VAN RUYSBROECK: LET GO AND LET GOD LEAD YOU

1. The spelling of his name may be seen as Jan van Ruysbroec or John Ruusbroec or, as in this chapter, Jan van Ruysbroeck.

2. See Evelyn Underhill, *Mysticism: A Study in the Nature and Development of Man's Spiritual Consciousness* (London: Methuen, 1941), for a superb analysis of the groundbreaking work of Ruysbroeck in describing these three stages of mystical experience.

3. See *John Ruusbroec: The Spiritual Espousals and Other Works*, trans. James A. Wiseman, O.S.B. (New York: Paulist Press, 1985), 152. Hereafter abbreviated *SE*, followed by the page number. In his preface to the volume, Louis Dupré says that Ruysbroeck is the "most articulate Trinitarian mystic of the Western Church," xi. His love for the Church obliged him to battle a number of heresies rampant in his day, especially one adhered to by a sect known as the Brothers of the Free Spirit. They held that humans and all beings are of the same substance as God—a pantheistic tenet. Since a person can be equal to God, he or she is freed from all ecclesial obligations, including fasting, confession, and prayer. Their leader, a charismatic woman, was amazingly popular in Ruysbroeck's time in Brussels and had a faithful following. In refuting her, Ruysbroeck met with such persecution and hostility that he and his companions had to retire to a nearby forest, where they established the hermitage of Groenendal.

4. *A Mirror of Eternal Blessedness*, in *The Spiritual Espousals and Other Works*, 199. Hereafter, abbreviated *SE Mirror*, followed by the page number.

5. *The Little Book of Clarification*, in *The Spiritual Espousals and Other Works*, 253. Hereafter, abbreviated *SE Little Book*, followed by the page number.

16. CATHERINE OF SIENA: ALWAYS SAY "YES, FATHER" WITH JESUS

1. Catherine of Siena, *The Dialogue*, trans. Suzanne Noffke (New York: Paulist Press, 1980), 33–34. Hereafter cited as *Dialogue*, followed by the page number.

2. For further insight into the life and legacy of St. Catherine of Siena, see Alice Curtayne, *Saint Catherine of Siena* (Rockford, IL: Tan Books, 1980); Raymond of Capua, *The Life of Catherine of Siena*, trans. Conleth Kearns (Wilmington, DE: Michael Glazier, 1980); Igino Giordani, *Saint Catherine of Siena: Doctor of the Church*, trans. Thomas J. Tobin (Boston: Daughters of Saint Paul, 1975); and Elizabeth A. Dreyer, *Accidental Theologians: Four Women Who Shaped Christianity* (Cincinnati, OH: Franciscan Media, 2014).

3. Though Catherine's life of prayer, heroic virtue, and love for the poor were exemplary, her practice of bodily mortification and certain corporeal penances, especially her dietary deprivations, came under question at the time of her death. For discussion of this, see Don Brophy, *Catherine of Siena: A Passionate Life* (New York: Blueridge, 2010).

4. See "Tears," in *Dialogue*, 88–169.

5. In a sense, the whole of *The Dialogue* is an answer to and an expansion of these four petitions. The prayer for her own spiritual needs, especially for the offering of herself to God in love, and for self-knowledge led to the doctrine of perfection. Her petition for the Church and its renewal and reform yielded her reflections on the mystical body of the Church. Her prayer for the whole world in need of divine mercy produced her doctrines of the bridge, of tears, and of truth. Praying that the sole concern of her spiritual guide would be for the good of others produced her doctrines of Divine Providence and obedience.

17. THE CLOUD OF UNKNOWING: BOW IN AWE BEFORE THE MYSTERY

1. Among these saintly souls were Julian of Norwich, Richard Rolle, Henry Suso, and Walter Hilton, all part of the English school of spirituality. For a vivid description of their times, see Barbara Tuchman, *A Distant Mirror: The Calamitous 14th Century* (New York: Random House, 1978), and Benedicta Ward, *Give Love and Receive the Kingdom: Essential People and Themes of English Spirituality* (Brewster, MA: Paraclete Press, 2018).

2. See *The Cloud of Unknowing*, ed. James A. Walsh (New York: Paulist Press, 1981). Hereafter cited as *Cloud*, followed by the page number. See also *The Pursuit*

of Wisdom, and Other Works by the Author of The Cloud of Unknowing, trans. and ed. James A. Walsh (New York: Paulist Press, 1988).

3. According to James Walsh, many writers in the genre of apophatic mysticism (the Cistercians, the Carthusians, the Carmelites) were "simply perpetuating the tradition and adopting the style of the first apostolic writers, beginning with SS. Luke and Paul, on the understanding that their writings would be passed from hand to hand, and read aloud in quasi-ecclesiastical gatherings: in this case, monastic refectories and chapter halls" (*Cloud*, footnote 11, 115). The footnotes to this edition detail in an excellent way the roots of this tradition and the lasting impact the *via negativa* has had on ascetical-mystical theology in the ancient, medieval, and modern classics of Christian spirituality.

4. Quoting "Saint Denis" (Dionysius the Areopagite), the author notes that "the truly divine knowledge of God is that which is known by unknowing" (*Cloud*, 161).

18. JULIAN OF NORWICH: TRUST IN DIVINE PROVIDENCE

1. An excellent study of Julian's life and times is that by Veronica May Rolf, *Julian's Gospel: Illuminating the Life of Revelations of Julian of Norwich* (Maryknoll, NY: Orbis Books, 2013). See also Julian of Norwich, *Showings*, trans. Edmund Colledge and James Walsh (New York: Paulist Press, 1978). Hereafter cited as *Short Text* or *Long Text*, followed by the page number.

2. See Rolf, 15–38.

3. See *Long Text*, 179. Julian always interprets her visions in Trinitarian terms. For instance, when she stresses repeatedly that God is love, she emphasizes that "life, love, and light" make up "one goodness of God" (*Long Text*, 339–40). In her words, "I had three kinds of understanding in this light of charity. The first is uncreated charity, the second is created charity, the third is given charity. Uncreated charity is God, created charity is our soul in God, given charity is virtue, and that is a gift of grace in deeds in which we love God for himself, and ourselves in God, and all that God loves for God" (*Long Text*, 341).

4. Julian summarizes the contents of these sixteen revelations in the first chapter of the *Long Text*, 175–77.

5. Her exact words are, "I wished that his pains might be my pains, with compassion which would lead to a longing for God. . . . I never wanted any bodily vision nor any kind of revelation from God, but only the compassion which I thought

a loving soul could have for our Lord Jesus, who for love was willing to become a mortal man" (*Short Text*, 129).

6. *Long Text*, 183. Julian's feminine-intuitive approach to the mystery of the deepest reality of divine love is comparable to that of Catherine of Siena and Teresa of Avila.

19. TERESA OF AVILA: LIVE IN HUMILITY, DETACHMENT, AND FRATERNAL CHARITY

1. See *The Book of Her Life*, in *The Collected Works of St. Teresa of Avila*, vol. 1, trans. Kieran Kavanaugh and Otilio Rodriguez, rev. ed. (1976; Washington, DC: ICS Publications, 1987), chaps. 7–10, 76–104. Hereafter abbreviated *BL*, followed by chapter, paragraph, and page number.

2. See *The Way of Perfection*, in *The Collected Works of St. Teresa of Avila*, vol. 2, trans. Kieran Kavanaugh and Otilio Rodriguez (Washington, DC: ICS Publications, 1980). Further references are taken from this edition, abbreviated *WP*, followed by chapter, paragraph, and page number.

3. See Thomas Alvarez and Fernando Domingo, *The Divine Adventure: St. Teresa of Avila's Journeys and Foundations*, ed. Patricia Morrison (Washington, DC: ICS Publications, 2015). See also *St. Teresa of Avila: The Book of Her Foundations: A Study Guide*, ed. Marc Foley (Washington, DC: ICS Publications, 2011).

4. See Susan Muto, *Where Lovers Meet: Inside the Interior Castle* (Washington, DC: ICS Publications, 2008). See also *St. Teresa of Avila: The Interior Castle: Study Edition*, ed. Kieran Kavanaugh and Carol Lisi (Washington, DC: ICS Publications, 2010).

20. JOHN OF THE CROSS: BEAR YOUR CROSS AND SEEK INTIMACY WITH THE TRINITY

1. *The Living Flame of Love*, 1:19:648, in *The Collected Works of St. John of the Cross*, trans. Kieran Kavanaugh and Otilio Rodriguez (Washington, DC: ICS Publications, 1991). Works from this edition (*CW*) are hereafter abbreviated as follows: *A*, for *The Ascent of Mount Carmel*; *DN*, for *The Dark Night*; *SC*, for *The Spiritual Canticle*; and *LFL*, for *The Living Flame of Love*, followed by book or stanza, chapter, paragraph, and page number.

2. Kieran Kavanaugh, introduction to *The Collected Works*, 26.

3. See Richard Hardy, *Search for Nothing: The Life of John of the Cross* (New York: Crossroad, 1982).

4. See Susan Muto, *Deep into the Thicket: Soul-Searching Meditations Inspired by Saint John of the Cross* (Pittsburgh, PA: Epiphany Association, 2001).

5. See *CW, DN*, 1, 1 to 7:361–75 for St. John's analysis of these impediments to a unitive life with God.

6. See Susan Muto, *Dear Master: Letters on Spiritual Direction Inspired by Saint John of the Cross* (Liguori, MO: Liguori/Triumph, 1999).

PART THREE: MODERN MASTERS

21. *FRANCIS DE SALES: RELISH THE RICHNESS OF THE ORDINARY*

1. See Francis de Sales, *Introduction to the Devout Life*, trans. John K. Ryan (New York: Image Books, 1966). Hereafter abbreviated *IDL*, followed by the page number. See also Francis de Sales, *Treatise on the Love of God*, vol. 1, books 1–6, and vol. 2, books 7–12, trans. John K. Ryan (Rockford, IL: Tan Books, 1974).

2. See *Francis de Sales, Jane de Chantal: Letters of Spiritual Direction*, trans. Péronne Marie Thibert (New York: Paulist Press, 1988).

3. In his preface to *Francis de Sales, Jane de Chantal*, Henri J. M. Nouwen writes that the Jesus-centered, affectionate friendship of Francis and Jane was "solidly anchored in their common love of God," which accounts for the "secret of their freedom and their fruitfulness," 3.

4. The Salesian method of meditation starts by placing the self in the presence of God, followed by an invocation and the composition of place—that is to say, imagining the mystery we wish to meditate upon. Then comes the consideration of this mystery by applying to it the powers of understanding, memory, and will. This application then gives rise to affections and resolutions: we raise our heart to the worship and work of God, and we resolve to love God and neighbor by cooperating with grace as fully as possible. We end with a spiritual bouquet, consisting of thanksgiving, offering, and supplication. For a description of this method, see the second part of *IDL*, 83–89.

22. BROTHER LAWRENCE OF THE RESURRECTION: CELEBRATE THE SACRAMENT OF THE PRESENT MOMENT

1. Lawrence of the Resurrection, *The Practice of the Presence of God*, trans. Salvatore Sciurba (Washington, DC: ICS Publications, 1994), 97. Hereafter abbreviated *PPG*, followed by the page number.

2. Brother Lawrence never mistook experiencing calmness in the presence of the Lord with the heresy of quietism spreading throughout France during his lifetime. Its emphasis on passive ways of prayer (mysticism without asceticism) was the opposite of Brother Lawrence's insistence on sacrificial presence and practice as conditions for doing works of love in imitation of Christ. For a thorough treatment of the "quietist turbulence" surrounding François Fénelon and Madame Guyon, see *PPG*, 155–92. See also Pierre Pourrat, *Christian Spirituality: From Jansenism to Modern Times*, vol. 4 (Westminster, MD: Newman Press, 1955).

3. Such sentiments may account for the fact that Brother Lawrence "belongs neither to Catholicism nor to Protestantism, but to all those who, regardless of their religious affiliation, try to make Jesus King in their daily life," *PPG*, xviii.

23. JOHN WESLEY: FOLLOW IN FAITH THE WAY, THE TRUTH, AND THE LIFE

1. See *John and Charles Wesley: Selections from Their Writings and Hymns*, annotated by Paul Wesley Chilcote (Woodstock, VT: Skylight Paths, 2011), 2.

2. The most famous of Charles Wesley's *Redemption Hymns* is "Love Divine, All Loves Excelling." According to Paul Chilcote, it "enunciates themes of his and his brother's life and maturity," namely, that God's unbounded love transcends all others, that faith consists in relationships of love, and that God offers us life abundant through the power of the Holy Spirit (*John and Charles Wesley*, 256).

3. *John and Charles Wesley*, 9.

4. Confirming Wesley's antislavery stance is the fact that his last letter was directed to his young abolitionist friend and admirer, William Wilberforce. See Stephen Tomkins, *John Wesley: A Biography* (Grand Rapids, MI: Eerdmans, 2003), 193. In this letter he says, "Go on, in the name of God and in the power of his might, till even American slavery (the vilest that ever saw the sun) shall vanish away before it." See also Tomkins, 194.

5. Introduction by Frank Whaling to John and Charles Wesley, *Selected Writings and Hymns* (New York: Paulist Press, 1981), 5. Hereafter abbreviated as *SWH*, followed by the page number.

6. *John and Charles Wesley*, 190.

7. Steve Harper, *John Wesley's Message for Today* (Grand Rapids, MI: Zondervan, 1983), 40.

8. Tomkins, 192.

24. THÉRÈSE OF LISIEUX: LET YOUR LIFE BE ONE ACT OF LOVE

1. See August Pierre Laveille, *The Life of St. Thérèse of Lisieux: The Original Biography Commissioned by Her Sister*, trans. Rev. Michael Fitzsimmons (Notre Dame, IN: Ave Maria Press, 2017).

2. See Joseph F. Schmidt, *Walking the Little Way of Thérèse of Lisieux: Discovering the Path to Love* (Frederick, MD: Word of God Among Us Press, 2012), 248.

3. *Story of a Soul: The Autobiography of St. Thérèse of Lisieux*, trans. John Clarke (Washington, DC: ICS Publications, 1975). Hereafter abbreviated *SS*, followed by the page number.

4. Thérèse wrote two Christmas plays focusing on the narratives surrounding the babe of Bethlehem. Moreover, the name she chose when she received her habit on January 10, 1889, was Sister Thérèse of the Child Jesus and of the Holy Face. See *The Plays of St. Thérèse of Lisieux*, trans. Susan Conroy and David J. Dwyer (Washington, DC: ICS Publications, 2008), "The Angels at Jesus' Manger," 101–30, and "The Divine Little Beggar at Christmas," 221–46.

5. See *The Poetry of Saint Thérèse of Lisieux*, trans. Donald Kinney (Washington, DC: ICS Publications, 1996). Titles celebrating Mary include "It's Close to You, Virgin Mary," "The Queen of Heaven to Her Beloved Child," "To Our Lady of Victories," and "To Our Lady of Perpetual Help."

6. *Poetry of Saint Thérèse of Lisieux*, 215.

7. *Poetry of Saint Thérèse of Lisieux*, 216.

8. Thérèse writes, "Jesus deigned to show me the road that leads to this Divine Furnace, and this road is the *surrender* of the little child who sleeps without fear in its Father's arms" (*SS*, 188).

9. See Thérèse's poem "Living on Love!" in *The Poetry of Saint Thérèse*, 89–92. In "The Eternal Canticle Sung Even in Exile," she says, "Jesus, I love you, / And

my life is but one act of love!" (142). She also professed that "abandonment alone guides me" (*SS*, 178).

10. See Patrick Ahern, *Maurice and Thérèse: The Story of a Love* (New York: Image/Doubleday, 1998).

25. JEAN-PIERRE DE CAUSSADE: ENJOY FULFILLING WHATEVER DUTY GOD GIVES YOU

1. Jean-Pierre de Caussade, *Abandonment to Divine Providence*, trans. John Beevers (Garden City, NY: Image Books, 1975). Hereafter abbreviated *ADP*, followed by chapter, paragraph, and page number.

2. Madame Guyon went so far as to teach complete indifference, even to eternal salvation. She said we should banish from the practice of contemplative prayer all thoughts, even of the attributes of God and the accounts of the life of Christ. Bishop Bossuet condemned her for her heretical teachings, whereas Fénelon defended her. Both seemed to embrace the works of Miguel de Molinos (1640–1697), the Spanish quietist. For an excellent treatment of heretical movements such as Jansenism and quietism, read Ronald Knox, *Enthusiasm* (London: Collins, 1950). For more recent explorations of the many factors involved in quietist controversy, see *Bérulle and the French School: Selected Writings*, trans. Lowell M. Glendon (New York: Paulist Press, 1989); *Miguel de Molinos: The Spiritual Guide*, trans. Robert P. Baird (New York: Paulist Press, 2010); and *Fénelon: Selected Writings*, trans. Chad Helms (New York: Paulist Press, 2006).

3. See Susan Muto, *Words of Wisdom for Our World: The Precautions and Counsels of St. John of the Cross* (Eugene, OR: Wipf and Stock, 1996), for an analysis of these three foes of faithful souls and their overpowering tactics.

26. ELIZABETH OF THE TRINITY: PRAISE AND GLORIFY FATHER, SON, AND HOLY SPIRIT

1. See *Elizabeth of the Trinity: The Complete Works*, vol. 1, *General Introduction and Major Spiritual Writings*, trans. Aletheia Kane (Washington, DC: ICS Publications, 1984), 162, which exemplifies the way she wove scriptural references into her reflections. Hereafter abbreviated *CW*, followed by the page number.

2. *Elizabeth of the Trinity: The Complete Works*, vol. 2, *Letters from Carmel*, trans. Anne Englund Nash (Washington, DC: ICS Publications, 1995). See letter 239,

where Elizabeth speaks of St. Catherine living in a little cell even in the "midst of the world," 216.

3. *Letters from Carmel,* letter 335, October 28, 1906, 360.

4. See Susan Muto, *Then God Said: Contemplating the First Revelation in Creation* (Eugene, OR: Wipf and Stock, 2014).

5. *Letters from Carmel,* letter 239, August 13, 1905, 215.

6. *Letters from Carmel,* letter 129, July 25, 1902, 57.

7. See letter 280, June 12, 1906, on the importance of remembering that "the kingdom of God is within you," 280.

8. See Adrian van Kaam and Susan Muto, *Living Our Christian Faith and Formation Traditions,* vol. 4 of the Formation Theology Series (Pittsburgh, PA: Epiphany Association, 2007), 41.

9. See Joanne Mosley, *Elizabeth of the Trinity: The Unfolding of Her Message,* vol. 1, *In the World & in Community,* and vol. 2, *In the Infirmary & After Her Death* (Oxford, Eng.: Teresian Press, 2012).

27. EVELYN UNDERHILL: CLEANSE YOUR PERCEPTION AND SEE WHAT IS REALLY REAL

1. See Evelyn Underhill, *Worship,* ed. W. R. Matthews and H. W. Robinson (New York: Harper, 1959), and Evelyn Underhill, *The Spiritual Life* (Homebush, Australia: Society of St. Paul, 1976).

2. Evelyn Underhill, *Practical Mysticism* (Columbus, OH: Ariel Press, 1942), 141. Hereafter abbreviated *PM,* followed by the page number.

3. See Evelyn Underhill, *Mysticism: A Study of the Nature and Development of Spiritual Consciousness* (London: Methuen, 1941).

4. See Evelyn Underhill, *The Mystic Way: A Psychological Study in Christian Origins* (London: J. M. Dent, 1913).

5. See Evelyn Underhill, *Abba: Meditations Based on the Lord's Prayer* (London: Longmans Green, 1940).

6. See Evelyn Underhill, *Modern Guide to the Ancient Quest for the Holy,* ed. Dana Greene (Albany, NY: State University of New York, 1988).

7. I am indebted for these points to Victor M. Parachin, "Evelyn Underhill: Practical Mystic," *Spiritual Life,* Fall 2014, 83–93. See also Susan Muto, *Gratefulness: The Habit of a Grace-Filled Life* (Notre Dame, IN: Ave Maria Press, 2018).

28. THOMAS R. KELLY: LET GOD LEAD YOU TO THE DAWN OF A NEW DAY

1. Thomas R. Kelly, *A Testament of Devotion* (San Francisco: Harper, 1992). Hereafter abbreviated *TD*, followed by the page number.

2. Thomas R. Kelly, *The Eternal Promise* (New York: Harper, 1966).

3. See Douglas V. Steere's introduction to *A Testament of Devotion* as well as his edition of *Quaker Spirituality: Selected Writings* (New York: Paulist Press, 1984), which contains works by both George Fox and John Woolman.

4. *Quaker Spirituality*, 140–42.

5. See Rufus Jones, *Spiritual Reformers of the 16th and 17th Centuries* (Boston: Beacon Press, 1959).

6. Michael L. Birkel, *Silence and Witness: The Quaker Tradition* (Maryknoll, NY: Orbis Books, 2004), 45.

7. Kelly, *The Eternal Promise*, 72.

8. Cited in "The Gathered Meeting," in *Quaker Spirituality*, 312.

29. DIETRICH BONHOEFFER: TAKE UP YOUR CROSS AND FOLLOW JESUS

1. See Dietrich Bonhoeffer, *The Cost of Discipleship* (New York: Macmillan Publishing, 1963), 64–66. Further references to this edition are identified as *Cost* followed by the page number.

2. Dietrich Bonhoeffer, *Life Together* (San Francisco: Harper and Row, 1954).

3. *Dietrich Bonhoeffer: Letters and Papers from Prison*, ed. Eberhard Bethge (New York: Macmillan, 1971). Hereafter abbreviated *LPP*, followed by page number.

4. *Life Together*, 35.

30. THOMAS MERTON: FOSTER THE CONNECTION BETWEEN SANCTITY AND SERVICE

1. Thomas Merton, *The Sign of Jonas* (New York: Harcourt, 1981), 5. Hereafter cited as *Sign*, followed by the page number.

2. See Thomas Merton, *The Seven Storey Mountain* (New York: Signet Books, 1948).

3. See Thomas Merton, *The Ascent to Truth* (New York: Harcourt, Brace, and Co., 1951); *Contemplation in a World of Action* (New York: Doubleday, 1973); *No Man Is an Island* (Garden City, NY: Image Books, 1967); and *The Seeds of Contemplation* (Norfolk, CT: New Directions, 1949).

4. Notable among these masters was St. John of the Cross. Merton says in *The Sign of Jonas* that he prepared for his profession by praying over *The Precautions and Counsels to a Religious* of St. John and that "for the rest of my religious life I would like, by keeping these *Counsels* [of resignation, mortification, the practice of virtue, and the seeking of solitude], to dispose myself for the work God wants to do in me and to which I am now completely consecrated," 32.

5. See James Finley, *Merton's Palace of Nowhere: A Search for God through Awareness of the True Self* (Notre Dame, IN: Ave Maria Press, 1978).

INDEX

Letters and Papers from Prison (Bonhoeffer), 297–299

Lewis, C.S., 275

Life of Macrina, The (Gregory of Nyssa), 27

Life of Moses, The (Gregory of Nyssa), 26, 28

Life Together (Bonhoeffer), 295, 300–301

light, 108
    glorious, 166
    more perfect light, 165–166
    ordinary, 165
    of Truth, 165–166
    Within, 283–291

literal examples, 107

Little Book of Clarification, The (Ruysbroeck), 158–159

little way, of Thérèse of Lisieux, 248–254, 318

Liturgy of the Hours, 48–49

logismoi (sources of sin), 18–21

Lord's Prayer, 201–202, 240

love, 108
    Bernard of Clairvaux on, 109, 112–117
    degrees of, 115–116
    divine, 89–93
    Maximus the Confessor on, 85–94
    ordinary, 180
    for others with detachment and humility, 197–200
    pure, 198–199
    self-giving (*agape*), 18, 30

supernatural, 180–181

lust, 210

Macarius, 13

Manicheism, 37–38, 40

Mary. *See* Blessed Mother

Maximus the Confessor, 85–94, 316

meditation, 279

Melania, 17

memory, 164–165

Merton, Thomas, 305–314, 319

metanoia (conversion of heart), 17, 297–298

Milton, John, 217

ministry, 169–170. *See also* pastoral care

Mirror of Eternal Blessedness, A (Ruysbroeck), 156–157

monasticism
    Benedictine, 55–63
    Egyptian, 7
    types of, 59

Monica, 38–39

monophysitism, 86

monothelitism, 86

moral examples, 107

more perfect light, 165–166

mystagogy, 88

Mystical Theology, The (Pseudo-Dionysius), 66–68

mysticism, 68–69, 174–175, 220, 276–281

Mysticism (Underhill), 275–276

SUSAN MUTO, executive director of the Epiphany Association, is a renowned speaker, author, teacher, and dean of the Epiphany Academy of Formative Spirituality.

Muto earned a master's degree and a doctorate in English literature from the University of Pittsburgh, where she specialized in the work of post-Reformation spiritual writers. Beginning in 1966, she served in administrative positions at the Institute of Formative Spirituality at Duquesne University and taught as a full professor in its programs, edited its journals, and served as its director from 1981 to 1988. An expert in literature and spirituality, she continues to teach courses on an adjunct basis at a number of schools, seminaries, and centers of higher learning.

Muto is a frequent contributor to scholarly and popular journals such as *Mount Carmel* and *Spiritual Life Magazine*, and she served as editor of Epiphany's online journals and courses, including *Growing in, with, and through Christ*. She is the author of more than thirty books, among them *Twelve Little Ways to Transform Your Heart* and the award-winning *Gratefulness*. She is the coauthor—with Rev. Adrian van Kaam, C.S.Sp. (1920–2007)—of more than forty books, including *Commitment: Key to Christian Maturity* and *The Power of Appreciation*.

Muto lectures and leads conferences, seminars, workshops, and institutes nationally and internationally. She has received many distinctions for her work, including a doctor of humanities degree from King's College, Wilkes-Barre, Pennsylvania. She was honored in 2009 with a lifetime achievement award by the Catholic Historical Society of Western Pennsylvania. Muto also was the recipient of the 2014 Aggiornamento Award presented of the Catholic Library Association. She lives in Pittsburgh, Pennsylvania.

epiphanyassociation.org

HALEY STEWART is a Catholic podcaster, blogger, and the author of *The Grace of Enough*.